AN INTRODUCTION TO THE
BOURDIEU

An Introduction to the Work of Pierre Bourdieu

The Practice of Theory

Edited by

Richard Harker
Reader, Department of Education
Massey University, New Zealand

Cheleen Mahar
Lecturer, Department of Social Anthropology
Massey University, New Zealand

and

Chris Wilkes
Senior Lecturer, Department of Sociology
Massey University, New Zealand

MACMILLAN

First published 1990

Published by
THE MACMILLAN PRESS LTD
Houndmills, Basingstoke, Hampshire RG21 2XS
and London
Companies and representatives
throughout the world

British Library Cataloguing in Publication Data
An introduction to the work of Pierre Bourdieu: The practice of theory.
1. Sociology. Bourdieu, Pierre
I. Harker, Richard II. Mahar, Cheleen III. Wilkes, Chris
301'.09'24
ISBN 0–333–52475–6 (hardcover)
ISBN 0–333–52476–4 (paperback)

Printed and bound in Great Britain by
Antony Rowe Ltd, Chippenham, Wiltshire

10 9 8 7
05 04 03 02 01 00 99 98

Contents

Acknowledgements

We are grateful to Richard Nice for his help and also to Yves Winkin for his careful reading of the manuscript. Our grateful thanks also to the Centre for European Sociology in Paris. We would like to thank Milson Neill and Anneke Visser for their kindness, competence and charity in processing all the words in this book – several times over! Finally our small, interdisciplinary group would like to thank the Massey University Research Fund Committee for providing that sufficient financial autonomy without which interdisciplinary groups almost inevitably founder.

R. H., C. M., and C. D. W.

Notes on the Contributors

Henry Barnard is Lecturer in Social Anthropology at Massey University, New Zealand. A graduate of Victoria University of Wellington, New Zealand and the School of Oriental and African Studies, London, he is on the editorial board of *Sites, a journal for radical perspectives on culture*. Mr Barnard carried out fieldwork in a village in Madhya Pradesh, India and is currently engaged in research on problems of cultural identity and politics in Bihar, India.

John Codd is Reader in Education at Massey University, New Zealand. His research is in philosophy and social theory in relation to curriculum design and educational policy. Dr Codd is the author of *Philosophy, Common Sense and Action in Educational Administration* and *Knowledge and Control in the Evaluation of Educational Organisations*, both published by Deakin University Press in Australia. Also, he has co-edited three books of essays on New Zealand education, and contributed to such journals as the *Journal of Curriculum Studies*, the *Journal of Education Policy* and the *Journal of Aesthetic Education*. Recently John Codd has conducted a national evaluation of craft education in New Zealand Polytechnics.

Ian Duncan is Senior Lecturer in the Department of Social Anthropology, Massey University. He has done fieldwork in a peasant village in central India. Current research interests: caste, untouchability, Hindu sects, social anthropology of religions.

Richard Harker is Reader in Education, Massey University. Co-author of *Education as Cultural Artefact* (Dunmore Press, 1985), co-editor of *Political Issues in N.Z. Education* (Dunmore Press, 1985), and foundation editor (with Chris Wilkes) of the journal *New Zealand Sociology*.

Cheleen Mahar is Lecturer at Massey University in the Department of Social Anthropology. Dr Mahar's major research interest is social class and its transformations within New Zealand rural communities. She has recently completed an ethnographic study of a rural village and has directed a national survey on rural women and their households.

Ivan Snook is Professor of Education at Massey University. He trained as a primary school teacher and taught in secondary schools before taking his Ph.D. at the University of Illinois. He is author of several books including *Indoctrination and Education*, *Philosophy of Education* (with Harry Broudy and others), *Education and Rights* (with Colin Lankshear), *More Than Talk: Moral Education in New Zealand* (with Colin McGeorge). He has published numerous articles in philosophical and educational journals.

Chris Wilkes is Senior Lecturer in Sociology at Massey University and Director of the University Social Research and Consulting Agency. Dr Wilkes has directed the New Zealand Class Project as part of Eric Wright's international project on class, and has recently completed a book on New Zealand class structure. His main research interests are the state and social class.

Editors' Introduction

The production of this book is the result of the collective effort of seven people, members of a study group that has been meeting regularly on Friday mornings since 1982. For the last few years, the Friday morning group has been involved in the discussion of the work of Pierre Bourdieu, the French sociologist, initially most familiar to the English-speaking world for his work on education. The group is an interdisciplinary collection comprising three anthropologists, three educationalists and a sociologist. Bourdieu's wide range of interests coincided with the wide collective interests of the group, though there were times when, even though the numbers favoured our side, we felt he outnumbered and outflanked us. Nonetheless, his original approach to many of the most interesting questions in social science was sufficiently compelling to continue to engage our interest over a considerable time. The anthropologists among us (trained on a diet of Lévi-Strauss and ethnographic methods), had become interested in the broader study of class and symbolic domination while retaining the powerful research tools of ethnography. In their work which concentrated on curriculum and learning, the educationalists had progressively moved away from positivist models of measurement and analysis to a consideration of class as a critical ingredient in the functioning of schools. For the sociologist, Bourdieu's comprehensive theoretical system, together with his empirical work, suggested a powerful post-structuralist research agenda in the fields of social class and ideology. While our initial interests were individual and within separate disciplines, we soon realised our shared research interests and decided to combine as a group to read Bourdieu.

In writing the book our aim has been to help the reader make sense of Bourdieu, not through a process of simplification or rendering down, but by an exploration of the complexity (and consistency) of his ideas and methods of working across a variety of subject fields. We have tried to avoid the two extremes of hagiography and *grande critique* – rather trying to take a middle road in providing an account of our own understandings as an introduction to his work, before concluding with a discussion of the problems we see as still unresolved. Bourdieu's is a theoretical model that derives its dynamic through a dialectical relationship with data gathered in specific

research enterprises. Such data provide the content for the various
conceptual entities that he uses, and hence it is inappropriate to try
to evaluate his work without *putting it to work*. Armchair non-
empirical critiques spectacularly miss the point. As Bourdieu says of
such critics: 'they cross the borders with empty suitcases – they have
nothing to declare'. (Schwibs 1985) What we try to do is to describe
Bourdieu's suitcase and the way he has filled it from his own experience and work in Algeria and France, while making the point that
other researchers must empty the contents and repack them with
their own experience and work. Notwithstanding the usefulness of
Bourdieu's work in interrogating (and formulating) fieldwork data,
we have reservations about its status as a unified theory of social
practices, and we conclude the book by detailing these arguments.

The book which results is therefore not a disparate collection of
papers, whose only claim to commonality is that they deal with
Bourdieu in some way. Rather, it is an integrated exposition of his
method, which begins with an introduction to his intellectual project
and his central ideas, before branching out in several directions
following the trends in his own empirical work. The book concludes
by reviewing the criticisms which have been addressed to his
analyses, pulls together what we have had to say relating his work
to some of the contemporary concerns of Anglo-American sociology,
and outlines his present projects. Each chapter was drafted by individual authors, redrafted in the light of criticisms and comments
from all contributors, and finally reviewed by the editors.

This introduction is followed by an exposition of his conceptual
apparatus and method in Chapter 1. Chapter 2, which provides an
introduction to Bourdieu through an analysis of both his work and
his career, is based on interviews between Mahar and Bourdieu, and
with various other sources, using the multi-level approach Bourdieu
often uses in his work, most notably in *Distinction* (1984). In line
with the strictures of Bourdieu's method, we then attempt to bring
this conceptual apparatus to life by applying it to specific fields of
practice in the following chapters. Indeed, we are in full accord with
Wacquant (1986) who argues that it is necessary to see the 'conceptual artillery' at work, as it were, in order to fully understand it.
Following the broad chronology of Bourdieu's own work, Chapter
3 reviews his ethnographic contribution, beginning with his early
work in Algeria. Chapter 4 canvasses his position on education,
again an early concern for Bourdieu, and an area in which he made
his early reputation. Chapters 5, 6 and 7 follow Bourdieu into three

persistent areas of concern to him, constituting three of the major themes which frame his work. Chapter 5 examines the connection Bourdieu's work on class has with the Marxist tradition; Chapter 6 follows Bourdieu into another field of analysis, looking this time at aesthetics; Chapter 7 looks at Bourdieu's interest in language and its relation to power. In Chapter 8, the story comes full circle. Using a new translation of the 1982 inaugural lecture Bourdieu gave to the Collège de France, it shows how reflexivity is at the heart of Bourdieu's sociological enterprise by providing a gloss of Bourdieu on Bourdieu. The book is concluded by a review of criticism, new work and commentary in Chapter 9.

Bourdieu's productivity is prodigious, and much of his work is yet to be translated into English, two problems of considerable importance for those writing about him. We list his major works as originally published in French in Section A of our bibliography. His major works can be separated for convenience into four main groups. The first grouping consists of work deriving more or less directly from his fieldwork experience in Algeria. These works are *Sociologie de l'Algérie* (Fr. ed. 1958), *Travail et travailleurs en Algérie* (Bourdieu et al., Fr. ed. 1963), *Le déracinement, La crise de l'agriculture traditionelle en Algérie* (Bourdieu and Sayad, Fr. ed. 1964), *Esquisse d'une théorie de la pratique* (Fr. ed. 1972), *Algérie 60* (Fr. ed. 1977), and *Le sens pratique* (Fr. ed. 1980). Three of these works have been translated into English: (Fr. ed. 1958) as *The Algerians* (1962); (Fr. ed. 1972) as *Outline of a Theory of Practice* (1977); and (Fr. ed. 1977) as *Algeria 1960* (1979). The last two are not complete translations, as there have been some materials omitted and others added from the original French editions. The development of this work has continued throughout his academic life.

A second grouping can be made from his collaborative work on education, for which most of the empirical work was confined to the 1960s. The major publications are *Les étudiants et leurs études* (Bourdieu and Passeron, Fr. ed. 1964), *Les héritiers, les étudiants et la culture* (Bourdieu and Passeron, Fr. ed. 1964a), *Rapport pédagogique et communication* (Bourdieu, Passeron and St Martin, Fr. ed. 1965), and *La reproduction. Eléments pour une théorie du système d'enseignement* (Bourdieu and Passeron, Fr. ed. 1970). A return to a direct interest in education has resulted in *La Noblesse d'Etat* (Fr. ed. 1989). Two of these works have been translated into English: (Fr. ed. 1964a) as *The Inheritors* (Bourdieu and Passeron, 1979); and (Fr. ed. 1970) as *Reproduction in Education, Society and Culture*

(Bourdieu and Passeron, 1977). In addition to these books there are a number of key articles that have also been translated and widely anthologised – see Bourdieu 1967; 1971; 1971b; 1973b; 1974. A third grouping derives from his early (and continuing) interest in the sociology of culture and cultural consumption. The major works here are *Un art moyen, essai sur les usages sociaux de la photographie* (Bourdieu et al., Fr. ed. 1965), *L'amour de l'art, les musées d'art européens et leur public* (Bourdieu et al., Fr. ed. 1966), and *La distinction* (Fr. ed. 1979). Of these, only the last has been translated, as *Distinction* (1984) and Bourdieu et al., Fr. ed. 1965 as *Photography: The Social Uses of Ordinary Art* (forthcoming).

We must point out that these three groupings are artificial and for our convenience only. The three groupings interrelate in complex ways in a continuous development of his underlying ideas, and are in turn related to a fourth group of works which reflect on his own professional practice as a sociologist. These books are *Le métier de sociologue* (Bourdieu et al., Fr. ed. 1968), *Questions de sociologie* (Fr. ed. 1980a), *Leçon sur la leçon* (Fr. ed. 1982a; 1982b), *Ce que parler veut dire* (Fr. ed. 1982), *Homo academicus* (Fr. ed. 1984), and *Choses dites* (Fr. ed. 1987). Of these, Fr. ed. 1982 has been translated as *Language and Symbolic Power* (1989); Fr. ed. 1982a has been included in *In Other Words* (1989a); and Fr. ed. 1984 as *Homo Academicus* (Bourdieu 1988).

We used the translated material, and all the relevant French sources, most of which were made available to us by Bourdieu and his colleagues at the Centre for European Sociology. New translations, the most notable of which is *Leçon sur la leçon* (1982a) were frequently made. References to all English sources, including many secondary sources, as well as all the available French sources, are included in the bibliography. Finally, Bourdieu published a great number of articles in French in the journal from the Centre for European Sociology, *Actes de la recherche en sciences sociales*, and these are listed in section B of the bibliography.

While the book concentrates on the work of one scholar, it is essential to an understanding of his work to appreciate the role of the setting he works in. Perhaps of most central importance is the collaborative work he has undertaken over the years, reflected in the list of collaborators with which books and articles have been completed. Of equal significance is the role of the Centre itself, and of the journal *Actes . . .* which he directs, where many of his ideas are first rehearsed. Among its pages are articles by a large group of highly innovative sociologists and other scholars, many with names familiar outside the group, including Foucault, Goffman, Raymond Williams, Gregory Bateson, Jack Goody, Howard Becker, and even little-known pieces of Wittgenstein. In this way, the Centre, through its journal and no doubt through Bourdieu's instigation, has served as a channel for bringing overseas scholarship to France. In the other direction, the journal has also been outward-looking, carrying articles by its own local writers on overseas issues, in Brazil, in New Caledonia, Algeria, the United States and Britain, often with overseas collaborators. In addition, its style has been highly original, and photography, bold graphics and varying styles of type have all served to present material in an evocative way, and as a challenge to more orthodox styles of scholarly review. These influences have not been without an effect on Bourdieu's own work, as a book like *Distinction*, with its photographs and different patterns of presentation, attests. The Centre has always tried to break away from the traditional divisions which have separated disciplines. In 1972, the report of current research from the Centre commented:

A collection of works whose very logic ignores the traditional division of sociology cannot easily be understood in terms of those divisions. Moreover, if these works are classified on the basis of the fields with which they are concerned, it is unlikely that the close interdependence which develops between different research projects and different researchers, both at the level of theoretical conception and that of practical activity, will be seen (Centre for European Sociology, 1972:7).

The team from the Centre consists of researchers who belong to various institutions both within and beyond Paris, as well as being affiliated with many workers outside France. It can be seen as a workshop, in which a broad theoretical and methodological logic connects work in various fields.

Bourdieu has also been heavily involved with the publishing house Minuit, as editor of the series *Le Sens Commun*, which publishes translations of 'fundamental works' in sociology, reissues of authors of the French school (Mauss, Hubert, Halbwachs) and which publishes work from present-day research in France and overseas. Its considerable list includes many of Bourdieu's books, as well as those of his collaborators. Of the translations from overseas contributors, some of the most familiar include Goffman, Bateson, Adorno, Marcuse and Richard Hoggart. In this way Bourdieu has been further involved with the dissemination of work from overseas intellectuals. It is important to emphasise that our purpose in writing this book is to provide an introductory text for English speakers, rather than an 'insider's' view of Bourdieu from a Parisian perspective, a goal we could clearly not achieve. This type of work has sometimes been attempted by outsiders, normally visiting scholars to Paris, but the work frequently suffers from the difficulties associated with all 'jet ethnography'.[1] It is impossible to reconstruct all the debates, the full intellectual environment, and the detailed exchanges which take place in Paris, and from which most English speakers are excluded, without a detailed ethnographic study directed to this specific purpose. Parisian intellectuals frequently complain that the 'debates' which are reported overseas are hardly typical of everyday intellectual life, but are merely the most newsworthy elements in a complex activity, whose reporting then obscures the more mundane events which are equally important to a full understanding. Thus instead, while we have sought to provide a contextual view where possible, we have concentrated on providing a critical translation of Bourdieu's ideas and draw attention to points of intersection with debates in the Anglo-American world.

We should add that this is by no means an 'authorised' biography and commentary on Bourdieu's work. While we spoke with Bourdieu about various matters (essential to the task), there were many points of disagreement between us, both as to the analysis of biography, and on the forms of interpretation which we followed. This is particularly relevant to our task of linking Anglo-American concerns to his work – and about which there were disagreements. Additionally, aspects of the biographical material were also discussed, and while open to correction on points of fact, we have stayed with our own interpretations.

R. H., C. M., C. W.

NOTE

1   For some examples of this form of work, see Lemert, 1981, 1981a, 1986, as well as Clark, 1973. For a vigorous reply (one might say demolition) see especially Jean-Claude Chamboredon, Sociologie de la sociologie et Intérêts Sociaux des sociologues, in *Actes*, no. 2, 1975, pp. 2–17.

1 The Basic Theoretical Position

Cheleen Mahar, Richard Harker, Chris Wilkes

INTRODUCTION

The contribution which Pierre Bourdieu has made to the social sciences has been in his attempt to construct a general theory of practice. This has been established through the creation of a method with which we may grasp the many levels of practical life, using an economic metaphor. Taken as a whole, his work provides novel and often persuasive alternatives for dealing with some of the major problems which beset the work of contemporary Anglo-American social scientists. In particular such problems are due to the (apparently) irreconcilable perspectives of objectivism and subjectivism. The intention of Bourdieu's work can be seen to transcend this opposition between two conceptions of scientific knowledge and to transform them into a dialectical relationship between structure and agency.[1]

Paris forms the centre of the intellectual field in which Bourdieu lives. There he is identified as a philosopher and as a sociologist. This can be explained by Bourdieu's own training and, perhaps more importantly, by the obvious connection between the two disciplines, in which philosophy is seen to raise questions which implicitly or explicitly constitute sociology, and which give sociology its theoretical and political purpose (Collectif 'Révoltes Logiques' 1984:8). Bourdieu's work is characterised as having emerged from diverse intellectual sources such as Marx, Durkheim, Weber, Saussure, Wittgenstein, Benveniste, Canguilhem, and from schools of thought ranging from phenomenology and structuralism to analytic philosophy. Rather than being characterised as merely eclectic, however, he is seen to have woven core ideas of Western thought into a synthesis of his own. For some reviewers the achievements of his work are seen as evidence of a new generation of intellectual thinking which is changing the conception of society (Encrevé Designe

1

1983:614–16; Pinto 1974:54–76). Others in the Parisian field describe Bourdieu's work as being created through the use of ideas (such as the notions of distinction and reproduction), which were already in existence, and 'whose time had come'. This new sociology is built upon the remains of a 'consumed world', which 'takes flight at the beginning of the 1960s with the great recapturing of rigorous theoretical marxism and the fires of revolution' (Collectif 'Révoltes Logiques' 1984:3).[2] The influence of Bourdieu's ideas upon schoolteachers, scholars and political activists is significant. This is because his work, while originating in the historical movements of the 1960s, explains the later illusions and failures of popular education through a methodology which tries to lay bare structures of domination and idealist illusions of liberation. For this reason even many years after the 1960s the impact of the work continues to grow.

   Conscious of the influence of history and the field upon intellectual practice, Bourdieu has often reflected upon his own position within the intellectual field and the genesis of his ideas. Since sociologists are producers of cultural work, the methods which Bourdieu has evolved for defining and studying the fields of cultural production can also be used to study academics. In this way Bourdieu argues, academics can better understand the genesis of their own ideas and master the effects of the social mechanisms to which they are exposed. Such reflexivity finds its fullest exposition in *Leçon sur la leçon* in which Bourdieu describes how a professor's position within the academic hierarchy is greatly dependent upon the structural context and the meanings which other participants bring to bear on the setting. (See Chapter 8, this volume; Fr. ed. 1982a; Fr. ed. 1984). In intellectual life, given these constraints, social scientists tend to be too easily satisfied by evidence obtained through commonsense experience or by familiarity with certain intellectual traditions. One of the most important consequences of this influence is that the structure of a field proposes (to those who are in the field) a problematic (or possible questions) which orients the activities and research that occur within the field, and serves to limit the range of possible legitimate research questions.[3] In a recent seminar given in the United States, Bourdieu explained his work, in part, by trying to convey to his American audience the fields which help define his work. Thus while sociology as a science may transcend national boundaries, the fact that Bourdieu is French and works in Paris means that he finds himself in a European field. This field is largely determined by the phenomenological and structuralist traditions, as well as important residues of Marxist thought. However, to classify Bourdieu as a post-Marxist, post-structuralist, Marxist or Weberian would be to partly misunderstand the nature of his work. Furthermore, such labels may play a harmful role in that they tend to monopolise and constrain the possibilities within the intellectual field. Such labels play the role of gatekeepers.

One of the first things to bear in mind when reading Bourdieu is that his ideas are written, presented and rewritten in a dialectical fashion. He works in a spiral between theory, empirical work and back to reformulating theory again but at a different level. Beginning with his work in the early 1960s Bourdieu has constantly reformulated his core ideas. This systematic development of the theoretical and methodological strategy can thus be traced through thirty years of work, which means that if you wish to understand the development of Bourdieu's ideas you may have to retrace the journey yourself.[4]

The following pages introduce the method and the theoretical base of what we have termed generative structuralism.[5] While providing a conceptual apparatus for the study of practical life, it is important to emphasise that these concepts are proposed as flexible and must be examined by the researcher in the empirical setting rather than being seen as a set of categorical boxes to which the data must conform.

THE METHOD

Generative structuralism describes a way of thinking and a manner of asking questions. Using such a method Bourdieu argues that he is trying to describe, analyse and to take account of the genesis of the person, and of social structures and groups (Bourdieu 1985c). Thus, returning to what we described in the first paragraph as a dialectical relationship between structure and agency, Bourdieu's method proposes a theory for the dialectical analysis of practical life. Such a perspective is said to offer the potential to exhibit the interplay between personal economic practice and the 'external' world of class history and social practice.[6] Such a task must use a relational mode of thought and go beyond what Bourdieu describes as the artificial opposition of objective structures and subjective representations, which may not be reduced to an examination of the concrete interactions between people. Bourdieu's approach is complicated; in defence, he argues that social reality itself is complex and that social science (anthropology, sociology, education and history) must inevitably create the concepts and methods to reflect and understand such a reality. The generative structuralism which Bourdieu proposes is designed to understand both the genesis of social structures and of the dispositions of the habitus of the agents who live within these structures. Chapter 4 discusses this argument further in relation to social change.

Two main conceptual tools which are crucial to Bourdieu's work are the terms habitus and field. These crucial concepts are supported by a number of other ideas, such as symbolic power, strategy and struggle (for symbolic and material power), along with various kinds of capital (economic, cultural and symbolic capital). We will come back to these concepts in more detail a little later, but it is important at this juncture to emphasise the lack of rigidity in what might be called the hierarchy of Bourdieu's conceptual apparatus. Thus, while an understanding of habitus is crucial to Bourdieu's work, an understanding of the role which *strategy* plays in overcoming a strict 'reproductionist' reading of habitus is also crucial.

In developing his position, Bourdieu sets out to make two breaks with modern Marxism, which he says is 'more Marxist than Marx' (Bourdieu 1985:195); and with the kind of phenomenological knowledge that seeks to 'make explicit the truth of primary experience of the social world . . . and excludes the question of the conditions of its own possibility' (Bourdieu 1977:3). Within Marxism Bourdieu says that first one must break with the 'economism' of Marxism, which reduces the social field to the economic field. Second, one must break with the objectivism of Marxism, which tends to ignore the symbolic struggles within the social world. These breaks are explored in greater detail in Chapter 5.

THE BREAK WITH MARXISM

Of particular concern to Bourdieu are those Marxist anthropologists who succumb to what is described as a subtle form of ethnocentrism (Bourdieu 1977:178). Working from a 'restricted definition of economic interest' (itself the 'historical product of capitalism') they 'apply the categories and methods of economics to archaic economies without taking into account the ontological transmutation they impose on their object' (ibid.:177).[7] Economism (Bourdieu's shorthand for

Marxist anthropologists and structural Marxists) 'can find no place in its analyses for symbolic interest'. While rejecting the economistic use of the concept of the symbolic, Bourdieu still retains the term. He defines the 'symbolic' as that which is material but is not recognised as being such (dress sense, a good accent, 'style') and which derives its efficacy not simply from its materiality but from this very misrecognition. Thus:

> Symbolic capital, a transformed and thereby *disguised* form of physical 'economic' capital, produces its proper effect inasmuch, and only inasmuch, as it conceals the fact that it originates in 'material' forms of capital which are also, in the last analysis, the source of its effects.
>
> (Ibid.:183)

The power of symbolic systems and the domination which they imply over the construction of reality, is of enormous importance in Bourdieu's work. For him, symbolic forms such as language, dress codes and body postures are important in understanding not only the cognitive function of symbols but the social function of symbols. Symbolic systems are instruments of knowledge and domination, which make possible a consensus within a community as to the significance of the social world, as well as contributing to the reproduction of the social order. The classical Marxist tradition emphasises the political functions of symbolic systems, and explains the connections between these systems in the interests of the dominant class, and the problem of false consciousness in the dominated classes. From Bourdieu's perspective this approach tends to reduce power relations to relations of communication. The real political function which he sees symbolic systems as fulfilling is their attempt to legitimate domination by the imposition of the 'correct' and 'legitimate' definition of the social world. The struggles between symbolic systems to impose a view of the social world defines the social space within which people construct their lives, and carry on what Bourdieu sees as the symbolic conflicts of everyday life in the use of symbolic violence of the dominant over the dominated, i.e. education, relationships in the workplace, social organisations, even in conceptions of good taste and beauty (Bourdieu 1977:115). The social space is a space of status groups which are characterised by different lifestyles.[8] Symbolic struggles over the perception of the social world can take two different forms. On the objective side one can act through the representations (both individual and collective) in order to demonstrate and valorise particular views of reality. On the subjective side one can act through using strategies of self-presentation, or by trying to change categories of perception and appreciation of the social world.[9] As an example of this argument, Bourdieu uses his field work done among the Berbers of Kabylia in Algeria. The manipulation of groups such as households, lineages, clans and even the tribe, can be seen to be both the instrument of strategies and the stake for which the Kabyle bargain, when they struggle for their individual and group identities both between themselves and with the dominant Algerian political and economic structures (Bourdieu 1979). From his analysis of an 'archaic' or 'ancient' economy where symbolic and economic capital are perfectly interconvertible and where it would be 'irreproachably' ethnocentric to introduce a distinction between them and subject them to different calculations, Bourdieu moves to an exploration of the relation between the two forms of capital in societies that are on the modern end of the transition which is called 'disenchantment'.[10] As his translator Richard Nice says:

> The essential concern of most of Bourdieu's recent work has been to explore the extent to which, despite capitalist 'rationalisation', the interconvertibility of economic and symbolic capital still persists and in fact fulfills an irreplaceable function in maintaining relations of domination.
>
> (Nice 1985)

We return to the discussion of 'capital' later in this chapter, and turn attention here to the second of the major theoretical breaks Bourdieu makes.

THE BREAK WITH PHENOMENOLOGY

The break with what he calls 'phenomenological knowledge' is a break with the naive humanism that is content to create a science on the basis only of 'lived experience' and the 'rights of subjectivity'. As we have mentioned earlier, the general aim of his programme is set within the dialectic between what we are in the habit of polarising as structure and agency (see note 1). He writes that his aim is to 'make possible a science of the dialectical relations between the objective structures . . . and the structured dispositions within which those structures are actualised and which tend to reproduce them' (Bourdieu 1977:3). In an interview he states:

In the sixties the main question was how to articulate the symbolic structure with the economic structure. This vision is now a fossil and can be surpassed by the use of fields and strategies (habitus). People play different games, which are autonomous, but at the same time, there are homologies between different games and, I think, there are general principles of the functioning of these games. What I want to write now is about the economy of symbolic goods . . . the core of the economy is, I think, culture.

(Bourdieu 1985c)

The analogy with games is an attempt to provide an intuitive understanding of the overall properties of fields. First, a sphere of play is an ordered universe in which not everything can happen. Entering the game implies a conscious or unconscious acceptance of the explicit and/or implicit rules of the game on the part of the players. These players must also possess a 'feel' for the game, which implies a practical mastery of the logic of the game – what Giddens calls 'practical consciousness'. Such competence is shared unequally by the players and determines their mastery of the game in proportion to their competence. On the subjective side of Bourdieu's dialectic, competence and mastery of the game are analogous to a person's habitus and possession of capital as they exist within the field. In order to proceed, Bourdieu, a non-linear thinker by his own description, has designed a formula. The formula replaces any simple relation between individual and structure with a constructed relation between habitus and field. The generative formula which explains social practice reads: (Habitus x Capital) + Field = Practice (Bourdieu 1984:101). A considerable note of caution must be sounded in relation to this formula. While it provides a useful heuristic device for summarising the relation between the major concepts at work, it should by no means be used as some sort of deified solution to analysis. The objectification of theory in this fashion is frequently rejected in Bourdieu's own writing. Rather, the use of the formula is to provide an explanatory device for exposition, and does not in any way offer a universal solution for social action, which would be antithetical to the general method. What we need to do now is to 'unpack' the elements of this formula before moving on to a description of the dynamics which drive it.

FIELDS AND THE SOCIAL SPACE

The conception of field which Bourdieu uses is not to be considered as a field with a fence around it, or in the American sense of domain, but rather as a 'field of forces', because it is required to see this field as dynamic, a field in which various potentialities exist. This conception is compared with Goffman's 'frame', 'rules of irrelevance', and so on. However, while Bourdieu has sometimes been called the French Goffman, he is sharply critical of such subjectivist –interactionist approaches, which concentrate on the individual level of analysis. And while Goffman is less guilty of subjectivism than other interactionists and is himself critical of the quasi-solipsism of some forms of ethnomethodology, he is still vulnerable to the criticism that social conditions play very little part in his sociological account. Randall Collins (1988:204) has suggested that Goffman's perspective is compatible with Marxist and conflict theory; this may be a reasonable assertion. However, Bourdieu's account is distinct from Goffman's in that social and economic conditions are embedded in the heart of his argument, rather than merely being implied at the periphery of his theory. Thus while Goffman and Bourdieu share a fascination with the exotic minutiae of everyday life, for Bourdieu, structural properties are always embedded in everyday events, while for Goffman, structures are distant echoes.

The field is therefore a partially autonomous field of forces, but also a field of struggle for positions within it. These struggles are seen to transform or conserve the field of forces (Bourdieu 1983:312). Positions are determined by the allocation of specific capital to actors who are thus located in the field. Positions once attained can interact with habitus to produce different *postures* (*prises de position*) which have an independent effect on the economics of 'position-taking' within the field.[11]

Fields are at all times defined by a system of objective relations of power between social positions which correspond to a system of objective relations between symbolic points: works of art, artistic manifestos, political declarations, and so on. The structure of the field is defined at a given moment by the balance between these points and among the distributed capital. This conception of field is used in particular substantive instances – indeed a great deal of this work can be said to be an attempt to identify the structure and uses of field as a method which constructs the object of research. Frequently, it 'sets the scene' for broad discussion (Bourdieu

1984:222ff; 1985:195ff). Fields thus identify areas of struggle – the field of Parisian intellectual life, the field of literary and artistic taste and so forth. The concept makes little appearance in *Outline of a Theory of Practice* (1977) or in the recent *Homo Academicus* (1988) although both of these works, especially the latter, are influenced heavily by the concept. Without analysing the field as a theoretical concept, *Homo Academicus* precisely delineates the field of French academic life, and seeks to analyse the strategies and struggles for position that take place within it.

One of Bourdieu's recent projects offers a good example of the use of the concept of the field. This is shown in his analysis of the system of higher education in France, which he considers as a separate field. (Bourdieu 1984; 1985a; Fr. ed. 1989; and (with M. de St. Martin), 1986; Actes 1987). This field includes all faculties, *grandes écoles*, *petites écoles* and technical colleges. The main aspect which characterises all of these establishments, as well as their students and the aspirations that the students have of their education is the integration between educational practice and objective structures (through the struggle over material and symbolic power). Thus, Parisian students, like their counterparts in many other parts of the Western world, face job prospects which are highly dependent upon the quality of their degrees, and the rank (symbolic and objective) that the schools have within the educational field. It is therefore important to remember that the construction of a conception of the field is not a completely theoretical construct imposed in an *a priori* way, but can only be determined through empirical research and through ethnographic investigation. Each field is thus treated as a special case and therefore lends itself to the use of comparative methods.

The implications of using the concept of field for methodology are taken up in Chapter 3, extended in Chapter 8 and the concept is discussed in relation to Education in Chapter 4. Its relevance to an analysis of art is shown in Chapter 6 while Chapter 9 uses the concept in a discussion of the relationships between sociology and philosophy, and compares its place in Bourdieu's work with the place of 'institutions' in Giddens' theory of structuration.

Social space refers to the overall conception of the social world. This concept views social reality as a topology (space). In this way the social space may be conceived as comprising multiple fields which have some relationship to each other, and points of contact. The social space of the individual is connected through time (life trajectory) to a series of fields, within which people struggle for various forms of capital. An example of Bourdieu's analysis of a social space is in his work in progress on Flaubert (1986b) (and earlier work on artists (Actes 1975)). In constructing the social space from *L'Education Sentimentale*, Bourdieu noted those who attended the different meetings, dinners and various gatherings. In doing so he located the two poles of power and the position of the key characters with reference to their two fields of power. Social space thus is also to be seen at a higher level of abstraction as a field of forces – more accurately, a series of fields of force. As with fields, and as Bourdieu shows with the work on Flaubert, the definition of a social space cannot be imposed in an *a priori* way, but the idea of a social space can make sense of empirical observation, its precise shape and configuration of forces being derived from the evidence at hand.

Coalitions (political groups, etc.) are created by people who have proximity in social space (Bourdieu 1985:195–220). Thus researchers can construct theoretical classes in order to designate the set of people occupying the same position united by objective similarities and real connections. To conceive of a social space in this fashion requires the breaks with Marxism and phenomenology that we discussed earlier, and the invocation of a new form of sociological method.

HABITUS

> The habitus is a system of durable, transposable dispositions which functions as the generative basis of structured, objectively unified practices.
>
> (Bourdieu 1979:vii)

Habitus refers to a set of dispositions, created and reformulated through the conjuncture of objective structures and personal history. Dispositions are acquired in social positions within a field and imply a subjective adjustment to that position. For instance, in the behaviour of a person, such an 'adjustment' is often implied through that person's sense of social distance or even in their body postures. Thus one's place and one's habitus form the basis of friendship, love and other personal relationships, as well as transforming theoretical classes into real groups.

It is also clear that habitus can be seen to operate at the subconscious level:

The schemes of the habitus, the primary forms of classification, owe their specific efficacy to the fact that they function below the level of consciousness and language, beyond the reach of introspective scrutiny or control by the will. Orienting practices practically, they embed what some would mistakenly call values in the most automatic gestures or the apparently most insignificant techniques of the body – ways of walking or blowing one's nose, ways of eating or talking – and engage the most fundamental principles of construction and evaluation of the social world, those which most directly express the division of labour . . . or the division of the work of domination.

(Bourdieu 1984:466)

Bourdieu's work on Flaubert provides us with another way to understand the integration between habitus and field. In this example Bourdieu likens the field to a game (as a site of struggle and strategy) with the trump cards being habitus (i.e. the assimilated properties of elegance, ease of manners, beauty, etc.), and capital (i.e. inherited assets). Both of these concepts define for the participants the possibilities inherent in the field. These trump cards determine the style of play, success and failure – in fact the entire *'éducation sentimentale'*.

Habitus also includes a person's own knowledge and understandings of the world, which makes a separate contribution to the reality of that world. Thus, that person's knowledge has a genuine constitutive power and is not merely a reflection of the 'real' world (ibid.:467). Because of its mode of development, habitus is never 'fixed', either through time for an individual, or from one generation to the next. As positions within fields change, so do the dispositions which constitute the habitus. However, the possibilities are far from infinite; to paraphrase the old dictum, we cannot make history just as we please. Bourdieu identifies two such constraints on agency. The first source is the habitus of the socialising agents (which is in its turn the product of the previous reproductive cycle).

Between the child and the world the whole group intervenes . . . with a whole universe of ritual practices and also of discourses, sayings, proverbs, all structured in concordance with the principles of the corresponding habitus.

(Bourdieu 1977:167)

Hence the child is disposed to see the world in the same way as the older generation of the primary group – 'to make the world conform to the myth' (ibid.). However, in a situation of relatively rapid change, the objective conditions of the material and social environment will not be the same for the new generation. This constitutes the second source of constraint of the habitus in each generation. Such objective conditions also durably inculcate dispositions, which in their turn engender both aspirations and practice (ibid.:77) in line with the objective conditions (see Chapter 4). Hence, Bourdieu argues, habitus changes with each sequence or iteration, in a direction which attempts a compromise with material conditions. However, the compromise is inevitably biased, as the perception of objective conditions is itself engendered and filtered through the habitus. The argument implies that the habitus itself is no more 'fixed' than the practices which it helps to structure.

So far as the creation of the habitus through socialisation is concerned, then, we have a set of objective conditions in the material world which tend to have a structuring effect on family socialisation practices. These practices durably instill in individuals principles which govern the generation of practice (what people do and think they are doing). The practices thus generated *tend* to reproduce the regularities in the original objective conditions, while adjusting to the habitus-governed perceptions of the continuously changing external circumstances (Bourdieu 1977:78). The central thesis to emphasise, then, is that habitus is a mediating construct, not a determining one. It is also 'a virtue made of necessity' (1984:372), particularly in relation to class habitus, where expectations (or lack of them) in relation to forms of capital are closely matched by objective probabilities. The idea of class habitus and 'valuing the necessary' are taken up and discussed further in Chapter 5, while Chapter 9 discusses the latter in relation to the notion of 'agency'.

Habitus is intimately linked to 'capital' in that *some* habitus (those of dominant social and cultural fractions) act as multipliers of various kinds of capital, and in fact constitute a form of capital (symbolic) in and of themselves.

The genesis and development of the concept of habitus in Bourdieu's work is elaborated upon in Chapters 2 and 6, and is related to inequalities in education in Chapter 4.

CAPITAL

As we argued earlier, a field may be conceived of as a field of forces and struggles for position and legitimate authority, and the logic which orders such struggles is the logic of capital. However, the definition of capital is very wide for Bourdieu and includes material things (which can have symbolic value), as well as 'untouchable' but culturally significant attributes such as prestige, status and authority (referred to as symbolic capital), along with cultural capital (defined as culturally-valued taste and consumption patterns) (Bourdieu 1986a). Cultural capital can include a broad range of goods such as art (see Chapter 6), education (see Chapter 4) and forms of language (see Chapter 7). For Bourdieu, capital acts as a social relation within a system of exchange, and the term is extended 'to all the goods, material and symbolic, without distinction, that present themselves as *rare* and worthy of being sought after in a particular social formation.' (1977:178).

Capital must exist within a field in order that the field may have meaning, but it can also be explained at another level through use of the generative formula. Such an explanation is slightly artificial but useful. The connection between the field, habitus and capital is direct. The value given to capital(s) is related to the social and cultural characteristics of the habitus (Bourdieu 1984). The field is bounded by objective power relations which have a material base. The types of capital that are recognised in particular fields and incorporated into habitus are also, in part, generated by the material base. Naturally the volume of capital, as well as the structure of additional capital, is also an important dimension in the field.

Capital is also seen by Bourdieu to be a basis of domination (although not always recognised as such by participants). The various types of capital can be exchanged for other types of capital – that is, capital is 'convertible'. The most powerful conversion to be made is to symbolic capital, for it is in this form that the different forms of capital are perceived and recognised as legitimate. To be seen as a person or class of status and prestige, is to be accepted as legitimate and sometimes as a legitimate authority. Such a position carries with it the power to name (activities, groups), the power to represent commonsense and above all the power to create the 'official version of the social world'.[12] Such a power to represent is rooted in symbolic capital. Perhaps one of the most powerful examples of the power to represent the 'legitimate' social world is through the law and the use of symbolic violence by the state to enforce this vision. The law guarantees to the state all forms of official nomination (such as titles of property, school titles, professional titles, etc.). This in turn gives individuals a known and recognised identity which in turn confers economic and cultural capital. In the struggle or conflict for the legitimate vision (the power to name), a state-named 'expert' (a doctor or a teacher) produces a point of view which confers universally recognised rights to others who hold certificates and who act in the legitimate (expected) way. This in turn produces a kind of consensus based upon the power relations between two different systems of presuppositions (those of the layperson and the expert) and results from the structure and functioning of the field. The law, Bourdieu says, is 'no doubt the form *par excellence* of the symbolic power of naming and classifying which creates the things named, and particularly groups' (Bourdieu 1987). One of the ironies of the logic of capital in practice is that the connection or the convertibility between different types of capital is not always recognised. Thus symbolic capital may not be recognised as a material form of power which is institutionally organised and secured.[13] Wacquant makes the point when he writes of:

(the) hidden processes whereby different species of capital are converted so that economically-based relations of dependency and domination may be dissimulated and bolstered by the mask of moral ties, of charisma, or of meritocratic symbolism (1984:9).

The work of constructing visions and divisions in the social world supposes a particular kind of capital (for some) which works effectively in the mechanisms of delegation and dispossession. The outcome of such mechanisms is what Bourdieu calls symbolic violence, because those who do not have the 'means of speech', or do not know how to 'take the floor', can only see themselves in the words or the discourse of others – that is, those who are legitimate authorities and who can name and represent.

The discussion of capital leads Bourdieu to the view that practice (as the outcome of the formula) can be largely conceptualised in terms of both individual and class trajectories.

PRACTICE

As we pointed out by way of introduction, Bourdieu's method is grounded in the mutual penetration of objective and subjective structures. As a dialectic it is an attempt to step out of the impasse of the structure/agency debate in social science, an attempt we will evaluate in Chapter 9. The core of the method is the process of 'the internalization of externality and the externalization of internality' (Bourdieu 1977:72). The practice of an individual or social group is thus to be analysed as the result of the interaction of habitus and the field.

While in this chapter we focus on the component parts of Bourdieu's conceptual apparatus, it is important to remember that the most effective way to assess how well the theory works is in relation to the ethnographic data of the case study. While the general argument works in an abstract way in different cultural settings, its flexibility (through the focus on processes) makes it possible to be tested in studies outside France. Indeed, it is only through the study of *particular* practices that a field can be delineated, the forms of capital perceived and the methodology assessed; that is, the generative formula as a methodology should be read from right to left. To help with this process of delineation and perception, we define in the next few pages the primary attributes of practice that Bourdieu uses. These are the concepts of relative autonomy, personal and class trajectories, and in particular, the nature of strategies and struggle for positions in the field. In order to appreciate the position of Bourdieu's work as being at a distance from simple reproductionist logic, the move from 'rule' to 'strategy' is of paramount importance and cannot be emphasised too strongly.

THE DYNAMICS OF THE GENERATIVE FORMULA

It is clear from the previous discussions of the component elements that Bourdieu's generative formula is powered by a number of 'enabling' ideas which both modify its effects in different fields, and make the outcome of practice relatively unpredictable for individual agents. Further, we have already suggested that for Bourdieu all practices have an economic edge if they involve goods (material or symbolic) that 'represent themselves as rare and worthy of being sought after' (1977:178). Related to this argument we should also remember that in archaic societies there is no differentiation of practices. That is, the objective structures are very stable and the mental structures are reproduced almost completely so that although they are arbitrary, their arbitrariness is not recognised and they are misconstrued as self-evidently correct. This conformity between mental and objective structures is called the *doxa* in Bourdieu's account since neither 'orthodox' nor 'heterodox' are meaningful in the absence of alternative accounts.[14] In these societies domination has to be direct and constantly renewed, for power comes from relations and in these societies there are only direct physical relations. Power is a multifaceted concept in Bourdieu's work and is best seen in relation to activities in particular fields.

As the result of crises and class division the homology between the subjective and objective structures is broken and there arise practices which break down the unanimity of the *doxa* and develop, so to speak, 'a life of their own'. They are not fully autonomous, for they are seen to exist only as variants of the accepted structure and depend on the relationship between 'authorised, authorising language and the group which authorises it and acts on its authority' (1977:171). Chapter 4 looks at power in relation to the power to define the field of education. Chapter 7 has an extended discussion of power in relation to language, and we offer a summary of Bourdieu's version of power in Chapter 9.

Bourdieu argues that the autonomy of the various fields has been partly created by the practice of intellectuals who by their 'ideological labour' construct a separate 'economic' field and set it against other fields. Nevertheless, the various practices do have a measure of autonomy. This 'relative autonomy' arises from the aspirations of the agents who, though part of the objective conditions, acquire the symbolic capital which masks the actual power relations and obscures the dominance of the economic. This symbolic capital enables the agents to 'recognise' what is occurring. This is a *misrecognition* of course, for it involves taking as true a set of opinions which are basically arbitrary. Yet it is also a real *recognition*, for without the symbolic capital it would not be possible to refer to the situation at all.

The relatively autonomous fields relieve the dominant classes of the need for direct control. They can control them much more adequately by indirect means such as access to education, artistic taste, living style and the like. Thus in the end the extent of the autonomy is a mark of how limited it is: the autonomy itself is finally and totally in the service of the economic. Given the idea that habitus is not totally determined by structures, and that an agent can take up a number of positions within relatively autonomous fields (and indeed can assume one of a number of possible postures within a position, once acquired), we have a situation which allows considerable room for manoeuvre through the employment of various strategies.

Bourdieu's important notion of strategy is one which breaks with both subjectivist and objectivist thinking. Such a notion has been used by Bourdieu from his early work to the present. As his concepts of habitus and the social field have become more highly developed, so has the notion of strategy, along with the idea of struggle (for positions within the field for capital of various sorts). In his earlier work Bourdieu wrote about strategies for the maintenance of 'honour' through challenge and riposte, and strategies of marriage and the power of parents. In his article entitled 'Marriage Strategies as Strategies of Social Reproduction' (1976), Bourdieu criticises the Lévi-Strauss paradigm of the kinship rule and the legalism it implies, and thereby attempts to impose a new manner of conceiving marriage. He has also written about the strategy of calculation of time, money and work in order to account for the movement of individuals from sub-proletarian positions to the proletariat (Bourdieu 1979). Such strategies are conceived to be intimately linked to objective structures and to habitus. 'Economy and ethos are so profoundly interdependent that the whole attitude towards time, calculation, and forecasting is virtually inscribed in the mode of appropriating the soil . . . ' (Bourdieu 1979:17).

In later work the concepts of strategy and struggle become tied together through the newly-introduced notion of the field, although Bourdieu says that in his earlier work there are still the same problems that he has today (Bourdieu, Fr. ed. 1987:33):

1 The idea that the struggle for recognition is a fundamental dimension of social life. Struggles are over the accumulation of capital. Therefore, there must be a specific logic of accumulation of symbolic capital, such as the capital which is founded on knowledge and recognition;

2. The idea of strategy, like the orientation of practice, is not conscious nor calculated nor is it mechanically determined. It is the intuitive product of 'knowing' the rules of the game;

3. The idea that there is a logic of practice – the details of which

depend on the specific time and place, or may, of course depend on a sequence of events over time.

Bourdieu comments that he came upon the idea of strategies to 'break from Lévi-Straussian discourse on 'indigenous rationalisations' which is incapable of clarifying the anthropology about the real causes or the real reasons of practices . . . . This is what compelled me to discover, about marriage for instance, that the reasons to accomplish the same category of marriage . . . could vary considerably given different agents and different circumstances . . . . I was on the track of the idea of strategy' (Bourdieu, Fr. ed. 1987:31).

Struggle and strategy are dependent upon *knowledge*, which has both active and materialist aspects. For Bourdieu knowledge is not idealist or passive. All knowledge and

> in particular all knowledge of the social world, is an act of construction implementing schemes of thought and expression, and that between conditions of existence and practices or representations there intervenes the structuring activity of the agents, who, far from reacting mechanically to mechanical stimulations, respond to the invitations or threats of a world whose meaning they have helped to produce (Bourdieu 1984:467).

The principle of such structuring is seen not as idealist or as a system of universal forms and categories but as a 'system of internalised, embodied schemes which, having been constituted in the course of collective history, are acquired in the course of individual history' (ibid.; see also Fr. ed. 1974). Agents, then, construct their social world and act to reproduce their positions and to gain position in the social world. Bourdieu has described two types of strategies to account for this process. The first 'type', *reproduction strategies*, are seen as sets of practices designed (and mediated) to maintain and improve position. They are mediated through dispositions toward the future, which are closely attuned to objective probabilities. Such strategies depend upon the volume of capital, the state of *instruments of reproduction* such as the inheritance laws, the labour market, the educational system and so on. The state of these instruments themselves depends on the state of the power relations between the classes (1984:125). By way of example, Chapter 4 gives a detailed analysis of the social and cultural reproductive consequences of schooling.

The second 'type', *reconversion strategies*, corresponds to movements within the social space which itself is structured in two dimensions; firstly, in that the overall volume of capital is structured, and second, through the structuring of the types of dominant and dominated capital. People are said to move sideways or up and down depending on capital, i.e. the reconversion of economic capital to educational capital – a strategy which enables business to legitimately maintain the position of its heirs (see Bourdieu 1984:125–68; and Chapter 4).

Strategy and struggle are also important because they are processes through which differences are said to be established and marked, for instance, as in the development of systems of social differences often labelled as 'taste'. 'Taste is an acquired disposition to "differentiate" and "appreciate" . . . to establish and mark differences by a process of distinction . . . (ensuring) recognition (in the ordinary sense)' (Bourdieu 1984:466; and Chapter 6 where 'taste' is further analysed in relation to art). Again, we come back to the same fundamental principles: strategy and struggle work within the logic of practice for the purposes of recognition, legitimation, capital and access to capital within the symbolic and material world. All these forms of practice are seen to be created and bounded by habitus, by the objective structures which define the social field, and by a whole host of other strategies to hide the fact of struggle for capital. Bourdieu often uses the term 'game' as a shorthand for this process. The game analogy is explored further in relation to language in Chapter 7 and in relation to sociology itself in Chapter 8.

Bourdieu suggests that it is not just the struggle over capital that societies may attempt to hide. Every society, he claims, conceals or masks the *calculations* involved in many social and cultural practices behind an ideological screen, the main purpose of which is to conceal from the participants themselves the economic basis of such calculations.[15] However, the term 'misrecognition', which is the usual translation of the word he uses in this context (*méconnaissance*), misses the subtlety of the original concept. The participants do not conceal a practice by dressing it up as something else (in the sense of disguising it), but rather render it invisible through a displacement of understanding and a reconstrual as part of other aspects of the habitus that 'go without saying'. The economics of gift-giving, for example, is rendered invisible by reconstruing it within such practices as family honour, generosity and so on. There may be a refusal to recognise (or a disavowal of) the economic calculation involved in gift-giving, since to 'see' it would destroy whole fields within the social space, by destroying the medium of exchange that *is* recognised – family honour, generosity (symbolic capital). Such a transformation also serves to legitimate the unequal distribution of *power* to the participants involved (Bourdieu and Passeron 1977:205), and hence reproduces existing power relations, and disguises the struggle for position, and the strategies for the acquisition of symbolic capital within the field. A minimal translation of *méconnaissance* would therefore be '(mis)recognition and reconstrual'. An example in the field of education is given in Chapter 4, and in the aesthetic field in Chapter 6.

TRAJECTORY

Using the generative formula and the attendant 'enabling' concepts that we have outlined, it is therefore possible to determine not only an individual's *position* in a social space, but, more importantly, how they arrived at particular positions, through the invocation of the concept of trajectory.

In *Distinction*, Bourdieu introduces the notion of trajectory in discussing the position of parvenus and people who are *déclassé*. People within a group (a position within a field) pick up on *jarring notes* – aspects of others' behaviour which indicate that they are of a different social origin than the members of the group in which they find themselves. In other words, they have *arrived* by a different route or trajectory from all the others. The most common route is what Bourdieu calls the 'modal trajectory', which he relates to a 'given volume of inherited capital'. A group sharing this capital may be expected to follow 'a band of more or less equally probable trajectories leading to more or less equivalent positions' (1984:110). However, because the relationship between starting point and present position is 'of very variable intensity' (ibid.:109) there is likely to be some divergence of individual trajectories from the modal trajectory, though the modal or, sometimes, collective trajectory is 'an integral part of the system of factors constituting the class' (ibid.:110). The notion of trajectory is thus seen to be something which results from the struggle for symbolic capital within fields, and may be decoded by carefully looking at the networks of economic, cultural and social relationships. It is discussed further in relation to class trajectory in Chapter 5.

CONCLUSION

It is obvious that there have always existed certain problems and core ideas in social science. The work of Bourdieu and others can be viewed as a struggle with classical ideas. For instance, like Anthony Giddens, E. P. Thompson and Raymond Williams, Bourdieu considers the dialectic between structure and agency. However, his work contributes a particularly 'European' view to the Anglo-American field in that he argues that their dialectic is false and owes its existence to, in part, the practice and methodology of orthodox social science. In attempting to untangle the complexities of social and cultural practice which have been identified as existing within the dialectic of structure and agency, Bourdieu offers a method, directed towards the analysis of social and economic practice, firmly anchored in ethnographic research. This focus upon practice and the structural features which set the conditions for determining practice is not, however, unique to Bourdieu, and itself is embedded in the work of past theorists such as Marx, Weber and Durkheim. As we know, Marx wrote about political and economic dominance, Durkheim about rules and norms, while Weber concentrated upon individual ethos and consciousness; all of which are echoed in the works of Giddens, who primarily looks at domination and social class by means of a broad synthetic theoretical initiative, and Sahlins who looks more concretely at what he terms 'practical reason and action' as it exists within the anthropological construct of culture. Bourdieu's contribution is, however, unique, in that the theory of practice which he proposes lies within the context of real lives – using habitus – and at the same time incorporates a theory of domination as existing within social fields. This method, which we argue is most suitably termed 'generative structuralism', provides useful openings to the contemporary social scientist, even if the opportunities they present are not without difficulties. Its difference from other approaches provides Bourdieu with a particular position in the field of social theory, a field constructed by the classical works, and by the work of contemporaries.

While Bourdieu's intellectual project spans work in several areas (literature, art, philosophy, education, and ethnography), his commitment in each of these areas is to a similar critical methodology. On the one hand, his method seeks to dissolve the division between objective and subjective perspectives in social science by the refinement and use of such concepts as habitus, field, the nature of symbolic power, capital and the notion of strategy. On the other hand, his considerable output of empirical work (which is not always apparent in the English translations of his work) emphasises his use of statistical and ethnographic evidence in the creation and use of his theoretical constructs. One might say that Bourdieu's methods lead him to attempt the ambitious goal of the creation of a science of practical knowledge. However, Bourdieu has always tried to make clear that he must be distinguished from those who consider the 'knowledge of practical knowledge' to be sufficient in completing the task of social science, and who reduce this knowledge to a simple description of what is taken to be 'real life experience', organised on the basis of universal principles. This distinction sets Bourdieu apart from the new trend of 'constructivists' in American sociology (the ethnomethodological vision) as well as separating him from the phenomenological approach taken by many anthropologists. The study of practical knowledge, according to Bourdieu, involves the social conditions which are at work in the construction of perceptions and which have a structuring effect on experience (personal communication). We can see then, that the perspective which Bourdieu offers is a far more complex method for the social sciences; but in doing so he is not setting out to make our work more difficult, but giving us the conceptual apparatus with which we can analyse a complicated reality. The success or otherwise of this attempt can be assessed in the wake of the following chapters.

NOTES

1. The structure/agency debate centres on the role that institutional and structural influences have in shaping society and how much part the actions of individuals (and groups) play in the same process; see, for example, Anthony Giddens, *Central Problems in Social Theory* (Macmillan, London, 1979). This debate, of course, is not new to social science, but can indeed be seen as a major theme in some disciplines, e.g. sociology. Marx, for example, in a famous dictum, argued that men can change the world through their actions, indicating the role of agency, but that they are not *free* to do so just as they please, indicating the social and economic limits to action in society. Marxist and functionalist accounts are sometimes therefore said to be structuralist accounts because they emphasise the structuring and determining quality of society over and against the voluntarist capacity of agents. Web-

erian and phenomenological accounts of society have sometimes, in contrast, been viewed as voluntarist, having centred too much on the actions of individuals to create and recreate the world, as if external constraints did not exist. One of Bourdieu's major contributions can be seen as an attempt to construct a method which accounts for both structure and agency, e.g. in his use of habitus. Some of the issues underlying the structure-agency debate are further elaborated in Chapter 9.

Structuralism can be considered a cul-de-sac since it has led to the 'death of agents', and in E. P. Thompson's view, excluded human subjects from history. Whether this view is reductionist is less clear. It is not reductionist in the normal use of the term, which generally refers to single-cause explanations, e.g. Marxist theories are considered reductionist when they stress economic explanations at the expense of other causes. However, structuralism in its Althusserian form was clearly not reductionist in this sense, since ideological, political and economic causes were frequently stressed together. Structuralism could be said to be reductionist in its limited use of levels of analysis, perhaps, reducing all cause to the level of the structure. See Chapter 2 for an account of Bourdieu's rejection of this position.

2. The Collectif goes on to discuss the 'moment' of both Bourdieu and Althusser: 'the critique of illusions in the Inheritors accompanied at its outset, the great Althusserian battle for revolutionary science against ideology. The theory of reproduction mixed the austere axioms of structuralism with the flavour of the cultural revolution . . . it accepted the theoretical and political heritage of critical marxism and it completed their interpretive scheme. In the university, as in journalism, it allowed the recovery of lines of division and of social classes in the most lowly inflexion of prose writers or in the posturing of politics. To the teacher or the activist as with reformers who try to resolve their problems, he (Bourdieu) explains the illusions and the failures of popular education. But at the same time he has taken away this interpretive capacity of the practical hypotheses of marxism and the naiveties of "hoping socially" (translator's commas). He allows denunciation both of mechanisms of domination and the illusions of liberation . . . ' (1984:6; trans. C. D. Wilkes).

3. In the book *Homo Academicus* Bourdieu analysed the debate between Barthes and Picard to demonstrate how the logic of the field structures the relationships between the position-taking of academics and how specialists are distributed amongst the *possible* approaches and different *possible* methods (Fr. ed. 1984:23–5).

4. Readers may find that *Distinction* (Harvard University Press, 1984) is a good place to begin their reading. The wealth of ethnographic detail is interesting and balances the 'weightier' theoretical passages. Another book, *Algeria 1960* (1979), is also a good place to begin because of the emphasis on ethnography. Then, the more theoretical works, such as *Outline of a Theory of Practice* (1977), *Le Sens pratique* or the many articles available (see bibliography), are more easily grasped.

5. However, in an attempt to situate himself within an arena known

to his American audience Bourdieu characterised his work as being *constructivist structuralism*. By 'constructivist' Bourdieu emphasises the subjective side of his methodology, which focuses upon the social genesis of mental structures. Through the use of the word structuralism (a different structuralism than that found in Lévi-Strauss) Bourdieu emphasises the objective structures which unconsciously act to orient and constrain social practice (there is an important break between Bourdieu and 'constructivists' which is discussed in the conclusion of this chapter).

6. 'The perception of the social world is the product of a double structuration' between objective and subjective aspects. (Bourdieu Fr. ed. 1987:158).

7. This refers to the process of reconstructing objects through the use of categories and methods inappropriate to the reality of the objects themselves. An extreme illustrative example of this would be asking an Indian group how many 'souls' they have, or attempting to enumerate the number of gods in Hinduism.

8. The world, however, does not present itself as being totally structured and totally imposing on all practice. It is open – available to the many possibilities and possible structurations which both create fields and are created by them. Thus the social world is open to change from those who struggle for the dominant vision such as those struggles between class divisions and between ethnic groups and between genders. There is always a degree of fuzziness and 'semantic elasticity' in the perception of the objects in the social world.

9. This process of symbolic power can be likened to the power of world-making (Nelson Goodman) or to Thomas Dewey's power of constitution which includes both philosophical and political meanings (Bourdieu: Actes 1986b). Perhaps a more interesting and comfortable connection can be drawn between Bourdieu's work on symbolic power and the influence of the work by Emile Benveniste (1969, 1974) on the development of this idea. The work of Benveniste was instrumental in developing Bourdieu's own thought. (Personal communication.)

10. Disenchantment (a term derived from Weber): to be enchanted is to be under a spell so that one fails to see (or misrecognises) connections. The 'transition' referred to is the historical transformation that occurs when the symbolic and the economic are separated and certain activities are seen as being political, religious, and others as being economic. Bourdieu's position on this question is deeply complex. For the rest of his work in fact, attempts to show how this separation expresses new forms of enchantment.

11. Bourdieu began to develop his idea of the field while teaching about Weber and his theory of religious agents (i.e. priests, sorcerers and prophets). In attempting to understand the relationship among these three agents, Bourdieu says that he realised that they were tied together in their own clerical world which had its own laws and forms of symbolic and cultural capital. While Weber's work is locked into the logic of functions he did write about specialists and their particular interests (i.e. the functions that their products, religious doctrines, juridical

corpora, etc., fulfill for them). It is in part through this development of the microcosm of the clerical world that Bourdieu came to write about the field. (Personal communication.) Other less important influences on the concept of the field come from Kurt Lewin and the anthropologists of the cognitive tradition (such as Conklin and Frake). The field is a relational concept and is expressed in speech though based upon objective relations (see *Ce que parler veut dire*, Fr. ed. 1982). This is an important point because it distinguishes Bourdieu's approach from the psychological/interactionist approach which is a dominant tradition in American sociology.

12. The most obvious example is afforded by members of the radical left who speak on behalf of the working class, thus generating an 'authority' to act as spokespersons for a group. In short, this is the capacity to name. In a sense they constitute the working class as a theoretical class, independent of whether or not the 'working class' is a mobilised and active group. Bourdieu (1985) covers this phenomenon in some detail, and it is discussed further in Chapters 3 and 5. The role that language plays is discussed in Chapter 7, and Bourdieu's self-analysis in these terms is discussed in Chapter 8.

13. In his inaugural lecture to the Collège de France, Bourdieu gives the example of the Roman *censor* who assigns people to their *societal* categories, thereby both defining and maintaining hierarchical positions – see Chapter 8 in this volume.

14. In *Outline of a Theory of Practice* (1977:164) Bourdieu introduces the word *doxa* to refer to those schemes of thought and perception which are produced by objective social structures but are experienced as natural and self-evident, and therefore taken for granted. *Doxa* is constituted of all those systems of classification which set limits upon cognition but also produce a misrecognition of the arbitrariness on which they are based.

15. For example 'etiquette' advice in women's magazines, assumes that learning the rules is all that is required. The point that Bourdieu would make, is that 'manners' deliberately learned signal a *lack* of symbolic capital which is only 'legitimate' if 'natural' – i.e. acquired from the family through primary socialisation.

2 Pierre Bourdieu: The Intellectual Project
Cheleen Mahar

INTRODUCTION

I think there are two versions of Bourdieu's past. One is the mythical one in which he is the peasant boy confronting urban civilisation, and the other one, which he actually thought through more seriously, is what it's like to be a petit bourgeois and a success story. And all this obsession with other people's language, and with the use of language to dominate and put down in non-rational ways is perhaps also the rethinking of his own experience.

(Nice 1985)

In Chapter 1 we formally outlined what we felt to be Bourdieu's major methodological themes and techniques. The intent of this chapter is to give a slightly more ethnographic approach to Bourdieu by providing the reader with an overview of the development of Bourdieu's work and the genesis of his ideas as drawn directly from himself and his reflections upon his intellectual past. The material for this chapter is drawn from personal observations and interviews with Bourdieu at the Centre de Sociologie Européenne in 1985 and 1986,[1] as well as from his written work from 1985 to 1989. In addition to the Bourdieu material, I have also included sections from a particularly interesting interview between Bourdieu and a group of German scholars (see Honneth and Schwibs 1985), plus impressions of Bourdieu's life and work by his first major English translator, Richard Nice. Finally, I would like to point out that the layout of this chapter differs from others in the book in that the text is interrupted by descriptive sections which take up particular ideas from the text. These sections are taken from an interview with Richard Nice and help illuminate certain points. Bourdieu has always maintained that it was imperative that the academic reflect upon his or her own practice. In this interpretive essay we have tried to allow him to speak for himself.

Before meeting with Bourdieu and seeing him at the Collège de France and at the Centre for European Sociology, I had not fully appreciated the power of his 'position', nor the formality which surrounded him in Paris. Bourdieu's position as professor at the Collège arguably provides him with the most prestigious chair in sociology in France.

In our interview, Nice offered a short description of the French educational system and tried to explain Bourdieu's position in it.

CM The French system seems very complicated. Can you tell me something about it, and Bourdieu's place in it?

RN Well, there are three, even four, different institutions or sets of institutions. The universities weren't always universities; they were faculties. What's happened historically is a kind of archaeology of the creation of the French educational system with splits and the formation of counter establishments . . . . The Collège de France has a group of professors, with minimal duties and is extremely prestigious. That's what Bourdieu was elected to a few years ago when he was in so many ways, at the peak of his career. He can't go any further in French academic life.

CM Who pays the salaries there? The state?

RN Well, it's financed by the government but it's very autonomous.

The Collège de France has no students; it's just open to the public. So it doesn't teach systematic courses – it's very much a matter of the exhibition of one's knowledge. On the sidelines people have research laboratories where they do their own work, which gives them resources to hire their own people so they can establish their own 'private cell'. Almost anyone who has really made it to the top of French academic life has done it that way . . .

What they represent very much sets the tone of French academic life. For example in the 1940s Hippolyte was Professor of Philosophy there. He was important because he was one of the translators of Hegel into French. Merleau-Ponty also made it. Aron became professor of Sociology in 1970. That was more in recognition of his total achievements than the content of his thought at the time. Foucault, in the same year, got a chair there; and that was important. Barthes in 1974 and Bourdieu in 1982. Bourdieu technically succeeded Aron after Aron's death which created an opening. I think the beauty of Bourdieu's own thinking is that it explains itself. It explains his life. I don't think that's true of everybody's thinking.

The emergence of a new chair always creates a succession struggle in which the clans fight for pre-eminence. Now Bourdieu's election was the outcome of a fight which he won essentially against Alain Touraine and Raymond Boudon. And again, another thing which one doesn't understand, about Bourdieu (I mean in order to understand Bourdieu, to look at his life as a sort of trajectory), you've also got to look at the intellectual field – indeed that's what he'd say or is part of the central content of what he's saying, anyway; the field determines the contents of each element. But he is extraordinarily conscious of that as a sort of over-determination of his own practice. He has an acute awareness of the field and therefore everything he says and does (I abstractly understand) is aimed at not just the readership but at the rivals.

The Collège de France serves as an elysian for the 'great academics'. The Ecole pratique des hautes études, a system of graduate schools, provides a base for those who direct others' research. Bourdieu established a niche for himself there which was accompanied by this curious institution called the Centre for European Sociology, which is partly financed independently. It was set up with the help of Raymond Aron.

However, when I finally saw Bourdieu give a lecture at the Collège and when we met for the interview, the prestige, status and formality of the French system fell away. Bourdieu was remarkable for his warmth, his energy and his sense of humour. I had previously arranged with Bourdieu that he would meet with me, but when I rang his office his secretary asked me to bring in my questions for him to see in advance. I delivered my questions to the secretary at the Centre, which is housed in the Maison des sciences de l'homme. The building is modern and elegant, with tall glass doors which give it a feeling of space. On Bourdieu's floor I found that he was surrounded by layers of workers; there were secretaries, the office for *Actes de la recherche en sciences sociales*, and a group of researchers. The next day the secretary called, and we agreed to a time for me to meet with Bourdieu, but before the meeting I was to meet with one of his senior research assistants. Again I went back to the Centre and talked for an hour. The researcher gave me copies of the interviews that Bourdieu had previously done, and suggested various books that I might read before my interview (which was to be held on the next day). She also mentioned that I should hear Bourdieu's lecture at the Collège at 10 a.m. the next morning.

The lecture was held in a very old theatre fitted out with modern sound and lighting equipment. This was Bourdieu's last lecture for the winter term. The room was packed with students and townspeople. The people in the front row had tape recorders all around the desk. At 10 a.m. Bourdieu was introduced by a man in a dark suit – '*Mesdames et Messieurs, Monsieur le Professeur.*' Bourdieu walked in through the door. There was an involuntary move to stand among the audience, a move which all quickly overcame and which was an echo of pre-1968 days when such deference was more common. He is a middle-sized man, about 55 years old, wearing an open-necked shirt and sports coat. He began the lecture quietly. He sat at the bench table, and while he spoke he used his hands for emphasis. He apologised to the audience for being off-colour (he had recently undergone a knee operation) but he hoped that the audience would find something worthwhile in his lecture. The lecture consisted of a discussion on the development of sociological knowledge and the career of the academic. As he spoke he began to project his voice more and more, and told a few jokes. The audience was with him and very keen. After 75 minutes Bourdieu closed the lecture and bringing his voice down, he said that he hoped that his talk had been of some interest, and thanked the audience for their attention. Then he walked off through the door.

When I arrived at his office in the afternoon, Bourdieu was seeing a journalist about the report of the Collège de France to President Mitterrand on the education system (Bourdieu 1985a). This had been in the news for the past three days. After a few moments of uncertainty, he stepped out, I introduced myself and was ushered into his office. He apologised for the mess. His office was surrounded by large glass windows, and had a desk and comfortable chairs around a coffee table. As we sat around the table, Bourdieu became animated about his work, using his hands and leaning forward for emphasis.

Within the field of French intellectual life the nature and object of intellectual discussions focus on the problem of structural constraints and practical actions. In the contemporary situation, the divisions between competing camps are blurred, and while Bourdieu and some others are important, the field is complex, and includes many writers less well-known in Anglo-Saxon circles – for instance the works of Canguilhem and Bachelard in the philosophy of science. Some commentators have argued that Bourdieu is attempting to be the last of the great sociologists, and that ideas from a variety of sources (Foucault, Derrida, Barthes, Lévi-Strauss and many others) now shape a highly ambiguous field. While they each work within their own specialised areas, their approaches have in common a negation of formalist structuralism and a refusal of reductionist logic. Each of the men and women clearly, work not, in isolation, but within a field in which their ideas and work develop, and they struggle to define a 'recognisable' intellectual space for name and career. For Bourdieu, that space was created through his own concept of the field which leads to his method, and also by his development of the concept of habitus.

In attempting to delineate retrospectively the development of Bourdieu's ideas there are two matters to keep in mind. The first is a point made in Chapter 1, that Bourdieu works and reworks the concepts central to his method in his successive books. A former theoretical situation generates the next, and so to understand the genesis of those concepts requires a specific self-consciousness. Bourdieu comments:

> In the case of social science, to understand the progress of knowledge, supposes a progress in the knowledge of the conditions of knowledge; it therefore requires a stubborn return to the same objects (here, l'Esquisse d'une theorie de la pratique and la Distinction) which offer opportunities to objectify more completely, the objective and subjective relation to the object. And, if it is necessary, we must retrospectively reconstruct in them the stages, because this work tends to make its own traces disappear.
>
> (Bourdieu, Fr. ed. 1980:7)

For Bourdieu the preface to work must always be that it is a 'work in progress'. What he is attempting to communicate would lose some of its meaning if the work were to be disassociated from the practice of the work. Theory must not be permitted to exist in an unreal and neutralised existence which is that of the theoretical 'thesis' or of epistemological discourses.

(ibid.)

The second matter to remember about Bourdieu's ideas and the intellectual field is that nothing is written in isolation. Bourdieu uses the 'tools' around him that he considers to be useful, with a good deal of *'humility but also with discernment'*. Bourdieu comments:

I think that one can only have access to really productive thought by devoting oneself to the means of having a really reproductive thought. To me it looks a bit like what Wittgenstein wanted to say when, in the *Vermischte Bemerkungen*, he said that he had never invented anything and that all that had come to him had been from somebody else, Boltzmann, Herz, Frege, Russell, Kraus, Loos etc. I would be able to produce a similar enumeration which would undoubtedly be much longer

(Honneth et al. 1986:47).

However I have never thought of myself in such terms as being 'a marxist' or a follower of Weber. I usually object to such questions. Primarily because, when one asks these questions . . . it is nearly always with the intention of polemic, to place me in a class, to catalogue me, *kategorisieren*, to accuse me publicly: 'Deep down, Bourdieu is a Durkheimian'. This is pejorative from the point of view of the one who says it: that means: he is not a Marxist, and that is bad. Or even: 'Bourdieu is a Marxist', and that is not right either . . . In any case, the answer to the question of knowing whether an author is a Marxist, a follower of Durkheim or of Weber produces hardly any information about that author.

(Bourdieu, Fr. ed. 1987:39)

RN Everyone raises the question, is he a Marxist or not? . . . I simply say, you have to understand the context. The essay I wrote in *Screen Education* (1978) was written in an extraordinarily unsympathetic environment, because it was dominated by structuralists who were not sympathetic to Sociology. I couldn't be bothered explaining why it was important to know about the audience and so on, but clearly someone ought to have gone ahead and done that. I just said 'OK'. They said that the readers were going to want to know whether or not

Bourdieu was a Marxist. I myself hadn't fully worked this out nor had he spelled it out. He hadn't taken a position until recently. So that's why I said 'If, dear reader, you wish to regard him as a Marxist, fine. But actually he's not.' It's very amusing to find that hesitation reproduced in an academic context. I think it is true to say that these people who pop up and say 'Is he or is he not a Marxist' are really posing a shibboleth. They want easy reassurance with the understanding that this man is friend or foe, which is not the point. But given the way things take shape, you see why people always ask the question. The answer I would now give is that he regards Marx as the most useful contributor to sociology but not a demigod and therefore not infallible, and above all, incomplete.

Bourdieu contends that one of the obstacles to research is the classificatory function of academic and political thinking. Often, this may slow or even inhibit intellectual invention. The classifying labels present, for Bourdieu, an obstacle against what seems for him to be the true relation between texts and past scholars. In fact Bourdieu treats those scholars as 'companions' who can be relied upon in difficult situations. This is particularly important, because it helps to reveal the way in which he works between political and theoretical categories, as well as explaining the very wide use he makes of diverse social thought. This diversity does not prevent him, however, from developing a highly original sociology of his own, though it is a sociology which self-consciously implicates many others.

Bourdieu takes the view that the intellectual field proscribes the authors who are likely to be useful to us (Bourdieu:Actes 1986b). In this field, the philosophical sense can be read like a political sense. Such a relationship between the text, current intellectual work, and the intellectual profession itself is structured by the profession's self-consciousness. Like any profession, it makes 'everything vanish that the majority of aspiring intellectuals feel obliged to do in order to feel themselves intellectuals.' (Bourdieu, Fr. ed. 1987:41). Professional intellectual life can be seen as having two important dimensions, those of display and of technical competence. A willingness to exert too much energy in either direction has negative consequences. Too much technical skill and too little display means rewards from the field are not forthcoming. On the other hand, too much display and too little competence means work is superficial. The self-consciousness which exists within a profession determines the social space of social scientific work, which consequently defines scientific problematics and the possible questions which science allows. Thus authors such as Marx, Durkheim and Weber represent the reference points in our own theoretical space, and of our perception of this space. One problem in sociological research is that at any given moment one must struggle against the inscribed constraints which are embedded within the theoretical space. False breaks, which are frequently being announced in order that stakes may be won in the intellectual field, are the product of a fight for recognition. False divisions are frequently evoked by reference to the canonical texts of Marx, Weber, and so on. One of the most typical examples is the false opposition between the individual and the society (Bourdieu 1985c). As pointed out in Chapter 1, Bourdieu's concept of habitus is aimed at surpassing such divisions and oppositions.

THEORETICAL PRELIMINARIES

This section introduces the theoretical work by examining some of Bourdieu's basic ideas.

CM What would you consider to be the core ideas around which your work has been written?

PB The main thing is that they are not to be conceptualised so much as ideas, on that level, but as a method. The core of my work lies in the method and a way of thinking. To be more precise, my method is a manner of asking questions rather than just ideas. This, I think is a critical point.

(Bourdieu 1985c)

Two central concepts of the method are habitus and the field:

PB If one wants to give a name to what I am doing, you could call it genetic structuralism. One can use this term in two senses. First, I am trying to describe and analyse the genesis of one's person. That is, habitus or the notion of habitus. The interest is in understanding how what we call the 'individual' is moulded by social structure. That is a problem of the internalisation of social structures and the production of habitus as a generative structure. The concept of habitus is a generative structure.

(Bourdieu 1985c)

Habitus was a way for Bourdieu to escape from structuralism which had no 'subject' and from the philosophy of 'the subject' which had no structure. Bourdieu says that from certain phenomenologists (Husserl, Merleau-Ponty and Heidegger), he found a way to analyse the relation between individual practice and the world, that was neither intellectualistic nor mechanistic. Bourdieu returned to the idea of habitus because it was always used as a way to break away from the dualism of Kant, and to reintroduce the permanent dispositions that constitute what is known as moral.[2] The use of habitus further indicates an effort to leave the philosophy of the 'conscience'. With Panofsky's work, Bourdieu recognised in habitus a way to recapture an earlier concept which accounted for scholastic thought (a point explored in greater detail in Chapter 6).

The history of Bourdieu's use of the notion of habitus begins early in his career (Fr. ed. 1967,) in an afterword which he wrote when translating the work of Erwin Panofsky, a professor of the history of art. In his book *Gothic Architecture and Scholasticism* Panofsky demonstrated the correlation between the development of Gothic architecture and the growth of scholastic philosophy. Thus, the style and structure of the architecture provided a parallel to the scholastic definition of order and thought.

When I wrote my first paper about structuralism it was a paper about Panofsky. I was young at that time and did not dare to write or to 'speak' in my own name. I translated Panofsky and in the postscript I wrote about habitus and my ideas but in such a way that it was about Panofsky. It was sort of a very generous interpretation of Panofsky. He used a notion of habitus, but in an ordinary older sense. He takes the notion of habitus from Saint Thomas Aquinas and he used it to understand the connection between the structure of the *summa* of Aquinas and the structure of the space of the Church. Panofsky says that the 'magic' between the two things is the habitus, the scholastic habitus. So that the idea of manner of thought or the permanent mode of thinking was illuminated for me; and I gained a broader sense of the idea at that time.

At that time structuralism was dominant in Paris. I had the vision that structuralists had of individuals. It was very mechanical, this structuralism of Lévi-Strauss and Althusser – especially Althusser. So, with my evolving idea of habitus as a generating principle of individual thought and behaviour, I wanted to show that the individual existed not just as an individual but as a social product and that a generative principle was at work. This idea will remind readers of Chomsky,[3] but you see at that time Chomsky was not translated into French. However once I began reading Chomsky I saw that there were similarities between my use of habitus as a generative principle and Chomsky's use of the 'deep structure' as a generative principle. In my view, although it's very pretentious to say this, it was a sort of simultaneous invention.

(Bourdieu 1985c)

Bourdieu's concern was to develop a method which could show active intention and inventiveness in practice; to recall the creative, active, generative capacity in individual social life and to demonstrate that the subject of practice was not as a transcendental subject in the idealist tradition. In order to apprehend and to reintroduce the practice of the individual as well as the capacity for individual invention and improvisation, Bourdieu states:

At the risk of being seen on the side of the most common forms of thought, I would like to recall the 'primauté de la raison pratique' ('primacy of practical reason'), of which Fichte spoke, and to explain the specific categories of that reason (what I have tried to do in *Le sens pratique*). In order to advance my thinking, rather than reflecting on it, I have been greatly aided by the famous Theses on Feuerbach, 'the principal defect of all previous materialisms, including the one of Feuerbach, lies in the fact that the object is solely conceived under the form of the object of perception, not as a human activity or practice.' It has to do with recapturing in idealism the 'active side' of practical knowledge from which the materialistic tradition had separated, especially with the theory of 'reflection'.

(Bourdieu, Fr. ed. 1987:23–4)

Bourdieu's development of the concept of habitus was an attempt to create social agents as individuals who construct the world around them. This process of construction, however, is completed through a system of acquired schemes. Such schemes function as categories of perception and appreciation, so that they act in a practical sense by organising action as well as classification.

The second aspect of Bourdieu's method is:

what I call field. In English it's an ambiguous word because it is often understood as a 'domain'. The closest conceptualisation that this has in English is Kurt Lewin's field theory, although I think that the way I use 'field' is still very different. To give you an idea, one can imagine society as a sort of system of fields, so you must think in terms of a system and relationships. This system of fields (within the social space) can almost be imagined, for simplicity, as a planetary system, because the social space is really an integral field. Each field has its own structure and field of forces, and is set within a larger field which also has its own forces, structures and so on. As it develops, it is weaving a larger field.

One of my lectures at the Collège is about the relations between habitus and field, and how action (practice) is a product of the relationship between habitus (which is a product of history) and field, which is also a product of history, and at the same time, a product of the field of forces. In a field, there are stakes. There are forces, and there are people who have a lot of capital and others who do not. Capital is a concentration of force, a specific force, which operates in the field. In the intellectual field, you must have a special, specific capital: authority, prestige and so on. These are things you cannot buy but are often conferred by economic capital in certain fields. The field is a field of forces but at the same time it is a field in which people fight to change the structure. For instance they see the field, they have opinions, they may say, 'He's famous, but he does not deserve it', and so the field of forces is at the same time the field of struggle.

Now these are the main attributes of habitus and field. However I would like to stress that in every different case, you must study how the situation works. So my ideas are not a general theory but a method. For instance, if I went to your country, I think that I might understand many things beforehand, because I am sure these are very general mechanisms which I might understand immediately. However, I must carefully observe the situation to weigh the different aspects of my method. So, what I would like readers to understand is that it's a very general manner of thinking while at the same time it obliges one to study each case . . . .

(Bourdieu 1985c)[4]

THE EARLY YEARS: ACADEMIC STUDY AND
INFLUENCES BEFORE ALGERIA

Bourdieu began his early studies at the Teachers College (the Ecole normale supérieure, Rue d'Ulm) during the early 1950s. His colleagues included such notables of the French intellectual field as Derrida, Pariente and Le Roy-Ladurie. During that time phenomenology in its existentialist form, was at its summit. In 1949 he read Sartre *L'Etre et le néant* and then went on to read Merleau-Ponty and Husserl (especially *Erfahrung und Urteil*). Bourdieu included Marx in his reading and was particularly interested in *Theses on Feuerbach*. In general, the approach that the university took was one of extreme conservatism and authoritarianism. Students were expected to read the classics, take their exams and to write a thesis. Bourdieu and others like him were forced to look outside of the ordinary courses, and to seek teachers who would help them 'to go a little beyond reading the classical authors and to give meaning to the philosophy' (Bourdieu, Fr. ed. 1987:14).

Bourdieu was interested in the history of science, philosophy and epistemology, and studied the history of science as well as mathematics. He was especially influenced by Canguilhem and Bachelard. These ideas were important for Bourdieu's studies, because they indicated the possibility of a new view and a new way to realise the role of the philosopher in intellectual life.

While some existentialist philosophy was important to Bourdieu's study (particularly Heidegger's *Sein und Zeit* (Being and Time) and Husserl's *Ideen II* (Ideas II)), he found what he calls the 'existentialistic mood' offensive to his taste for scientific rigour and his political consciousness (what he calls his social feeling). Bourdieu's decision not to write a thesis while at Teachers College is another aspect of the uncomfortable position that he felt himself to be in *vis-à-vis* the conservative administration.

THE ALGERIAN WORK: BECOMING AN
ETHNOGRAPHER AND SOCIOLOGIST

Like many of his generation, Bourdieu was conscripted to serve in the French Army in Algeria. While there, he became an ethnologist, more or less reluctantly. In the early 1960s, the reputation of Lévi-

Strauss contributed to the scientific reputation that ethnography was gaining in the intellectual field. Bourdieu at this time still viewed himself as a philosopher, and was captivated by what he defines as the scientific rigour of science and philosophical research. Before he went to Algeria, he had researched the question of the temporary structures of emotional experience. However,

> When I went to Algeria I did an 'apprentissage sur le tas', an apprentice who learns by doing.
>
> (Bourdieu 1985c)

After two years of soldiering, during which research was not possible, Bourdieu decided to write a book that would intellectually make the reality of that country known and understood. Bourdieu comments:

> I came to Algeria when I was in the army. After two arduous years during which there was no possibility of doing research I could do some work again. I began to write a book with the intention of high-lighting the plight of the Algerian people and, also that of the French settlers whose situation was no less dramatic, whatever else had to be said about their racism, etc. I was appalled by the gap between the view of French intellectuals about this war and how it should be brought to an end, and my own experiences; the army, the embittered 'pieds noirs', as well as the military coups, insurrections by the colonisers, the inevitable recourse to de Gaulle, etc. I did of course agree with the actions of some intellectuals – I am thinking here of Sartre, Jeanson, Vidal-Naquet – against torture and for peace, and I tried to contribute in my own way. I was however concerned about the associated utopianism since in my view it was not at all helpful, even for an independent Algeria, to feed a mythical conception of Algerian society. Here again I found myself between camps as far as intellectual life was concerned.
>
> (Honneth et al. 1985:38).

Of Bourdieu's first Algerian work Nice mentions the following:

> Bourdieu wrote some articles that have never really been translated – more journalistic things. He argues with Franz Fanon. He's unable to subscribe to the romantic idea of Third World revolution, precisely because he is too aware of the conditions for what

he calls a rational project, and he is rewriting those ideas in *Algeria 1960*.

(Nice 1985)

I wanted to do something useful and then return to philosophy. Maybe I wanted to be useful in order to overcome my guilty conscience about being merely a participant observer in this appalling war. Something similar happened to me at the Ecole normale: I just did not feel right within myself. It was only much later that I found in Nizan, and in Sartre's brilliant foreword to *Aden Arabie*, in the minutest detail what I had felt in this 'school'. After my agrégation I could have stayed a further year at the Ecole but decided instead to enter teaching right away. I did not go to Aden, but to a provincial town. I wanted to do something useful and earn a living. As far as the education system was concerned I was half 'in' – I had its blessing and recognition and was shaped by its ideals, and half 'out' without knowing why. I was deeply attached to it and rebelled against it just as much . . . I could not be content with reading left wing newspapers or signing petitions; I had to do something concrete as a scientist . . . .

(Honneth et al. 1985:39)

After this period Bourdieu returned to philosophy and wrote the book *Sociologie de l'Algérie* (in the *Que sais-je?* series), which was expanded in English as *The Algerians* (Bourdieu, 1962), but which had no effect on the field. He comments that such a book, and its translation was a 'bad strategy' for an outsider. In a sense, the book was written against the popularity of utopian revolutionary writing among Algerian intellectuals; Bourdieu felt that such work could be fatal for their future.

I wanted to understand the specificity of the Algerian revolution by clarifying the difference between proletariat and sub-proletariat. To my mind this had never been clearly determined. I also wanted to analyse the economic and social conditions in which the appearance of economic calculation occurred, in matters of economy and also of fertility, etc. Also, through my analyses of the temporal consciousness, I wanted to understand what the conditions were for the acquisition of the 'capitalistic' economic habitus that was formed among the people in the pre-capitalistic cosmos. I have tried to show that the principle of this difference is situated at the level of the economical conditions of possibility, (having to do with dispositions and strategy), and of the directions of rational expectation, of which the revolutionary aspirations are a dimension.[5] I wanted to make a sociology of the forms of the experiences of the future, that allows us to understand the different forms of revolutionary consciousness. The magical millenarianism of the sub-proletariat, or the more realistic revolutionary purpose of the proletariat which, paradoxically, becomes apparent among those who are wrenched out of insecurity and total inability, and who have minimal economic security and the necessary social status to produce an organised representation of the future.

(Honneth et al. 1985:148)

During this period I read all the texts of Marx again . . . and even Lenin's study of Russia. I also worked on the Marxist idea of relative autonomy in relation to the investigations that I began on the artistic field (a small book, *Marx, Proudhon, Picasso*, written in French between the two wars by a German immigrant by the name of Marx was very useful to me). All of that was before the strong turn towards structural Marxism . . . . At the time the books of Fanon, notably *The Wretched of the Earth*, were in fashion and it seemed to me that they could be both wrong and dangerous.

(Bourdieu, Fr. ed. 1987:17)

In his interview with me, he returned to his experiences as a young anthropologist in Algeria:

In one sense, in a personal sense, *Algeria 1960* is my favourite book. In my lecture this morning I said that academic people don't have biographies, they have careers. Well, I have a little biographical story about when I was in Algeria. Initially I was there as a soldier, sent by the French government to help with a pacification programme against the revolutionaries. While I was there I began to be interested in Algerian culture. When my tour with the army was completed, I stayed in Algeria to become an anthropologist, even though I was conducting my research during the war. So, I was in my car, driving along roads that had burned-out cars all along the sides, looking for a particular group of people which I wanted to study. And because it was such a personal experience, that research is very important to me. I was so very happy in the field that I wasn't conscious of the danger – now I don't think that I would do it, but then I was not afraid. And the people were really wonderful in this revolutionary situation. It's a naive thing to say and I can't explain it in scientific terms, but I feel very strongly that people in this situation are better. They are more generous and oh, it's wonderful! I was protected only because people liked me. One time − −, my research assistant (who is still with me), and I went to a region where the French army did not go, because it was completely occupied by the liberation army. But we wanted to go there because it was so interesting. One day, we asked a man about these people and he told us that they were very nice. We were three at the time − myself and two Algerian students of mine. Well, we were walking and walking, it was drawn out like a Western gun fight. There was a huge group of people sitting under the olive trees and they had machine guns under their burnous (dress). Of course, we were feeling tense because of the guns and because some of the young men took drugs like cannabis or hashish, and they seemed tense and angry too. Then someone yelled out 'What are you doing here?' (*laughs*). Well, I gave him a good answer and said that the French army was very, very far away: 'You may do what you want. Come and sit down', someone said. It was wonderful and later when we left, the people gave us gifts − even during the war. So, in that sense the Algerian work was something very important. But I think that the work itself is not so good, although the part about time and its structure is good, because it works for other areas. But in general I think that as a researcher I was too involved personally and politically and so perhaps it's a little naive.

(Bourdieu 1985c)

When Bourdieu returned from Algeria in 1960 he followed the seminars of Lévi-Strauss at the Collège de France and worked as an assistant to Raymond Aron. Because Lévi-Strauss had gained prominence at that time, social science was being established as a respectable and even dominant discipline. While Bourdieu has never considered himself to be a structuralist,

I have resisted with all my power, the fashionable forms of structuralism and was not inclined to be indulgent to the mechanical transpositions of Saussure or Jakobson to anthropology . . .

(Bourdieu, Fr. ed. 1987:16)

he was keen to bring the method of structural or relational thought into play in sociology.

After I came back here I was a student of Lévi-Strauss – I think it was very important because he made old things new. For example many things that you find in Lévi-Strauss you can find in Durkheim, and Mauss. In hindsight, it's easy to say that all of Lévi-Strauss has already been said, but it's not true. At that time they were invisible. It was impossible to see, so he made them new. Lévi-Strauss made these ideas understandable and accessible, for example, in the study of ritual. I could see that I was in opposition to Lévi-Strauss vis-à-vis his objectivism.[6] But at the same time the best things I did came from Lévi-Strauss. You know, this kind of sensitivity to objective structures and so on . . . .

CM Have you returned to Algeria?

PB Yes, I have returned often and I have many students working with me here. Algeria is a wonderful country and I have personal and political reasons for saying that.

CM I wondered how you integrated your life as a professor with the political aspect of your work.

PB I feel very strongly that good social science is important politically. My conviction is that, especially in countries like Algeria in which you have a huge sub-proletariat, a lumpen proletariat, a little petite bourgeoisie, half taught . . . , a society which tends to mix everything up, mystical vision, and so on, social science is a very important political instrument – so we had a sort of plan of development in Algeria and we wanted to help Algeria to develop a strong sociology. It was important because Algeria is seen as the 'mother' of so many Third World countries.

But the problem was that in the situation after the war, all the good people were put into the government. They became ministers and ambassadors – all my best students disappeared. Well, there are five very good sociologists working on problems of educational sociology and problems of bilingualism which is extremely important, because the main debate in Algeria and in many Middle Eastern countries is between the people who speak French and the people who speak Arabic. There is a fight in the ruling class between people who studied in France and who speak French, and people who studied in Arabic-speaking countries, for example in Egypt, and who speak Arabic. The French-speaking people are, in social terms, higher, and in political terms more *progressistes* (progressivist) which implies internationalism, and so on . . . . Arabic-speaking people come from the lower strata, but at the same time speaking Arabic they are all very ambitious and traditionalist in politics. It is a very interesting problem in which social conflicts are related to cultural capital; that is language as a cultural capital.

(Bourdieu 1985c)

DEFINING A POSITION

Bourdieu's serious concern with methodology, particularly with respect to the question of positions in the field, and the struggle for such positions, began with his essay on honour[7] and was followed by a gradual tendency to work in opposition to the structuralist position. While interested in solving properly anthropological problems, those problems were, by and large, presented to him through the structuralist approach. In writing the *Esquisse d'une théorie de la pratique* he developed the view that the structuralist approach to marriage rules could not account for the statistical data. The data demonstrated that it was not possible to integrate the facts into a system of the constituent oppositions of ritual logic.

It took me a very long time to really break away from some of the fundamental presuppositions of structuralism (which I made to work simultaneously in sociology, by considering the social world as the space of objective relations, transcendent with respect to agents and irreducible to interactions between individuals). I had to discover the untenable objectivistic presuppositions. I did this by returning to familiar observation areas, on the one hand the Béarnais society from which I originated, and on the other hand the university world, like the privilege of the observer with respect to the unconscious naivety of the subject; which are embedded in the structuralistic approach. And subsequently I think that it was necessary that I left ethnology as a social world when becoming a sociologist, so that certain unthinkable problematics become possible. So I do not simply talk about my life in these two settings: I deliver a contribution to the sociology of science. Belonging to a professional group demands an effort of censorship,

which goes far beyond institutional or personal constraints: there
are questions that one does not ask and that one cannot ask. That
is what Wittgenstein indicates when he recalls that radical doubt
is so deeply identified with the philosophic attitude, that a well-
educated philosopher would not even dream of doubting this
doubt.[8]

(Bourdieu, Fr. ed. 1987:18)

One of Bourdieu's main preoccupations in his writing at this time
was the attempt to reintroduce the agents that Lévi-Strauss and
Althusser had tended to abolish. In his work on marriage patterns
and the struggle for positions of honour, the action of the agents in
using the appropriate or available strategies to cement their position
within the field, became more and more obvious. Individual action
was not a matter of the simple obedience to a rule or to quasi-
mechanical laws but to engage the principles of generative habitus.

In the most complex systems of matrimonial exchanges, or ritual
practices, one finds the principles of generative structuralism or
habitus to be engaged. Habitus can be thought of in an analogous
way to the generative grammar of Chomsky, and can be contrasted
with those dispositions which are acquired through one's experience
as to time and place. This *sens du jeu* or 'feel for the game' is what
allows habitus to generate an infinity of strategies which are adapted
to an endless number of possible situations. In view of this, Bourdieu
has substituted matrimonial strategies for what in structuralist terms
would be called the 'rules of relationships'. Bourdieu came to his
original insight, and also moved away from structuralism (from 'rule'
to 'strategy'; see 1986b) as a consequence of his observations in
Béarn, which were reinforced by his further work in Algeria. Rules
were broken when the shape of the 'game' changed through the
inclusion of new forms of capital. Exceptions to the rules could only
be explained by a change in theoretical approach away from rules
to the idea of strategy.

In rethinking marriage strategies, Bourdieu by inclination and by
the necessity implicit in his method, denied the previously acceptable
'bird's-eye-view' of the anthropologist that allowed the 'professional'
to speak about rules, maps and scientific analysis in relation to
indigenous practices. Anthropology, Bourdieu says, makes plans
which are an inevitable consequence of the objectivism of the anthropological task. However his challenge to anthropologists and generally to the structuralist school was the relation of agents to the social

world. It was necessary for Bourdieu to develop a theory of the non-theoretical, partial, commonplace practice in the social world. The ideas which developed out of these consecutive works, the *Esquisse*, *Outline of a Theory of Practice* and *Le sens pratique*, focused on a theory of habitus, strategies and positions as well as on a consideration of the relationship of the theoretical world to common experience. It is clear, then, that his developing theory and the necessary method to engage his ideas put Bourdieu in a position of having to part company with structuralist logic, and the detached position of the 'scientist' at that time. Also, because Bourdieu felt a personal closeness between himself and French peasants, the artifice of general theories to account for Kabyle peasants did not 'feel' true. Along with his scientific baggage, Bourdieu carried with him from childhood an acceptance of a kind of intellectual practice which collided with the way mainstream sociology was practised.

Given the fact that from his early days in school Bourdieu was always outside of the ruling educational élite (both in a structural and emotional sense), there was a tension in his relationship to the intellectual world which still exists today. For him there was no easy and 'natural' acceptance of academic life.

Of the English translation of this work and the development of Bourdieu's ideas Nice says:

> *Outline of a Theory of Practice* had a very tortuous publishing history, because I took a long time to translate it. I wasn't entirely satisfied and he, in the meanwhile, expanded the text by adding more and more pieces and by the time we submitted it to the publisher they said 'What is this?' When he cut it, he further rewrote it and the translation was actually part of the process of moving beyond the French 'Outline' to a new version which he then subsequently published as *Le sens pratique*, which is supposed to be translated by the end of next year. In the rewriting, he started rethinking some aspects of the book and exploring new areas; those of the relationship between thought and consciousness, and reality and language.
>
> (Nice 1985)

The theoretical intentions in Bourdieu's work, which are seen in the concepts of strategy and habitus, were present in a semi-explicit form from the very beginning of his work.

Bourdieu's early position in the intellectual field is connected to his interest in education, and its impact on the lives of students (which is discussed in Chapter 4), as well as his later study of French intellectuals and their positions in the field of Parisian intellectual life (see Chapter 8). Bourdieu has remarked that his vision of the culture and system of education owed much to the position that he occupied in the university and to the early course along which he was guided to the university. In fact, Bourdieu mentioned that part of the conditions which contributed to the development of his thinking was a kind of auto-analysis; his university training was due to his success (as a child) in the educational system, and not to a privileged position of class.

In an early paper (1967) titled 'Systems of schooling and systems of thought', Bourdieu tried to demonstrate how mental structures in literate societies were inculcated by the school system, and that the organisational divisions of schools were the principal forms of classification. The task was not a parallel to a Durkheimian 'sociology of the structures of the mind', because the problems of language and classification are forms of domination.[9] Bourdieu states:

> the sociology of knowledge (*connaissance*) is inseparable from a sociology of recognition (*reconnaissance*) and of the failure to recognise (*méconnaissance*) – in other words, symbolic domination (in reality, this is true even in the less differentiated societies like Kabyle society); the classifying structures that organise the whole vision of the world in the final analysis come down to the division of work between the sexes. The fact of asking traditional ethnological questions about our societies, and of pulling down the traditional barrier between ethnology and sociology was already a political act . . . . The classifying schemes which may be fundamental oppositions of thought such as male/female, right/left, east/west, (and also theory/practice), are also political categories. The critical theory of culture leads very naturally to a political theory.
>
> (Bourdieu, Fr. ed. 1987:35–6)

The emphasis in Bourdieu's work, away from the universal rules of structuralism and the norms of Anglo-American sociology, is a key to the implicit historicism in the conceptions of habitus and field. Rather than deducing 'the universal', Bourdieu asks, 'who is interested in the universal?' (or who has a stake in certain named universals) and 'what are the social conditions which must be fulfilled so that certain agents are interested in the universal?' (This is particularly so in Bourdieu's work on the artistic or scientific field and in *Distinction*). For him, it is most valuable to accept the fact that reason is a product of history. This is not to say that reason is confined to history but that there are historical conditions for the appearance of the social forms of communication which makes the production of trust possible. It is truth and the legitimacy to the right to name that is at stake in struggles in every field.

> To say that there are social conditions of the production of the truth, is to say that there is a politics of truth, a ceaseless action to defend and improve the functioning of the social worlds where the rational principles are active and where truth is developed.
>
> (Bourdieu, Fr. ed. 1987:44).

In *Homo Academicus*, Bourdieu claimed to have 'objectified' the university even though he is part of that world. Such a claim in a world in which claims are proved to be 'universals', exposed Bourdieu to counter-claims about the legitimacy of his attempt. In Chapter 7 this argument is examined in detail, particularly as it relates to language.

Bourdieu argues that what he discovered is that one has an absolute interest in the universe of which one is part, and that the question of distance and the 'divine' and detached intention of the sociologist is a 'formidable principle of error'. Knowing that he himself invests part of himself in his research, and that this is connected to his history, allows him to be aware of the limits of his version. This is a task which (in *Outline of a Theory of Practice*, 1977) he urges all social scientists to take up, and one in which he confronts himself in *Homo Academicus* (1988) and in his inaugural lecture – see Chapter 8. For Bourdieu, the reflexivity necessary to develop one's research is not the *point* of research and can only be successful to a degree. To tear oneself free from the 'relative', one of the most important instruments is the analysis of knowledge and the way knowledge and 'points of view' are defined by history.

DISTINCTION[10]

Like his work on the intellectual field, Bourdieu's work in *Distinction* (1984) is inspired by the concern to focus on the genesis of dispositions and individual history and in this sense, he is redeveloping old themes. The direction is away from the ideological and anti-genetic focus of structuralism. In *Distinction*, the study of taste and cultural consumption is undertaken by bringing together 'culture' in the normative sense and 'culture' in the anthropological sense, and demonstrates that cultural needs and practices are the product of history, habitus and the field. In the final chapter, Bourdieu tries to show how 'classes' in the ordinary sense of the term, are the objectified product of the class struggle, at a particular moment in history.

While Nice thinks that *Distinction* is a major work, there is a general criticism to be made regarding the use of empirical data. He says:

RN The major political science journal in France devoted half of a whole issue to *La Distinction* when it came out in 1980 or 1981. Most of the articles said 'wasn't it wonderful'. One or two were more critical and one looked at his use of statistics and demonstrated that his method is capable of proving anything. And that all this marshalling of data is essentially a bluff. The empirical stuff is neither here nor there – it's interesting that the ideas convince you by their theoretical self-evidence once you've grasped them.

CM He seems, in the preface to *Distinction* to very much want to show that his methodology is sound – so obviously he must think of that as a critical point.

RN It's rather more than a critical point, it's actually enacting the way he thinks that all social science needs to be conducted – in other words a sort of crab-wise movement or something that is simultaneously theoretical and empirical. It's the original theory that seeks the data and the data then calls for revision of the theory. In a number of his prefaces, he says that that is what it's all about. In the closing passages of *Distinction* there are more reflections on the method.

(Nice 1985)

The problem of symbolic structures and their connection to fundamental aspects of social (ideological and material) reality is one which is not solved either in *Distinction* nor as yet in his present work.

But, for a long time Bourdieu has been struggling with this problem of the relation between symbolic structures and social structures. This discussion dominated arguments between structuralists and Marxists during the 1960s. Clearly he is not one to argue that symbolic structures create social structures, but he would argue that the 'symbolic' is much more than simply an instrument of knowledge. Rather, symbolic structures must be understood like principles of vision and division, which allow us not only to create a reality, but to believe in that reality, even before it may exist. Within certain limits, symbolic structures have an extraordinary and, Bourdieu would argue underestimated, power of constitution. Such a power is realised in philosophy as well as in political theory.

CM Do you make the connection between the economy and culture and so on?

PB Asking the question in this manner is something that I have abandoned. In the sixties I had this in mind; that is, the main question was, How does the symbolic structure articulate with the economic structure? Now, in my view, this is a survival of a Marxist vision of the social structure – much like Althusser's conception of society. Using the concept of field is a way of getting into and around this problem, because there are fields and strategies and people 'play' different games. These games (to use an easy expression) are relatively autonomous. At the same time, there are homologies between different games, and I think that there are general principles to the functioning of these games.

(Bourdieu 1985c)

The fundamental problem of the relationship between symbolic structures and social structure are further explored in Bourdieu's new work. As of 1989 Bourdieu is engaged in at least three new pieces of research. As well as publishing in *Actes*, he has completed a long-term study of the field of higher education and the state in France. In *La Noblesse d'Etat* (1989) Bourdieu offers a theory of the state through a study of the nobility that comprise it. He is also engaged in a study of how taste and style are important in housing preferences, and a third study which examines the work of Flaubert and Manet in relation to the genesis of the intellectual field (Bourdieu 1988b). In each of these studies there are common themes which characterise Bourdieu's overall project. First, there is the continued use of statistical and ethnographic material, which he blends together in his own unique way. Secondly, there is the continued general interest in how symbolic power articulates with objective structures in order to create the social space of specific fields. (These twin ideas are more thoroughly canvassed in Chapter 1. Bourdieu's new work is further discussed in the concluding chapter of this volume.)

ON REFLECTION

In this section I was concerned to explore Bourdieu's own intellectual practice, and the work of his group.

CM Some people have written that your method is the new paradigm for French sociology. Your main books are now all being translated into English, and more of your work is now quoted in the English-speaking academic world. After some twenty years as a sociologist you now have a large research group, you are the Professor of Sociology at the Collège de France, and are requested to write reports for President Mitterrand. What do you think about your career? Are you pleased or surprised that you have been so successful?

PB Well, I don't think like that (*laughter*)! I mean my vision is very different. I see the research group as a very little group, in comparison with others. Also, the people who work with me are very modest. There are some of us who think that it is a strength of the group that they work so much, and that they are also modest. They will accept and do things that arrogant people would not do and that is very important. There is a theory about the importance of 'modesty' in a paper by David Ben-David and Randall Collins. It looks at the main inventions in the social sciences during the 19th century. They say that very often, the important inventions were by people who originally were trained in prestigious disciplines like physics, and who, for some reason or other were dropped and had to take-up a 'lower' discipline like psychology, for example. Very often these people were Jews, like Freud, and they had a strong commitment to their work and are also very modest. They are willing to do work that others despise and they create something from it. So we had masters like Freud, or even Durkheim who, at the time when France was a culture of literature, wrote about ritual.[11]

I believe that I have always been strongly motivated in my choices by resistance to the phenomena of fashion. For instance at the time that I had read and taught Saussure from 1959 to 1960, I was exasperated by the fashionable use of Saussure's work by the structuralists. Similarly, many of the strategies in my papers are inspired by the concern to refuse the great totalising thought which is ordinarily identified with philosophy. Thus, for instance, I have always maintained a sufficiently ambivalent relationship with the Frankfurt School: the affinities are evident, but nevertheless, I felt a certain nervousness in the face of the 'fashionable' side of that holistic criticism which kept all the features of the great aristocratic theory no doubt true because of the concern not to get entangled in the tricks of empirical research. It's the same with regard to the followers of Althusser, and to his interventions which are at the same time simplistic, and peremptory. I wanted to try and ask big questions about restricted objects, which were therefore capable of being analysed empirically.

(Bourdieu 1985c)

The problem of translating Bourdieu's work was taken up by Nice in his interview. About meeting Bourdieu and taking on the job of translation Nice says:

I floated around various institutions in Paris and occasionally went to Barthes' seminars and I went to listen to Foucault. I wasn't actually satisfied. Structuralism didn't correspond to my expectations, and then I happened to hear of Bourdieu and he turned to me as another possible translator, because he had been dissatisfied with his previous translations. The reason was that he's almost impossible to translate anyway – no one can do it well – perhaps he sensed that no one was doing it well. But also (others) weren't very interested in doing it well. It was just another job of work for them. The difference with me was that though I thought that it was not easy to translate, I was willing to do my best because I found it very interesting. It virtually went to the heart of questions that had always been problematic for me. He showed me the limitations of structuralism. There are passages in *Outline of a Theory of Practice* which perfectly dismantled the great confidence trick worked by – well, by lots of people and it starts with Lévi-Strauss, the whole unjustified extrapolation of Saussure, and so on.

(Nice 1985)

Bourdieu's argument is that there are several problems related to meaning between English and French. For example, when he visited the United States some years ago, discussing his ideas of repro-duction, he was constantly being confused with the American writers Bowles and Gintis (Bowles and Gintis, 1976). It is crucial to an understanding of Bourdieu's work that Anglophone academics con-ceive of his work more broadly to include his Algerian work on habitus and to connect that analysis to education and class (see Chapter 4 of this volume where the point is taken up in detail). In some ways the work of Bourdieu's group is important because it challenges the dominant sociologies in the Anglo-American world.[12] The work in fact, is involved in a struggle for legitimacy and domin-ation in sociology, since the dominant positions are still held largely outside France. This conceals several other problems involving politi-cal rivalries within academia, as well as a widespread ignorance outside France of the many important figures who shape the field of French sociology, philosophy, linguistics and history.

Bourdieu's position in relation to sociology in particular and to the intellectual field in general has been one in which he is seen much as an outsider, as one whose career is firmly embedded within the field. His political convictions on the use and misuse of power and personal 'unease' with the status of authority is an aspect of his work which has consistently been in evidence since his days at Teachers College. At that time Bourdieu decided not to write a thesis; the decision was, in part, politically motivated in that he saw his decision as a kind of revolt against the misuse of academic power and a refusal to participate in the traditional career pattern of the educational elite in France.

I can remember clearly an incident during my preparation for the *Agrégation* in Philosophy. I attended, with other *Normaliens*, a lecture by Georges Davy, the last survivor of the Durkheim school, who was then president of the panel. At the beginning of the year he distributed seminar topics and anyone who wanted to be highly regarded was interested in getting one. A female student applied and was asked: 'Mademoiselle, do you fulfill the prerequisites?' – 'Which ones, monsieur le President?' – 'Are you, or have you been a *sèvrienne*' (member of the Ecole Normale Supérieure de Sèvre) – 'Non, Monsieur le President' – 'In this case I can't give you an exposé.' I was appalled and tried to get the other Normaliens to join in a boycott of the seminars; they considered me too 'excessive' – as usual. I could never bear it when professors misused their authority to exercise academic power . . . . There was, no doubt, a political aspect to this indignation. I sensed a discrepancy between professorial statements with their universalistic claims and opposition to external powers, and the toleration of academic misuse of power.

(Honneth et al. 1985:37)

Bourdieu appears to have never stopped resisting the use of the statutory authority of the Professor as an intellectual authority. Such resistance is part of his rebellion against *homo academicus* even today.

CM Can you tell me something of Bourdieu's politics? For instance is he a socialist?

RN Socialist, no. Well, if that means supporter of the French Socialist Party, as it is now, no. He situates himself outside conventional politics. Clearly his heart does warm to certain syndicalist or cooperative ventures in France. When there are cases of workers' self-organisation for self-defence or anything, he is sympathetic, and he has taken a stand on certain anti-racist questions.

CM But he's not very political in his everyday life?

RN Absolutely not. He used to make it a rule never to sign petitions, . . . precisely because that world in which people sign petitions was the object of his study. I mean he raises in very acute form the question of where intellectuals situate themselves, and he doesn't really have an answer to that. But at least he does think about the question. Well, there is a sense in which he has always thought about it. I can't say exactly where it is in the *Outline* but in the *Esquisse* the actual theoretical part starts by posing the question of the relationship of theory to practice. It's somewhere in the *Outline* and also in the very opening paragraphs of *Distinction*, in a way.

(Nice 1985)

While Bourdieu is not the sort of political actor who is in evidence in street demonstrations, or in open political struggles, or a signatory to every petition, his work has never been anything other than deeply political. The volumes of *Actes* which have been devoted to political action are numerous, and many can be seen as nothing other than political interventions (see numbers 36/37, 38 in 1981; 41 in 1982; 56 in 1985; and 61 in 1986). One of the important aspects of Bourdieu's project is his attempt to destroy the distance between science and politics, that is, to seek to create a methodological balance between what is known as the 'detached observer' and the 'completely involved' bias. It is his feeling that while from the left science may be defined as bourgeois, and from the right the politics of the left are seen as hopelessly biased, there is methodological middle ground which, while more scientific, also has more political effect. Thus, for instance, the work produced in *Actes* sought to maximise political effect by being especially scientific. The higher the scientific profits, the greater the political effect.

The last question that I asked Bourdieu to comment on, in my interview with him in 1985, was directed towards self-reflection. I wanted to know what he felt his major contribution would be to the sociology of France. His answer revolved around the report that he and others at the Collège de France had given to President Mitterrand in March 1985.[13] The report argued that the evaluation of teachers should not be based solely on their educational degrees, but on the work that they produced in the schools. Bourdieu felt that the greatest contribution schools could offer was to do *less* of what they do so well now, i.e. the reproduction of class differences. The position that Bourdieu took in the report was one in which he used his position of authority to describe and sometimes denounce the structure of authority and positions of authority. This form of reflexivity is everywhere in his work, especially in the first lecture he gave at the Collège (Fr. ed. 1982a; 1982b). In the interview he commented:

I think my optimism is that there is some little power of ideas.

Before I held the conviction that said 'don't believe it, don't believe in the power of ideas'. But now, I say that under some structural and political conditions, there is some power to ideas. So, we must use it. If not, the power structure is so terrible and so complete.

(Bourdieu 1985c)

Nothing stays the same, however. A problem of doing life histories is that what is constructed in a linear, rational fashion often belies the underlying confusion of a lived biography; so too interviewing a scholar over several years reflects changes and ambiguities. In September 1986 I was again in Paris. In October one could say that the mood in Paris at least in sociological circles, appeared despondent, both in the political sense of a sadness at the failures of the Mitterrand government, and in the sociological sense as a reaction to a dearth of new ideas. Bourdieu could not help but be affected by this mood. There was no action taken with regard to Bourdieu's *Report on Education* due in large part to bureaucratic stubbornness; hardly a problem unique to France. Bourdieu's response was to dig back into his sources, his '*compagnons*', to discover new strategies and perhaps provide innovations for future struggles. However, by early December the mood was buoyant, due to the student demonstrations for educational reform and against Chirac's proposed changes to university admissions. At this time Bourdieu was very much in evidence, as his interview with *Libération* (4 December 1986) was read and discussed across faculties and schools. The text was published by certain unions (notably the CFDT) and even published in an Italian newspaper. This type of political activity is the model of Bourdieu's political intervention, as was previously evidenced by the reaction that he and his research group took against the Polish government's actions toward the Solidarity movement. This latest youth movement, Bourdieu said, gave everyone hope but one worry was that it could be used by the right as an excuse for a fascist intervention. As of May 1987, the *Report on Education* was again a central point of discussion for government ministers. In May 1989 Bourdieu had completed a further report as convenor of a committee to change the secondary school programme.[14] It is probably not too much to say, that as he develops his own intellectual project he is changing some of the understandings social science has of the world, and inevitably therefore, some of the understandings the world has of itself.

NOTES

1. These interviews were conducted over two years, amounting to some ten hours in French, English and Spanish, with English predominating.
2. Here Bourdieu refers to the use of habitus by Hegel, Husserl, Weber, Durkheim and Mauss.
3. Readers interested in the parallels to Chomsky's work may find the section in *Outline of a Theory of Practice* called 'The Objective Limits of Objectivism' interesting reading (Bourdieu 1977:1–30).
4. This contrasts strongly with reductionist criticisms made by education writers. See Chapter 4 for further comment.
5. In *Algeria 1960* one of Bourdieu's main points is to show the connection between class, temporality and expectations. In the preface he writes:

> 'The relation to a future objectively inscribed in the material conditions of existence contains the basis of the distinction between the sub-proletariat and the proletariat – between the uprooted, demoralised masses' disposition to revolt and the revolutionary dispositions of organised workers who have sufficient control over their present to undertake to reappropriate the future.' (Bourdieu 1979: viii).

6. 'I believe that I was guided by a kind of theoretical feeling, but also and maybe above all by the rather deep-seated refusal of the ethical posture which implicated the structuralistic anthropology. This means, the noble and distant relation which was established between the scientist and his object, as being simple lay persons. This led me to favour the theory of practice, which is explicit among the followers of Althusser who transform the agent to a simple "support" (Träger) of the structure (the idea of the unconscious fulfilled the same function with Lévi-Strauss). Thus, I stubbornly keep on asking the informants the question of why, by breaking away from Lévi-Strauss's discourse about the indigenous "rationalisations" which are totally incapable of clarifying the anthropological task, related to the real causes or the real reasons of the practices. This is what compelled me to do research, about marriages for instance.' (Bourdieu, Fr. ed. 1987:31–2.)
7. See 'The Sentiment of Honour in Kabyle Society'. This particular essay was included in the English translation of *Algeria 1960* (Bourdieu 1979) and is also available in English in J. Peristiany (1965).
8. 'Wittgenstein is undoubtedly the philosopher who has been the most useful to me in difficult moments. He is a kind of life-saver in moments of great intellectual distress. When it is about questioning things as self-evident as *"obéir à une règle"* (to obey a rule). Or when it is about saying things as simple (and simultaneously nearly inexpressible) as to practise a practice.' (Bourdieu, Fr. ed. 1987:19).
9. See Chapter 4 and Chapter 5.
10. The reference is to the book *Distinction* (Harvard University Press, 1984). It may be of interest to readers that the interview with Nice began with a brief discussion of *Distinction*, which was described by him as being an enormously important book, though difficult and

definitely not 'mainstream'. We discussed the problems that he and Bourdieu had had with the publishers, the difficulty of translating and publishing other work by Bourdieu, and the fact that the publishers would not add a complete bibliography of Bourdieu's work at the back of *Distinction*.

11. Bourdieu's research group publishes *Actes de la Recherche en Sciences Sociales*. It was originally set up as a counter-cultural sociological magazine. In one of the issues an article by Luc Boltanski focused on road accidents. Nice (1985) describes the article as follows.

> And one of the funniest things by Boltanski was a correlation between road accidents and social class showing that rich people don't have so many accidents. (I think there's a lot more to be said about that because if you drive around faster you do have more accidents.) But, it explains how the rich are able to run bigger and safer vehicles which get them out of trouble and their aggressive driving tends to push other people off the road into ditches! – with accompanying photographs to show them pushing cars off the road! It is the class war on the roads!

12. The whole result of the domination exercised by American science, and also the more or less disgraceful or unconscious adhesion to a positivist philosophy of science, leads to insufficiencies and technical errors passing unnoticed in all the stages of research, from the sampling until the statistical analysis of the data. This is the positivist conception of science: one does not count the cases where experimental designs, imitating the experimental rigour, dissimulate the total absence of a real sociologically constructed object. (Honneth and Schwibs, 1985).

For Bourdieu, this domination of false technological impeccability hits upon an absence of genuinely theoretical problematics. This does not mean, however, that he has no sympathy for American social science. On the contrary he has shown considerable interest in Goffman, Cicourel, Geertz, Chomsky and many others, though his own work is so singular as to remain quite distinct.

13. *Propositions pour l'enseignement de l'avenir: Elaborées à la demande de Monsieur le Président de la République par les Professeurs du Collège de France*, by Pierre Bourdieu. Paris, Collège de France, 1985. 36 pp. NPL paper.

14. In 1989 Bourdieu was asked by Prime Minister Rocard (the ex-president of the Socialist Party), to convene a committee of other prominent scientists which would submit a report on the transformation of secondary school programmes. It may be important to note that this report was for the Prime Minister himself, and not specifically for the Ministry of Education. The report was published in May 1989.

3 Bourdieu and Ethnography: Reflexivity, Politics and Praxis

Henry Barnard

The last two decades have witnessed an increasing sense of crisis in the central practical[1] activity of the discipline of social anthropology – the creation of ethnographies. The impasse that seems to have been reached has resulted in what one recent commentator (who is also a 'participant') has been led to call a 'failure of nerve' (Geertz, 1985:624). This chapter surveys the crisis, examines one peculiar development which pretends that the crisis does not exist, and then explores the work of Pierre Bourdieu. It will be argued that by 'working on the working subject' (1984:511) in the very act of dealing with the objects of his scientific work, Bourdieu partially overcomes a series of obstacles that have stood in the way of other ethnographers. He has shown how ethnography can be reflexive without being narcissistic or uncritical; how to generate a critical ethnography of modern societies which overcomes the problem of defining an 'authentic' group for the application of the ethnographic method; and he provides the theoretical apparatus appropriate for the new mode of analysis necessitated by his innovations in ethnography.

THE CRISIS IN ETHNOGRAPHY

Until the early sixties, the production of ethnographies and the related activity of fieldwork were considered largely unproblematic within social anthropology. The ground rules, established and given mythological charter by Malinowski in the 1920s, had been, over the course of three decades, refined and worked into the tradition of the discipline so that they had taken on an almost conventional status for the discipline as a whole. These rules were roughly as follows: a person aspiring to become a professional social anthropologist was required to select a 'closed' community – tribe, caste, village community, or urban ghetto – in one of the colonial or neo-colonial territories for 'in-depth' study. He or she (and there were quite a few women involved, especially from Malinowski's seminar) was then expected to reside for a period of time (the length was never formally established but it was expected to be 'considerable') 'amongst' (a much favoured word) the chosen people to study their social and cultural life so that on return from the field, the now neophyte anthropologist could produce an ethnography or series of ethnographies which would capture this life as a whole.[2] There were tacit rules concerning linguistic competence, length of residence and degree of involvement which constituted a kind of symbolic capital of the discipline[3]: recognised as being essential but considered 'bad form' to be questioned in any depth with regard to particular investigators.[4] It was, in other words, a form of 'obsequium' (Bourdieu 1977:95).

In the 1960s this complacency began to be shaken. Attention was drawn to the 'social' as opposed to the 'intellectual' advantages of fieldwork for the discipline. The initiatory and hence 'tribal' character of the experience was adduced in an attempt to demythologise it. There were pleas for a return to the nineteenth-century division of labour between theoreticians (who 'stayed at home') and ethnographers (who went into the field to 'test' the theories developed in the metropolitan centres) (Jarvie 1964:28–35). More important than this, however, was the critique of fieldwork, ethnography and the discipline of social anthropology as a whole launched by those who had been the objects of the anthropologist's gaze. As decolonisation progressed, the work of anthropologists was subjected to a critique aimed at colonialism and the various activities, intellectual as well as political, which constituted it. It is said that a cartoon framed and given prominent position in the office of a leading African nationalist of the time showed a scene with a raised black fist in the foreground clenching a gun symbolising national independence and freedom, and in the background three retreating, white, pith-helmeted figures with the captions 'colonial administrator', 'missionary' and 'anthropologist' under each.

This critique from outside the discipline engendered an auto-critique, and in the early 1970s a spate of works appeared which examined the 'collaboration' of social anthropology with colonialism and social anthropologists with colonial administrators.[5] These initial studies varied immensely in quality and some were fairly naive attempts at trying to establish guilt by association and assertion. The response to them was often equally naive.[6] In defensive reactions, social anthropologists who had carried out fieldwork in the colonies denied the charges laid against them using a variety of arguments: that settlers and administrators more often than not found their activities subversive; that their work was highly critical of colonial regimes; that colonial governments never read anything they wrote anyway; that theirs was a 'scientific' activity and of not much use to colonial regimes; and so on.

Fortunately, the level of debate, argument and counter-argument did not remain at this level. Another assault was launched on the political dimension of the way social anthropology constitutes its object, this time by feminists and feminism. The emphasis here was not simply on the *distortions* produced by the social conditions of the production of anthropological knowledge but the *absences* in anthropological discourse created by those conditions. The sexist dimensions of such classics as *The Nuer* (Evans-Pritchard, 1940) were revealed, and questions of gender relations were placed in the forefront of theoretical debate in the understanding of social formations.

The consequences of these critiques and auto-critiques were far reaching. On a practical level, social anthropologists began to find it much more difficult to carry out their researches. Newly-independent nations and ethnic groups asserting their independence questioned the right of social anthropologists to carry out research in the manner they had done hitherto.[7] This questioning began to extend to bans and the denial of visas, to the insistence that local people be involved in the research project at all stages, to the demand that the subjects of research be the final arbiters of what was to be done with research findings, etc. Many people find these 'impediments' onerous (see the debate in Crick et al. 1984). These factors and others, such as the growing emphasis on free-market values in the world of intellectual production, have made the business of doing fieldwork in the conventional sense a much more difficult task.

Related to these developments has been a growing unease over how anthropology, at the methodological level, constitutes its object/subject. The 'natural science' model began to lose its hold in the fifties and early sixties. Lévi-Straussian 'structuralism' seemed to offer an alternative model which retained the naturalism of the earlier structuralism (studying 'men as if they were ants' (Lévi-Strauss 1966:246)) but which turned its attention away from social organisation as an object in itself to a study of the sign systems that lay at the root of it. Sign-systems became the new object of description and analysis – an object which seemed at a safe remove from the tricky questions of politics and economics yet an object which seemed to offer something distinctive for anthropology to investigate. However, structuralism failed to address the critical issues confronting anthropology, or more accurately, having faced them, offered an answer that attempted to sidestep them. It never saw anthropology itself as a sign-system amongst others. Lévi-Strauss's anti-ethnography *Tristes Tropiques* was a very early attempt to articulate consciously the situation of the observer in the act of creating ethnography. It recounts his travels through the devastated tropics of South America in search of 'the extreme limits of the savage' (Lévi-Strauss 1973:436). He encountered one culture after another contaminated by contact with European civilisation but finally when he does find himself with 'charming Indians whom no other white man had ever seen before and who might never be seen again', he finds 'Alas! they were only too savage': he could not speak their language. Out of this impasse is born structuralism, because:

> Even though I was ignorant of the language and had no interpreter, I could try to grasp certain aspects of the Munde way of thinking and social organisation, such as how the group was made up, the kinship system and vocabulary, the names of the parts of the body, and the colour vocabulary, according to a chart I always carried with me. Kinship terms and those used for parts of the body, colours and shapes . . . often have common characteristics which put them halfway between vocabulary and grammar: each group forms a system, and the way in which different languages choose to arrange or confuse the relationships expressed by means of it allows us to make a certain number of hypotheses, even though they may relate only to the distinctive features of the particular society (ibid.:435).[8]

It is interesting to compare Lévi-Strauss's account of the key or critical experience of his fieldwork with that of Bourdieu (see Chapter 2 above). Both are recounted in a narrative that is structured like a journey into the unknown ('like a gunfight' says the vulgar Bourdieu; Lévi-Strauss's allusions are more cultured – Conradesque!). However, the contrast in mood is enormous. When Bourdieu steps out and meets the people he says: 'It was wonderful and later when we left the people gave us gifts' (ibid.). For Lévi-Strauss, although he 'had set off on the adventure with enthusiasm it left me with a feeling of emptiness', and rather than laden with gifts *Tristes*

Tropiques recounts the plundering and horsetrading that Lévi-Strauss had to undertake in order to collect his hoard for the museums of France. The resulting ennui resonates with the austere, withdrawn, almost ascetic methodology of structuralism or 'Zen Marxism'. Bourdieu's sociology, on the other hand, is engaged; almost self-consciously an intervention.

In the last analysis, therefore, confronted by issues central to the anthropological enterprise, Lévi-Strauss sidesteps them. Instead of realising or construing the issues of 'doing ethnography' as political ones, he constructs them as, on the one hand, 'scientific' difficulties, and on the other as 'personal difficulties' and offers the objectivist approach of structuralism as a solution to the one, and ethnography-as-autobiography to the other. Even the question of the relation of 'native' models to the anthropologist's models is formulated in purely 'scientific' terms and not in terms of the political relationships underlying the construction of these models. There is a failure of nerve of classic proportions and it is this failure that was recognised at the barricades of May 1968 in the slogans that proclaimed that 'structuralism is dead'. The 'is' here is used in both the general present and the perfect senses.

CLIFFORD GEERTZ AND INTERPRETIVE ETHNOGRAPHY

In response to the obstructed path of structuralism various forms of 'semiotic' or 'interpretive' anthropology were put forward as solutions to the impasse. They too reconceptualised the object of anthropology – on this occasion by exploring the concept of culture. It is necessary here to discuss in detail one of these solutions (Geertz) for two reasons: firstly, because there is a real danger that Bourdieu's work might be assimilated to it, especially as Geertz's language echoes some of the major arguments contained in Bourdieu's work; secondly, because the work of Geertz has been extremely influential in relation to discussions concerned with the crisis in ethnography.[9]

In some early papers Geertz (reprinted in 1973 as Chapters 2, 3, 4) attempted to arrive at reformulations of the concepts of culture, mind and ideology which moved beyond the ritualistic opposition of 'subjectivism' and 'objectivism' (1973:56ff). In relation to the concept 'mind' he says:

It is a term denoting a class of skills, propensities, capacities, tendencies, habits; it refers in Dewey's phrase to an 'active and eager background which lies in wait and engages whatever comes its way'. And, as such, it is neither an action nor a thing, but an *organised system of dispositions* which finds its manifestation in some things (ibid.:58 – emphasis added).

Geertz attempts to move away from the mentalistic conceptions of mind, culture and ideology and towards what he calls an 'extrinsic theory' of these concepts, a theory which sees their referents as a 'public reality'. He wants to move away from any connotations they might have of being part of a 'dim and inaccessible realm of private sensation' and to point out that they belong to the 'well-lit world of observables' (ibid.:96). Of ideology he says:

> Asking the question that most students of ideology fail to ask . . . gets one very quickly into quite deep water indeed: into, in fact, a somewhat untraditional and paradoxical theory of the nature of human thought as a public and not, or at least not fundamentally, a private activity (ibid.:213–14).

and of 'culture':

> Culture, this acted document, thus is public . . . . Though ideational, it does not exist in someone's head; though unphysical, it is not an occult entity. The interminable, because unterminable, debate within anthropology as to whether 'culture' is 'subjective' or 'objective', together with the mutual exchange of intellectual insults ('idealist!' – 'materialist!'; 'mentalist!' – 'behaviourist!'; 'impressionist!' – 'positivist!') which accompanies it, is wholly misconceived. Once human behaviour is seen as symbolic action . . . the question as to whether culture is patterned conduct or a frame of mind, or even the two somehow mixed, loses sense (ibid.:10).

In such passages Geertz seems to lay the ground for the development of a theory of symbolic forms that is similar to that developed by Bourdieu. The points of convergence are manifold. Bourdieu also speaks of transcending the perennial oscillation between subjectivist and objectivist modes of theoretical knowledge. Part of his success in breaking from this debate lies in the development of the concept *habitus*, a concept that has strong links with the concept of culture but which he prefers because of dangers of misinterpretation. As

Nietzsche said: 'Terms that have histories cannot be defined.' Bourdieu has, however, in the course of a series of works that dialectically transcend each other, reformulated the concept and renamed it so as to take it away from the semiological conception developed by Lévi-Strauss (drawing on Saussure) which posits it as some kind of unconscious mechanism which governs conduct, towards a 'transubstantiated' concept, a concept where the implicit dualism of mind and body is transcended so that even the body can be seen as 'a memory' (Bourdieu 1977:94; and Chapter 8 of this volume). This movement from a mentalistic conception towards a concept which overcomes earlier dualisms seems to follow the same path that Geertz followed.

The points of convergence seem to be particularly strong in relation to their use of the concept of *disposition*. Geertz sees the individual as being inducted with

> a certain distinctive set of dispositions (tendencies, capacities, propensities, skills, habits, liabilities, pronenesses) which lend a chronic character to the flow of his activity and the quality of his experience. A disposition describes not an activity or an occurrence in certain circumstances . . . . The virtue of this sort of view of what are usually called 'mental traits' or, if the Cartesianism is unavowed, 'psycho-logical forces' . . . is that it gets them out of any dim and inaccessible realm of private sensation into the well-lit world of observables. (Geertz 1973:95–6)

Bourdieu sees other virtues in the word:

> It expresses first the *result of an organising action*, with a meaning close to that of words such as structure; it also designates a *way of being*, a *habitual state* (especially of the body) and, in particular a *predisposition, tendency, propensity* or *inclination*. (Bourdieu, 1977:214, emphasis in original)

Both of them try to distance themselves from any Cartesian conception of the relation of mind to body, and they find the answer in conceiving of habitus (read 'culture' for Geertz) as a set of dispositions, inscribed in the body and not as 'ghosts in the machine.'[10]

Both go further and converge in a critique of semiology conceived of as a mode of knowledge that constitutes sign-systems (languages, kinship-systems, myths, etc.) for the purposes of internal analysis (Bourdieu 1973:188). Major portions of *Outline of a Theory of Practice* (1977) can be read as a negative critique of Saussurean linguistics and the importation of concepts and models based on it into social anthropology (ibid.:24ff) and every chapter of Geertz's *The Interpretation of Culture* (1973) embodies critiques of the concept of 'culture' current in anthropology. Geertz says of Lévi-Strauss that he:

> seeks to understand (symbolic forms) entirely in terms of their structure, independent de tout sujet, de tout objet, et de toute contexte.

Whereas he, Geertz, attempts to understand them

> in terms of how they function in concrete situations to organise perceptions, meanings, emotions, concepts, attitudes. (1973:449)

And finally, in such essays as that on the Balinese cockfight, Geertz's analyses of the strategies of the game recall Bourdieu's discussion of the strategies of honour (ibid.:433).

Given these convergences, how then do Geertz and Bourdieu differ? They do so in at least three fundamental ways, all of which are closely linked to each other. Firstly, in the list of 'influences' on the two the name of Marx is noticeable by its absence in the work of Geertz. In fact, he seems to have a strong allergy to Marx and makes no reference in his work to recent interpretations within a Marxist framework. As an initial guess this aversion may be explained by the circumstances of a social scientist coming to maturity in the fifties in the United States.[11] Secondly, Geertz appears to have an allergy too to any attempt to develop a general theory of culture or symbolic forms. My argument here is that given his attempt to take the study of symbols in a 'materialist' direction, and given his aversion to Marx, it would have been impossible to develop any such general theory.[12] That is, in order to develop such a theory he would have had to confront the Marxist tradition – and as he appears to have been congenitally incapable of doing this, there was no question of any such theory being developed.[13] In addition to this, in spite of his attempt to define culture in terms of *systems* of dispositions, Geertz never takes the systematic nature of sets of dispositions seriously. His approach to the study of cultural phenomena refuses to explore the systematicity of these phenomena.

Thirdly, Geertz, in spite of his espousal of a *semiotic* (as opposed to a semiological)[14] conception of symbols, makes no room in his analyses for social structure. This may sound strange, but in spite of all his professions of faith in a semiotic concept of culture, in the last analysis Geertz's own analyses treat symbolic systems as systems divorced from the political contexts in which they have their being. 'Power' is not a concept that plays any significant part in his 'theory', such as it is. As a corollary of this he has a tendency to treat cultural activities as texts that need interpreting. As Bourdieu (1977:2) has warned us to expect of anthropological approaches to social phenomena, Geertz introduces into the objects he constructs for analysis his own relationship to them. Thus, for example, having constituted the cockfight as 'text' that needs interpreting he imputes this relationship to the Balinese themselves:

> Like any art form – for that, finally, is what we are dealing with – the cockfight renders ordinary, everyday experience comprehensible by presenting it in terms of acts and objects which have had their practical consequences removed and been reduced to the level of sheer appearance, where their meaning can be more exactly perceived . . . . The cockfight is 'really real' only to the cocks – it does not kill anyone, castrate anyone, reduce anyone to animal status, alter the hierarchical relations among people or refashion the hierarchy; it does not redistribute income in any significant way. What it does is what for other peoples with other temperaments and other conventions, *Lear* and *Crime and Punishment* do; it catches up these themes – death, masculinity, rage, pride, loss, beneficence, chance – and ordering them into an encompassing structure, presents them in such a way as to throw into relief a particular view of their essential nature. It puts a construction on them, makes them, to those historically positioned to appreciate the construction, meaningful – visible, tangible, graspable – 'real', in an *ideational* sense. An image, fiction, a model, a metaphor, the cockfight is a means of expression; its function is neither to assuage social passions nor to heighten them . . . but, in a medium of feathers, blood, crowds, and money, to display them. (Geertz 1973:443–4, emphasis added)

and he concludes:

> It (the cockfight) provides a metasocial commentary upon the whole matter of assorting human beings into fixed hierarchical ranks and then organising the major part of collective existence around that assortment. Its function is interpretative: it is a Balinese reading of Balinese experience, a story they tell themselves about themselves (ibid.:448).

So finally when pressed to take the direction of his own thought seriously Geertz retreats from a materialist conception of 'culture' to the very position from which he wants to distance himself – namely that 'culture' and all that it stands for are fundamentally ideational objects, figments of the imagination in the literal sense. In the final analysis then, far from being reflexive and politically engaged ethnography, Geertz's solution to the problems of praxis in anthropology is no different from the disengagement of Lévi-Strauss's structuralism. If Lévi-Straussian analyses construct social phenomena in such a way that the analyst can treat them as musical scores, as objects, therefore, of and for aesthetic appreciation, Geertzian analyses, retreating from a confrontation with materialism, construct them as texts on the literary model for the same purposes.

Geertz has recently taken this approach to its extreme by arguing for an almost completely literary approach to the evaluation of ethnographies. If his prescriptions are followed we would be doubly distanced from any social reality. These realities would be interpreted and constructed as texts within texts for the purposes of comparative criticism! This approach is just the opposite of the direction that underlies the recent discussions initiated by Marcus and Cushman (1982) and carried forward in such works as Marcus and Fisher (1986), Clifford and Marcus (1987) and Clifford (1988). Superficially, the latter works may appear to be developing the same argument as Geertz but in actuality they do not, because they still embrace the aim of 'producing realist descriptions of society' (Marcus and Fisher, 1986:14). The purpose of drawing attention to the 'literary' aspects of ethnographic work is, for the latter authors, in order that they are able to utilise them more consciously. This allows them to achieve the aims outlined above, and not to become trapped into the never-ending circle of textuality conjured up by Geertz.

We shall see that Bourdieu does not retreat from the confrontation that I have referred to above, and, in fact, through a fundamental break with traditional conceptions of materialism constitutes a new kind of materialism, one which asks the reflexive question that materialism itself seems reluctant to ask: what are the material and social conditions for the emergence of materialism? Furthermore, he quite explicitly engages with the issues of representation raised by Clifford, Marcus, Fisher and others working in the field of anthropology as cultural critique (see Wacquant 1989).

ETHNOGRAPHY IN CULTURAL STUDIES

This discussion of the crisis in ethnography and responses to it has restricted itself to the discipline of social anthropology. Bourdieu's work is an intervention in this field, at present dominated by structuralism and various semiotic alternatives to structuralism, most notably the interpretive anthropology of Clifford Geertz. However, there is one further field that we need to explore, if only briefly, before we examine the work of Bourdieu in relation to ethnography; the field of Cultural Studies. This newly emergent approach has appropriated ethnography as one of its most important strategies to realign the empirical work being done on the sociology of culture. Moving away from methods based on survey techniques, it has used ethnography as a way of grasping the lived experience of social groups in society. It is crucial therefore, in a discussion of the impact of Bourdieu's work on ethnography, to situate his method in relation to this field. It is even more crucial because, in one of the most accurate and sympathetic accounts of Bourdieu's work, Garnham and Williams set out 'to indicate what in particular Bourdieu's work has to offer us at this moment in what he could call the field of British media and cultural studies'. (1980:209).

They fail, however, to bring out the implications of Bourdieu's work at the methodological level. Their failure in this respect is in contrast to their success in relation to other aspects of Bourdieu's work – his theories of class and the appropriation of cultural goods, his philosophy of history – is symptomatic of the relationship of Cultural Studies to the ethnographic tradition as a whole and calls for comment.

Williams in a different but also recent statement has called Cultural Studies a 'sociology of a new kind' (1981:14). A branch of sociology 'more in the sense of a distinctive mode of entry into general sociological questions' than a specialised sub-field, Cultural Studies

> requires new kinds of social analysis of specifically cultural institutions and formations, and the exploration of actual relations between these and, on the one hand, the material means of cultural production and, on the other hand, actual cultural forms (ibid.:14).

Cultural Studies works with a concept of culture which merges

the anthropological and sociological senses of culture as a distinct 'whole way of life' . . . (with) the more specialised if also more common sense of culture as 'artistic intellectual activities', though these, because of the emphasis on a general signifying system, are now much more broadly defined, to include not only the traditional arts and forms of intellectual production but also all the 'signifying practices' . . . which now constitute this complex and necessarily extended field (ibid.:13).

In the rest of this work, however, Williams is once again strangely silent on questions of methodology. This silence can perhaps best be explained in the following terms: Cultural Studies has unconsciously reproduced the division of intellectual labour that is and was characteristic of the sociological tradition it is trying to supersede. It gives *theoretical* lip-service to the unity of theory and method – and in this respect goes beyond sociology – but reproduces the division at the level of practice. There are two important reasons for this – the origins of Cultural Studies in literary criticism, social history and British sociology, and the trajectory it has followed in its appropriation of the ethnographic method. As we shall see, the origins and trajectory of Pierre Bourdieu's work are quite different, resulting in a more sophisticated praxis.

Cultural Studies originated in attempts to fill the 'absent centre' of a totalising perspective on society that British sociology failed to provide (unlike its Continental and American counterparts).[15] Cultural Studies began in that part of the British intellectual field, literary criticism, where attempts to establish such a perspective had already been made. However, this discipline's perspectives on culture had to be enlarged to incorporate a notion of 'culture' which it had hitherto denied. The other discipline which also provided a totalising perspective, social anthropology, was 'raided' for this concept without too much attention being given to a critique of the discipline itself. This was the first missed opportunity in relation to methodological issues; whereas the concept of 'culture' was borrowed in a critical spirit from anthropology, the methodology at the heart of the discipline – 'ethnography' – was not examined seriously.

Ethnography, in fact, entered Cultural Studies through responses to already existing 'ethnographic' studies of British sub-cultures. These, in their turn, had been the result of the application to the British scene of naturalistic methods derived from the Chicago School. This is not the place to review in detail the way Cultural Studies reacted to and appropriated the methods of this school. What it is important to note is the irony of the fact that an already established tradition of 'ethnography' and 'theory of ethnography', as Leach called it (1957:119), within the British intellectual field, was ignored; this was doubly ironic because the Chicago School itself – through the influence of Radcliffe-Brown's period in Chicago – had already been exposed to and influenced by this British tradition!

All of this would be an amusing footnote to an intellectual history but for the fact that in the process of transference, key issues in relation to the method itself were filtered out. It has also meant that developments in relation to a critique of ethnography from within the discipline of anthropology (such as I have outlined above) have been passed unnoticed by Cultural Studies and it has also meant that we find people like Willis (the person who has most consistently applied and thought about ethnography within Cultural Studies) offering to his public as innovations ideas that had already been rehearsed decades before and, in fact, superseded.[16]

The most damaging aspect of this lack of dialogue, the lack of an engagement with the political questions at the heart of the ethnographic method, is (once again ironically) a result of the very reason why Cultural Studies chose to ignore the discipline of social anthropology in the first place. As Baron says in a review article:

> Anthropology, developed in the context of colonial rule, necessarily asked questions of the total social system, how it worked and how it could be controlled, but it asked these questions of people safely distant geographically and culturally – 'useful to colonial administrations and dangerous to no domestic prejudice'. . . . (Baron 1985:72).

When the decolonisation of anthropology took place (see Bourdieu 1976) questions were raised in relation to ethnography which were *not* asked by the ethnography of Cultural Studies because it had, indirectly, adopted the theory of ethnography of the colonial period. These questions were not placed at the centre of its discourse and methodological issues remained just that; issues that were best left for discussion in methodological 'appendices' (see Willis 1978; Hall and Jefferson 1976) or even confined to silence (Williams 1981). This explains why I have not chosen to discuss Cultural Studies through the work of its central figure, Stuart Hall. His silence on these matters of methodology is deafening.

Thus, in the end, the responses to the crisis in ethnography from within the discipline of social anthropology which I have discussed, and the methodology of Cultural Studies, converge. Whereas in the case of Lévi-Strauss and Geertz the refusal of the political dimension is almost deliberate, in the case of Cultural Studies it is due to 'limits of naivety'.

If Cultural Studies is to realise what Baron calls its 'critical potential', it cannot afford to continue to treat these issues as marginal. Its 'theoretical definition' must include, simultaneously, a 'methodological definition'. This is why it is critical to emphasise that what Bourdieu's work has to offer Cultural Studies is more than just a theory of practice, as Garnham and Williams' (1980) otherwise excellent review would imply; it is a theory of practice which is at the same time a theory of intellectual practice. As we shall see, the reasons for Bourdieu's success in this field is a result of the different trajectory he has followed in arriving at his current position.

BOURDIEU AND ETHNOGRAPHY

I have stated, though not argued, the case that from the point of view of the present crisis in ethnography, Bourdieu's work represents a way out of the cul-de-sac that ethnographers and theorists of ethnography have created for themselves. This crisis centres around the politics of interpretation and representation: what is the position of the researcher in relation to the objects of research? What questions of power arise out of the constituting discourses that constitute ethnography?

The theorisation effect and epistemological rupture

Distinction (1984)[17] is the work that best exemplifies the novelty of Bourdieu's approach to these questions but it is perhaps not the best place to begin in order to understand it. I will return to it later. From works available in English the work which most explicitly discusses fundamental breaks with received ethnographic practice is *Outline of a Theory of Practice* (1977). Though certain key concepts are given less prominence here (for instance, the concept of 'field') it, nevertheless, contains an extended discussion of one aspect of Bourdieu's work from which many of the other methodological breaks derive; this is his 'theory of the theorisation effect'[18] (1977:178) or the theory of 'intellectualocentrism' (1983:5).

The practical privilege in which all scientific activity arises never more subtly governs that activity (insofar as science presupposes not only an epistemological break but also a *social* separation) than when, unrecognised as privilege, it leads to an implicit theory of practice which is the corollary of the neglect of the social conditions in which science is possible (1977:1).

His translator, Richard Nice, sums up the aim of the *Outline* as follows:

> a 'reflection on scientific practice which will disconcert both those who reflect on the social sciences without practicing them and those who practice them without reflecting on them', [the *Outline*] seeks to define the prerequisites for a truly scientific discourse about human behaviour, that is an adequate theory of practice which must include a *theory of scientific practice*. (Emphasis added. Ibid.:vii.)

The important idea here is that the 'epistemological break' which constitutes a scientific practice is also a 'social break' and that, as Bourdieu points out on many occasions, the epistemological obstacles social scientists face are also social ones. Here we can sense the strong influence of two of the most important figures in the development of Bourdieu's thought, Gaston Bachelard and Georges Canguilhem.[19] In particular they developed two concepts – that of 'epistemological break' (*rupture épistémologique*) and 'epistemological obstacle' – which Bourdieu has adopted and placed at the centre of his discussions of methodology (see Chapters 1 and 5).

Intellectuals, and in the *Outline* he singles out anthropologists in particular (1977:1–2, 10, 109–110; 1976:425), make a 'virtue of necessity' and 'transmute into an epistemological choice' their 'objective situation', that of the 'impartial observer'. They are the people 'who are so used to saying what they think they think that they no longer know how to think what they say' (1984:510). In *Outline* we are given a graphic discussion of the theoretical consequences of the theory of practice which results from the position of the anthropologist in the 'field' (the double meaning is intended). The model they construct, and the very term itself are instructive, of the relationship between theory and practice, one which sees the connection as one of some form of 'execution'. Hence the predilection for terminology which relies on words such as 'rules', 'norms', 'constraints', 'performance', and so on.

So long as he (*sic*) remains unaware of the limits inherent in his point of view on the object, the anthropologist is condemned to adopt unwittingly for his own use the representation of action which is forced on agents or groups when they lack practical mastery of a highly valued competence and have to provide themselves with an explicit and at least semi-formalised substitute for it in the form of a *repertoire of rules*, or of what sociologists consider, at best, as a 'role', i.e. a predetermined set of discourses and actions appropriate to a particular 'stage-part'. It is significant that 'culture' is sometimes described as a *map*; it is the analogy which occurs to an outsider who has to find his way around in a foreign landscape, and who compensates for his lack of practical mastery, the prerogative of the native, by the use of a model of all possible routes (1977:2).

This extended critique of the limits of objectivism could be read as an, albeit exemplary, theoretical exercise. The presentation of the argument in *Outline* leads to such a reading and therefore we have to be careful to take heed of both Bourdieu's own warnings and those of Richard Nice.

a text which seeks to break out of a scheme of thought as deeply embedded as the opposition between subjectivism and objectivism, is fated to be perceived through the categories which it seeks to transcend . . . (Nice in Bourdieu 1977:vii).

This questioning of objectivism is liable to be understood at first as a rehabilitation of subjectivism and to be merged with the critique that naive humanism levels at scientific objectification in the name of 'lived experience' and the rights of 'subjectivity' (1977:3–4).

On the contrary what we are presented with here is a novel type of critique (cf. 1983:5): one which not only shows the limits of objectivism but which also constructs 'a theory of the theoretical and social conditions of the possibility of objective apprehension'. The *Outline*, therefore, has to be read at two levels: as an outline of a theory of practice which is, simultaneously, a theory of scientific practice. In other words, the *Outline* should be seen not simply as a critique of scientific practice, but also as a theory of why it is that that practice takes the form it does.

Having said all that, it must be pointed out that we are presented with an incomplete account in the *Outline* and that for a more thorough treatment we have to wait until *Distinction*. Bourdieu himself says:

> the critique of intellectualism . . . is at one and the same time epistemological and sociological (1983:5).

In the *Outline* he has erred towards the epistemological side and only given hints of the sociological critique underlying it. In *Distinction*, we are presented with a detailed ethnographic and sociological account, amongst other things, of the dominated fractions of the dominant class, which include the intellectuals who have been the subjects of the critique in the *Outline*. In this 'barbarous' work (see Chapter 6, note 4) Bourdieu shows how there are 'intelligible relations which unite apparently incommensurable "choices"', such as preferences in music and food, painting and sport, literature and hairstyle', and, one may add, in the case of sociologists, their modes of analysis. The 'inner-worldly ascetism' of intellectuals, their 'interest in disinterestedness', reflected in the kinds of theories of practice to be found in their work, is reflected too in their 'taste' – in their relation to objects of consumption such as food and music, newspapers, films; in their activities, and so on. Their lifestyle is all of a piece with their scientific activity. This orchestration is not brought about by the 'action of a conductor' but by the coming together of two histories – the objectified, institutionalised history of their positions in a variety of fields – intellectual, scientific, political, art, etc. – and habitus, the incarnated, embodied history appropriate to their class.

Distinction is an 'ethnography of France' and it does 'emphasise the particularity of the French tradition' (1984:xi). It would be a mistake to seek out in it an analysis of the habitus of intellectuals that could be applied everywhere (see Chapter 4 for further details), though as Bourdieu himself points out 'At the level of the "international" pole of the dominant class', certain obvious substitutions can be made.

It is important to note that this critical reflexive methodology does not succumb to the narcissism of recent attempts at reflexivity in ethnography. The absence of such rhetorical and stylistic devices as the use of the first person is a symptom of the unflagging critical stance of all of Bourdieu's work. If he is sharply critical of objectivism, he is merciless in relation to subjectivism – whether in Sartre (Bourdieu 1977:73–6) or Touraine (Bourdieu and Reynaud 1974). Reflexivity is not achieved by the use of the first person or by the expedient of constructing a text which situates the observer in the act of observation. Rather it is achieved by subjecting the *position* of the observer to the same critical analysis as that of the constructed object at hand.[20]

AUTHENTICITY AND THE FIELD

If there is no question that the careless borrowing of methods and concepts developed in the study of societies with no writing, no historical traditions, which are relatively undifferentiated socially and have had little exposure to contacts with other societies, can lead one into absurdities (think, for example of some 'culturalist' analyses of stratified societies), it is nevertheless all too clear that we have to be wary about taking these conditional limitations as inherent limitations of validity in ethnological method. There is nothing to stop us applying the methods of ethnology to modern societies, provided that, in each case, we submit to epistemological reflection the implicit presuppositions of these methods concerning the structure of society and the logic of its transformations.

(Bourdieu, Fr. ed. 1973:67)

One of the corollaries of the fundamental rupture that constitutes the reflexive side of Bourdieu's methodology is that it overcomes the problem of authenticity that ethnography has created for itself. Expressed most clearly by Lévi-Strauss but implicit in the writing of all those who use ethnographic methods, ethnography seems appropriate only for so-called 'authentic' societies or groups – societies or groups where relationships are direct and face-to-face, uncomplicated by intermediaries. Lévi-Strauss went so far as to say that there was a radical difference in types of existence characteristic of archaic and primitive societies as compared to modern ones. *The Savage Mind* (Lévi-Strauss 1966) argued that 'Both science and magic . . . require the same sort of mental operations' and constituted a frontal attack on 'theorists of primitive mentality' like Lévy-Bruhl and even Sartre. But it gave a new authority to the idea that there was fundamental difference between modern historical societies and others, and that the methods and techniques of social anthropology – that is, ethnography – were strictly appropriate only to non-modern societies. At the crudest level he distinguished between 'hot' and 'cold' societies, between societies where entropy is unknown or exists only in a very weak form, and which functions at a temperature of absolute zero – not zero as understood by the physicist, but in the 'historical sense' . . . these societies have no history (in Charbonnier 1969:38–9).

On the other hand there are

Societies like our own, which have a history, (which) operate . . . at a higher temperature, or, to be more exact, there are greater differentials . . . which are caused by social differences (ibid.).

He argued that ethnographic methods were only appropriate for 'cold' societies, not 'hot' ones. In other discussions he used the concept of *authenticity*, the idea that societies could be distinguished on the basis of the degree to which they permit or are based on 'authentic' relations between individuals, on direct face-to-face relations. Lévi-Strauss argues that in our own society 'actual people' are, by and large, cut off from each other or are interconnected only through intermediary agents or systems of relays, such as administrative machinery or ideological ramifications (ibid.:54). Only 'authentic' relations can be the subject of ethnographic research.

Not all social anthropologists subscribed or subscribe to these ideas explicitly, but, in practice there are few if any who have not worked with some variant of them. As a result, it became increasingly difficult for anthropologists to see how they could develop or produce an ethnography of modern societies.[21] Certainly it was possible to produce ethnographic descriptions of 'sub-cultures' or groups within modern society. Even Lévi-Strauss conceded that though modern society as a whole was inauthentic there were 'levels of authenticity' within it which were appropriate objects for anthropological methods: thus studies like that of James Agee (Agee and Evans 1960) provided new insights into marginal groups in the United States, and Willis has discovered his authentic groups in the form of 'sub-cultures' among the youth of Britain.

To see how deep-rooted this search for authenticity is, we need only turn to an essay by Paul Rabinow (1985). This piece is particularly instructive because the essay as a whole also invokes the work of Bourdieu in an attempt to critique the ethnographic tradition in a way not dissimilar to that presented here. Rabinow concludes his essay:

Where do we go from here? I have no general prescriptions or proscriptions to offer. I have emerged from this immersion in textuality feeling inchoately anthropological. Anthropology for me has meant pursuing criticism of the *barbarism of civilisation, an openness to otherness*, and a commitment to and great suspicion of Reason. These have been foregrounded in epistemological and ethical issues for me. Given the constraints of the contemporary historical situation, *what kind of subjects do we want to be? What kind of relations do we want to have with other subjects?* How much can they be forged? How? How does writing connect with these projects? What are the relations of ethics and politics at different conjunctures? What is the place of reason in these activities?

Being temperamentally more comfortable in an oppositional stance, I have chosen to study a *group* of elite French administrators, colonial officials as well as social reformers (within one branch of French socialism) all concerned with urban planning in the 1920s. By 'studying up' I find myself in a *more comfortable position* than I would be were I 'giving voice' to dominated or marginalised groups, or playing the role of universal intellectual, spokesman for the Truth. *I have chosen a group* who, while *unquestionably* holding positions of power and privilege, were nonetheless highly critical of racism in the colonies and class oppression at home. But these men were no heroes; better than some, worse than others, they invented and carried out some of the initial programs of the welfare state. *They seem to afford me an anthropological difference; separate enough so as to prevent easy identification* yet close enough to afford a *charitable* but critical understanding (1985:12).

I have quoted this at length in the same spirit as Bourdieu quotes from Sartre and Lévi-Strauss; it is a specially good illustration of the epistemological (which is at the same time sociological) unconscious at work. It brings to life the foregoing discussions of intellectualocentrism, the theorisation effect and the epistemological/social obstacles that impede social science; we could find few better examples of a virtue being made of necessity than in Rabinow's 'choice' of his subject, his relation to his subject, his voluntarist account of it, his choice of and his emphasis on 'difference' – a notion that the whole of Bourdieu's work works against.[22] But this is not the only point that can be made from the text. What is instructive as well is the choice of object – a *group*, a group which in fact was fairly 'authentic' in as much as they were all 'social reformers' and 'all concerned with urban planning in the 1920s', a concern that must have brought them into direct relationships with each other. Thus, in spite of an encounter with Bourdieu's work, Rabinow seems not to have learnt one of the most critical lessons from it; the radical transformation brought about by constructing, not groups as objects for analysis, but *fields* (within which, of course, groups occupy positions). From the field of marriage strategies (in the analysis of which we find the most explicit discussion of the part the category of 'group' plays in anthropological thought), the field of honour, to the fields of intellectual production of politics and science, Bourdieu's analyses have never been directed at groups per se but a completely different constructed object, the field.

As pointed out in Chapter 2, the sociologist also occupies a position, willy-nilly, and is thus not outside the game: 'There is no way out of the game of culture' (1984:12; and see Chapter 8). The objects of analysis within the field are the stakes in the game (capital), the strategies, the objectified histories of the agents (their positions and habitus) including, ineluctably, that of the sociologist.

> To think in terms of fields is to think of the space of production as a system such that the characteristics of each of the intellectual producers are defined by their position in this system. A field is a universe in which the characteristics of the producers are defined by their position in the relations of production, by the place they occupy in a certain space of objective relations. *It is this space which must be analysed, in each case, at the same time excluding the study of isolated individuals like the practice for example of literary history of producing 'Men and their works' series. One is better off knowing little things about many people, systematically bound together than everything about an individual.* (Bourdieu, Fr. ed. 1976:420)

Rabinow fails to grasp the shift in the foci of analyses and still searches desperately for an authentic group to devote his energies to. One may ask the question that Bourdieu asks of Sartre:

> Can one avoid attributing to the permanence of a habitus the constancy with which the objective intention of the . . . philosophy (despite its language) asserts itself against the subjective intentions of its author? (1977:215)

THE PRIVILEGED INDIGENOUS OBSERVER

A further corollary and consequence of Bourdieu's position is that it provides an answer to the claim that indigenous researchers or observers are privileged in relation to their own societies.

Nothing is less neutral, therefore, than the relationship between the subject and the object, researchers and the objects of their research. But to put the question in this form is completely different from asking whether there is such a thing as a privileged relationship with the object. Must one be native born to understand the native? That is the masquerade of ideology. Lévi-Strauss's lectures on the privileged status of the outside observer are a good example of the ideological expression of the interests of the ethnologist. In its less extreme form this position does at least countermand the opposite and nowadays more frequently held position which attributes a privileged position to the native born. But when someone takes one or other of these opposing positions we have to ask ourselves, what interest does he have in talking like this. In every case it is important to know that behind these so called 'epistemological' problems there are 'interests', and that the whole field is a place for the monopoly of a specific stake (which changes from field to field; when it is a matter of science, it is the monopoly of scientific authority) (Bourdieu, Fr. ed. 1976:425).

In other words, 'the problem of the outside observer and the native is a false and dangerous one' (ibid.:424). This 'naive problem' hides in fact a real one, that is that the claims to privilege from one or the other are in fact strategies in a field and are to be understood in terms of the state of the field at a particular moment. There are no 'privileged' positions in and of themselves. Some of Bourdieu's *bêtes noires* are the spokespeople for various groups – classes, ethnic minorities, and others, mentioned briefly in Chapter 1. He elaborates:

> The *narodniki* of all times and all lands, by identifying with their objects to the point of confusing their relation to the working-class condition with the working-class relation to that condition, by speaking and writing as if it were sufficient to occupy the workers' positions in the relations of production for a brief while, as observer or even as participant, in order to understand the

worker's experience of the position, present an account of the working-class condition that is statistically improbable, since it is not the product of the relation to that condition which is ordinarily associated with the condition, precisely because of the conditioning which it exerts (1984:372).

These *narodniki* and others, through the use of phrases such as 'my people' or 'the working-class', etc. in a sense create for themselves representations of the groups they create in the act of representing them. The process is disguised and the very hiding of the process is a part of the strategy they employ in the field – whether of politics or intellectual production. A more detailed discussion of *narodniki* is taken up in Chapter 5.

The point here is that sociologists cannot step outside of this game. But neither must they allow themselves to participate in it in such a way as to either mystify their relationship to the field or those of others.

THE ETHNOGRAPHIC STATUS OF BOURDIEU'S WORK

One final question remains: the ethnographic status of Bourdieu's work. I have taken at face value his claims for this status for the work he produces but it is the case that many people would not recognise his work as ethnographic. Here we confront a problem that deserves separate treatment in its own right: what constitutes an ethnographic text as such? In recent years this question has been much-aired and a variety of positions have been taken by those working in this area.

There seems little doubt about Bourdieu's earlier work on Algeria: *The Algerians* (1962) and parts of *Esquisse* (Fr. ed. 1972) are recognisably ethnographic in the traditional sense – dealing with aspects of the culture of the Kabyle and others, based on 'fieldwork' amongst them. Here we find the analyses of the symbolic and value systems of various peoples of the Maghreb. Even *Algeria 1960* (Bourdieu, 1979), which represents the reworking of the 'ethnographic' studies which formed parts of larger works such as *Travail et Travailleurs en Algérie* (Bourdieu et al., Fr. ed. 1963) is also recognisably ethnographic. But already in these latter works we begin to see the presence of data which indicate reliance upon techniques that are less recognisably ethnographic, especially the survey questionnaire.

These works contain extensive documentation in the form of tables of statistics, a form of documentation not relied upon by the majority of anthropologists. These are important exceptions; the work of the Manchester School in Central Africa, in particular, relied heavily on the presentation of statistical materials. But once again contrasts are instructive; whereas the latter used statistical tables to present data elicited through censuses, Bourdieu and his colleagues used questionnaires to elicit data on the cultural values and orientation of their respondents. In this early work the integration of this 'statistical' work with the 'ethnographic' studies was, at least textually, incomplete. In the translation, for example, of his work on education in France, large portions of his statistical work were omitted as if to suggest that they were secondary. This approach is rejected in *Distinction*. This book is 'dense with the machinery of "hard" sociology: graphs, charts, survey, interviews, and maps' (Warner 1985:1134).[23] Yet the book also contains excerpts from magazines, photographs and the data obtained from participation in the milieu being described. Furthermore, in this work like no other, all these elements are fused into a whole, so that there is no sense of priority being given to one mode of textual production or the other. If this is ethnography – and it certainly has elements which could not be thought of as otherwise, such as descriptions of the kinds of foods, styles and interiors that are favoured by different classes and class fractions – it is certainly ethnography of an entirely novel kind.[24] But this is only appropriate because what Bourdieu has attempted is to provide an analysis 'which differs from the blind insight of the participants without becoming the sovereign gaze of the impartial observer' (1984:511).

NOTES

1. See, for example, Marcus and Fischer (1986) and Clifford and Marcus (1987).
2. Marcus and Cushman (1982) discuss in detail the conventions that shaped the final written ethnography.
3. 'Every field of scholarly production has its own "rules" of propriety, which may remain implicit and only be known to the initiate' (Bourdieu, 1984:601). That this symbolic capital is utilised explicitly on occasion can be little doubted by a close reading of a passage like the following:

Armchair Marxists have accused those of us *who lived close* to the
'people' in the 1950s in African, Malaysian, and Oceanian villages,
often for several years, of 'using' structural functionalism to provide
the 'scientific' objectification of an unquestioned ideology (colonialism in prewar anthropology, neoimperialism now).

These dour
modern 'Roundheads' – an infra-red band on the world's spectrum
of Moral Majorities – have become so obsessed with power that
they fail to sense the many-levelled complexity (hence irony and
forgiveability) of human lives experienced at first hand (Turner 1982,
pp. 8–9, emphasis added).

For good measure Turner adds in the next paragraph:

In the field my family and I *lived in no 'ivory tower'*; we spent
nearly three years in African villages (Ndembu, Lamba, Kosa, Gisu),
mostly in *grass huts* (ibid., p. 9: emphasis added).

Needless to say, many famous anthropologists did not live up to the
stringent requirements implied here. Claude Lévi-Strauss's grand tour
of South America, though adventurous, did not involve any long stay
with any one society. A. R. Radcliffe-Brown's fieldwork experience
has also recently been the subject of searching and sceptical scrutiny
(see Needham, 1974 and the ensuing debate in the journal *Oceania*
from 1981).

4. The recent controversy and some of the reaction surrounding the publication of Freeman's analysis (Freeman 1984) of Margaret Mead's
Samoan ethnography is partly symptomatic of this attitude.

5. The literature, though not large, continues to grow. Some crucial texts
are Said 1979; Asad 1973; Moniot 1976; Copans 1974; Fabian 1983.

6. See, for example, the remarks in Note 2.

7. In New Zealand there is, at the time of writing, a vigorous debate at
a variety of levels about the relationship of non-Maori researchers, film
producers, etc. to 'Maori' topics and subjects. Thus, for example, the
historian Michael King, who has written and edited a large number of
works on 'Maori' subjects, has felt it necessary recently to abandon
the field and to take up Pakeha themes – such as l'Affaire Greenpeace!

8. Bourdieu (1977:2) discusses the reliance of anthropologists on models
of culture which borrow metaphors from cartography. Here Lévi-
Strauss provides a concrete example of this reliance.

9. the influence is wider than this:

Few anthropologists in recent years have enjoyed wider influence
in the social sciences than Clifford Geertz. Sociologists, political
scientists, and social historians interested in popular culture have
turned increasingly to anthropology, and the anthropologist most
often embraced is Professor Geertz (Roseberry 1984:1013).

10. In his early work Geertz was influenced by Ryle. Bourdieu acknowledges convergences between his ideas and those of Wittgenstein. The
parallels between a certain tradition of analytic philosophy and the
work of these two anthropologists would be worth exploring if only

because Bourdieu's work represents an opportunity for the analytic tradition to escape its sterility. See also Snook's comments in Chapter 7 below.

11. See Bloch, Maurice, 1983, especially Chapter 5, 'Marxism and American Anthropology'.

12. It is interesting to note that Geertz's early work showed strong influences from the American tradition of materialism. He seems to have left this far behind and his recent work hardly shows any vestiges of it.

13. This is not to say that Bourdieu's materialism is a Marxian one. It nevertheless grew out of and developed in relation to it.

14. See Singer (1984:4–6, 32ff.) for one of the clearest discussions of these distinctive approaches to the study of symbolic forms. Semiological approaches are, generally speaking, those that construct symbolic systems in such a way that the analysis of them is seen merely as a matter of internal analysis, of recovering the logic of the system itself. Semiotic approaches on the other hand, emphasise the relationship between symbols and 'symbolising' subject.

15. This account of Cultural Studies relies heavily on the review by Steve Baron 1985.

16. Thus, for example, he argues in 1978 and 1980 that 'the specific and finally irreducible problematic of the Participant Observation method should be used as a resource in a "self-reflexive" analysis – not regarded as the implicit limits of "scientific inquiry".' This merely repeats what Lévi-Strauss had said in his inaugural lecture to the Collège de France in 1960, in its turn merely reformulating ideas already current in ethnology and social anthropology.

17. *Leçon sur la leçon* is at once a more sustained and yet more narrow meditation on this subject. Taking as his focus his own location in the social space Bourdieu subjects it to a critique which he initially develops in *Outline* and *Distinction*. See Chapter 8 in this book.

18. Marxist theory in particular suffers from this effect: 'The historical success of Marxist theory, the first would-be scientific social theory to have realised itself so fully in the social world, thus helps to bring about a paradoxical situation: the theory of the social world least capable of integrating the *theory effect* – which Marxism has exerted more than any other – nowadays no doubt represents the most powerful obstacle to the progress of the adequate theory of the social world, to which it has, in other times, contributed more than any other.' (1985:744).

19. The importance attached to and the prominent position given to Canguilhem and Bachelard in his collaborative work *Le métier de sociologue* (Fr. ed., 1968) justifies this claim (see also Fr. ed., 1987:13–14).

20. This reflexiveness is reflected too in Bourdieu's style of work. A large number of works have appeared with him as joint author indicating his devaluation of the notion of the self. Furthermore the continual return to the same objects of research (see Chapter 1) indicates his 'scientific' spirit, his critical evaluation of his own work. This contrasts strongly with the style of work of someone like Lévi-Strauss: singular and

constantly in search of new subjects to show his skills. Lévi-Strauss speaks of his intelligence as being neolithic, slash-and-burn; Bourdieu has the patience of a peasant to cultivate the same plot year after year yielding different crops.

21. This is a task becoming increasingly urgent from another point of view because the 'traditional' societies which have been the grist of anthropological mills have begun to disappear both theoretically and historically.

22. In another context there is trenchant critique of this notion by someone whose work comes close at times to Bourdieu's position:

> The more the European anthropologist shows himself to be respect-ful of differences (and we should not forget here the current vogue that the cult of difference enjoys . . .), the more Hountondji informs us, he credits 'the generally implicit theses that non-western societies enjoy a complete specificity, the unspoken postulate that there is a difference in *nature*. . . . a qualitative difference . . . between so-called primitive societies and 'developed' ones.
>
> (Augé 1982:82)

In Augé's account of his work Hountondji comes close to Bourdieu. Hountondji has coined the term 'practical ideology' – 'the set of prac-tices, rituals and behaviours that seem to constitute both schemes of conduct and schemes of thought (not a "philosophy")' and he suggests the following procedure for the 'prudent analyst':

> What first strikes one as being a group's dominant ideology (in the singular) is never just its *dominant* practical ideology. Instead of hastily extending it to all the group's members, instead of naively taking it at face value, instead of forging a philosophical theory out of it that is presumed to have the support of the entire community, the prudent analyst will strive to uncover, behind the surface una-nimity, the whole gamut of non-dominant ideologies, or, at any rate, relations at a tangent to the dominant ideology (ibid.:86).

Here Hountondji comes close to various concepts used by Bourdieu – 'habitus' (practical ideology) and 'field'. The missing element is the reflexive analyses of the analyst's own position.

23. A note on Bourdieu's statistics: typically, Bourdieu uses an innovative and 'French' technique of statistical analysis (see Bourdieu 1984:571–2). This technique is associated with the 'Analyse des don-nées' school whose key figure is Jean-Paul Benzecri. Lebart, Morineau and Warwick (1984) have recently made available an English text on the techniques and methods of this school. They write (ibid.:165):

> Benzecri (1974) doubts that purely analytical data reduction (i.e. explanation of complex phenomena by simple phenomena) can be possible (as they are in physics), because in . . . social sciences, 'The order of the composite phenomenon is worth more than the elementary properties of its components'.

They argue for the virtues of the new analytical tools they develop, and especially their 'maps' of correspondence.

Presenting the results as maps is in itself a methodological innovation – although the rules for reading these maps are more complicated than they would appear to be. In fact, common language, by its linear and sequential character, makes it easy to express non-symmetrical relationships such as *implications*, whereas the relationship of covariance, which is symmetric, is more difficult to translate into language that implies a causal relationship. This is why the two-dimensional pictures that represent the factorial planes are very useful tools for analysis and communication. (ibid.:165–6).

Bourdieu echoes these sentiments:

One of the difficulties of sociological discourse lies in the fact that, like all languages, it unfolds in strictly linear fashion, whereas, to escape oversimplification and one-sidedness one ought to be able to recall at every point the whole network of relationships found there. This is why it has seemed useful to present a diagram which has the property, as Saussure says, of being able to 'present simultaneous complications in several dimensions . . . ' (1984:126).

Bourdieu (see also p. 107) however, goes on to warn us of the pitfalls of an over-reliance on statistical description and on 'maps'. We have to beware the statistical unconscious as much as any, and therefore epistemological analysis of the tools of analysis is not, says Bourdieu following Bachelard, a mere scruple.

24. See *Le sens pratique* (Bourdieu, Fr. ed. 1980) for further commentary on ethnography, especially Chapter 2. The journal *Actes* (see Section B of the bibliography in this book) also contains work by Bourdieu relevant to this discussion of ethnography. See especially No. 59 (September 1985) which includes a discussion with Darnton and Chartier making reference to the work of Geertz. Another issue (No. 62, June 1986) entitled 'L'illusion biographique' is also particularly relevant. In one respect Bourdieu's ethnography, though novel, nevertheless gives expression to a suppressed tendency in French ethnography. Clifford (1988) has argued that we need to see the close relationship at its origin between French ethnography and surrealism and in his essays calls for surrealistic ethnography. Bourdieu's work, though not surrealistic, nevertheless adopts the methods of montage and collage in its construction.

4 Bourdieu – Education and Reproduction[1]
Richard Harker

INTRODUCTION

Many English-speaking commentators seem to assume that Bourdieu's fundamental work on education is to be found in two major books (Bourdieu and Passeron 1977; 1979) and a number of articles (Bourdieu 1967; 1971; 1973b; 1974: Bourdieu and St Martin 1974).[2] But those who think this are mistaken. To the extent that these works constitute the limit of reading they constrain a proper understanding of Bourdieu's theoretical enterprise, which has blossomed from a continual reworking of his ethnographic material from Algeria (Bourdieu 1962; 1963; 1973; 1977; 1979), and from France itself (Bourdieu 1984). The essential point is that it is inappropriate to extrapolate Bourdieu's theoretical enterprise solely from the educational writings, since they predate the intensive development of his theory of practice during the 1970s. Hence evaluations of Bourdieu that appear in the educational literature and which do not take into account these later theoretical developments, are inadequate and misleading. This chapter attempts to overcome such difficulties.

The theoretical issues addressed by Bourdieu's educational critics (Giroux 1983; Willis 1983; Jenkins 1983) are covered elsewhere (see particularly Chapter 9), but some specific aspects will be taken up later in this chapter. First, however, an outline of Bourdieu's views on education will be given, together with an attempt to relate these views to his more recent theoretical work.

EDUCATION – INCLUSION AND EXCLUSION

Bourdieu's work is one of the few coherent accounts of the central role that schools have in both changing and in reproducing social and cultural inequalities from one generation to the next. He achieves this analysis in relation to education through an exploration of the tension between the conservative aspect of schooling (the preservation of knowledge and experience from one generation to the next (*re*-production)), and the dynamic, innovative aspect (the generation of new knowledge (*pro*-duction)). This tension is exacerbated in a plural society by considerations of which particular cultural past (and present) is to be 'conserved' or reproduced in the schools. Bourdieu (1973b:80; 1974:39) has argued that it is the culture of the dominant group (the group (or groups) that control the economic, social and political resources) which is embodied in the schools, and that it is this 'embodiment' that works as a reproduction strategy for the dominant group. Such a reproduction strategy is never complete or perfect, but is an element of the process of class reproduction which is discussed further in Chapter 5. Bourdieu's early work on education attempted to show how this reproduction strategy worked out in relation to school practice.

He asks us to think of *cultural capital* in the same way we think of economic capital, as outlined in Chapter 1. Just as our dominant economic institutions are structured to favour those who already possess economic capital, so our educational institutions are structured to favour those who already possess cultural capital, in the form of the habitus of the dominant cultural fraction. The schools, he argues, take the habitus of the dominant group as the natural and only proper sort of habitus and treat all children as if they had equal access to it.

> The culture of the élite is so near to that of the school that children from the lower middle class (and *a fortiori* from the agricultural and industrial working class) can only acquire with great effort something which is *given* to the children of the cultivated classes – style, taste, wit – in short, those attitudes and aptitudes which seem natural in members of the cultivated classes and naturally expected of them precisely because (in the ethnological sense) they are the *culture* of that class (1974:39).

In this way the dominant habitus is transformed into a form of cultural capital that the schools take for granted, and which acts as a most effective filter in the reproductive processes of a hierarchical society. Poor achievement for some groups (and success for others) in a society, then, is not something inherent in cultural difference *per se*, but is an artifact of the way schools operate. Those with the appropriate cultural capital are reinforced with 'success', while others are not. This is shown in Figure 4.1.

For an individual from a non-dominant background to succeed, a

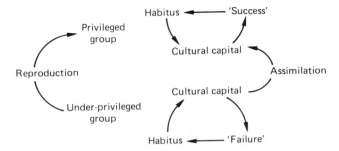

Figure 4.1   The cycle of reproduction

shift from the bottom cycle to the top cycle in Figure 4.1 is required
– the appropriate cultural capital has to be acquired, with inevitable
consequences for the habitus. Theorists of social class call this
embourgeoisement; theorists of ethnicity refer to it as *assimilation*.
But for Bourdieu this is not enough. He wants to show how the
system of schooling works to maintain social order amidst all this
potential for conflict.

> The educational system, an institutionalized classifier which is itself
> an objectified system of classification reproducing the hierarchies
> of the social world in a transformed form . . . transforms social
> classifications into academic classifications, with every appearance
> of neutrality, and establishes hierarchies which are not experienced
> as purely technical, and therefore partial and one-sided, but as
> total hierarchies, grounded in nature, so that social value comes
> to be identified with 'personal' value, scholastic dignities with
> human dignity. The 'culture' which an educational qualification is
> presumed to guarantee is one of the basic components in the
> dominant definition of the accomplished man, so that privation is
> perceived as an intrinsic handicap, diminishing a person's identity
> and human dignity, condemning him to silence in all official situ-
> ations, when he has to 'appear in public', present himself before
> others, with his body, his manners and his language.
> Misrecognition of the social determinants of the educational
> career – and therefore of the social trajectory it helps to determine
> – gives the educational certificate the value of a natural right and
> makes the educational system one of the fundamental agencies of
> the maintenance of the social order (1984:387).

The part played by the school system may be conveniently reviewed through an examination of his writing, which identifies five levels of practice through which inequalities are perpetuated. They may be summarised as follows.

Level 1: For under-privileged children there is a lower success rate – expectations are adjusted accordingly, and become part of the habitus.

Level 2: Where some success is attained, under-privileged children (and their families) tend to make the 'wrong' option choices.

Level 3: Learned ignorance of schools and selection agents – recognising only those who recognise them.

Level 4: Denigration of the academic – style over content.

Level 5: Devaluation of certificates – in favour of habitus. Where selection now turns on habitus (style, presentation, language, etc), these things then become a form of *symbolic capital*, which acts as a multiplier of the productivity of educational capital (qualifications).

At Level 1 the schools, by naturalising the culture of the dominant group, immediately place at a disadvantage all those children from groups other than that whose habitus is embodied in the school. For these individuals 'the school remains the one and only path to culture [in his special use of the term], at every level of education' (Bourdieu and Passeron 1979:21). As such, he adds, schooling could be 'the royal road to the democratization of culture if it did not consecrate the initial cultural inequalities by ignoring them' (ibid.).[3] One of the more obvious of the cultural inequalities is the complex and academic variant of language embodied in educational practice which is treated by teachers as *natural* to the gifted, and is used to rationalise academic judgements 'which in fact perpetuate cultural privilege' (1974:40) since language has its origins in the social milieu.

By defining education as the transference of culture from one generation to the next, classical theories tend to mask the function of *social* reproduction – that is, they treat the cultural heritage as being the undivided property of the whole society, rather than as belonging only to those endowed with the means of appropriating it for themselves (1973b:72–3). Such appropriation involves the mastery of a code of interpretation which is the result of systematic education – facilitated by an appropriate socialisation in the family. Thus the school tends to reinforce and consecrate the initial inequalities (with regard to cultural appropriation) that are engendered by families – 'cultural capital is added to cultural capital' (ibid.:79). In this way the subjective elements of class are embodied in the objective structures of society, and serve as an example of the general themes outlined in Chapter 5. There would appear to be, then, an homology between the structure of relations amongst social classes and the structure of achievement within schools. In spite of this, however, there is movement –

> the controlled mobility of a limited category of individuals, carefully selected and modified by and for individual ascent, is not incompatible with the permanence of structures (of relations between classes) (1973b:71; see also 1974:42).

Bourdieu examines this particular phenomenon from two major directions – attitudes of pupil and parent, and 'learned ignorance' on the part of selection agents. Attitudes toward school, its culture and the various futures to which it leads are based, Bourdieu argues, on class-derived value-systems which are incorporated within the habitus (1974:33). Parents appear to be objectively aware of the probabilities for their children and make educational choices accordingly. Habitus must, of course, be seen as merely a source of choices, rather than a lock step prescription. The potential strategies to which it is connected vary according to circumstances. However,

> everything happens as if parental attitudes towards their children's education . . . were primarily the interiorization of the fate objectively allotted (and statistically quantifiable) as a whole to the social category to which they belong (1974:33).

Within this argument objective probabilities are intuitively perceived and internalised as subjective hopes adjusted accordingly (ibid.). This is a specific example of a more general theoretical proposition Bourdieu makes in his *Outline of a Theory of Practice* (1977:164):

> Every established order tends to produce . . . the naturalization of its own arbitrariness. Of all the mechanisms tending to produce this effect, the most important and the best concealed is undoubtedly the dialectic of the objective chances and the agents' aspirations, out of which arises the *sense of limits*, commonly called the *sense of reality*, i.e. the correspondence between the objective classes and the internalized classes, social structures and mental structures, which is the basis of the most ineradicable adherence to the established order.[4]

The children's attitudes parallel those of the parents and are objectified in school-leaving rates. Further, he argues there are some groups for whom 'success' in school would imply an individual's rejection of their social origins. Hence all sorts of quite subtle (and not so subtle) influences are at work which have the effect of discouraging excessive ambition (1974:35):

> Objective limits become a sense of limits, a practical anticipation of objective limits acquired by experience of objective limits, a 'sense of one's place' which leads one to exclude oneself from the goods, persons, places and so forth from which one is excluded (1984:471).

People come to want, and to value, what is objectively allotted to them, which Bourdieu has called 'making a virtue of necessity' (see Chapter 5 of this volume). At Level 2, the argument based on attitudes indicates a 'double selection' process at all levels of the educational system: first, a lower 'success' rate at any specific point; and second, even with 'success' for the few, a different pattern of options from the range made available by the 'success'. Disadvantaged families tend to make choices which do not capitalise on the initial 'success' – thus advantages and disadvantages become cumulative. These option choices are not necessarily made out of ignorance of the range of possible options, but may be due to a family opting for known 'security', which for many families is a synonym for 'success'. Habitus is thus incorporated possibilities, and must be seen quite differently from socialisation. The strategies which closely accompany habitus would be meaningless without its dynamic quality. But, the choices available to parents at any particular time are nonetheless constrained. Hence Bourdieu is arguing that the perception of success is very much a factor of the structural location of the perceiver.[5] The implications of this argument for the structure–agency debate will be taken up in Chapter 9.

A qualitative shift occurs with Level 3. The further up the system, the greater the tendency for the schools to recognise only those who recognise them – what Bourdieu calls the *learned ignorance* of the schools and selection agents. Even if the student 'succeeds' and makes the right choices for further success, the habitus engendered by the school operates in such a way that at each cut-off point, those who succeed come to accept the criteria which recognised their success (see proposition 3 and its extensions, Bourdieu and Passeron 1977:31–54). Hence the students become more like each other, and less like their diverse backgrounds, so at the next cut-off point the agents of selection (teachers, examiners) have even less cause to question the social neutrality of the selection procedure (Bourdieu and St Martin 1974:345).

This demonstrates nicely the objective structure of the relationship between the dominant class and the school, which

> dominates the mechanisms by which the educational system repro-
> duces itself by recognizing those who recognize it and by giving
> its blessing to those who dedicate themselves to it . . . (ibid.:358).

These structures of relationship serve to transform *social* advantages or disadvantages into *educational* ones through choices which are linked to social origins, thereby duplicating and reinforcing their influence (1974:36).

The learned ignorance is exacerbated by the conflating of the cultural capital of the dominant group with the educational capital supported by the school. The assumption that the habitus of the dominant or élite group constitutes the only proper criterion of scholastic success gives *de facto* sanction to initial cultural inequalities by ignoring them, and treating all pupils, however unequal they may be in reality, as equal in rights and duties (1974:38; Bourdieu and Passeron 1979:21). Hence formal equality masks an indifference or a dismissal of cultural differences, and teaching techniques take for granted a background in pupils which is true only for some.

For the underprivileged student who does succeed despite the structures of inequality described so far, there is still a further hurdle. This fourth level in the practice of inequality is constituted when the school devalues its own culture 'by denigrating a piece of academic work as being too "academic"' (Bourdieu and Passeron 1979:21), and thereby gives favour to 'the inherited culture which does not bear the vulgar mark of effort and so has every appearance of ease and grace' (ibid.). And elsewhere:

> Those who have by right the necessary *manner* are always likely
> to dismiss as laborious and laboriously acquired values which are
> only of any worth when they are innate (that is, acquired from
> family and class) (1974:38).

This mechanism is analysed in relation to social structure when he later writes of the distinction between the easy 'brilliance' of a student from a cultivated background, and the pedantic 'plodders' from underprivileged backgrounds (Bourdieu and St Martin

1974:347–51). "'Pedantic" and "limited", their too exclusively scholastic interest and knowledge show that they owe everything to the school' (ibid.:355).

More specifically Bourdieu describes the relationship between social class and prestige linguistic forms, schooling, and taste, as a 'triadic structure', in which the working class is simply dispossessed through lack of an appropriate habitus, the ruling class simply actualises what is the norm for it, while the middle classes strive anxiously 'for correctness which may lead them to outdo bourgeois speakers in their tendency to use the most correct and the most recondite forms . . . the subtly imperfect mastery obtained by entirely scholastic acquisition' (1977b:658–9). This triadic structure involves ambiguity in the unique nature of the French school system and the kind of intellectual tradition which it fosters – described in some detail in the final section of his paper on 'Systems of Education and Systems of Thought' (1967:352–8) – characterised as a 'tendency to prefer eloquence to truth, style to content' (ibid.:355). The ambiguity surfaces when examination candidates are often criticised by their examiners for their over-didactic approach 'when in fact that is really why they are there' (Bourdieu and St Martin 1974:353). Bourdieu and St Martin also add wryly that the criticism is for 'usurping too soon one of the privileges of the teaching profession and exposing too clearly the reality of the exercise'. The style, wit and brilliance which the examiners appear to be looking for are attributes of the habitus of the cultivated classes and are objectified in the ideas of 'precocity' and 'giftedness' which are the 'ideological mechanisms by which the educational system tends to transform social privileges into natural privileges *and not privileges of birth*' (ibid.:346) – misrecognition in action – see Chapter 1.

The fact that schools may take as an aim the 'happy medium' between brilliance and pedantry merely acts as a cover for a dictatorship of 'good-sense', 'tact' and 'taste' which is the basis of the infallible and final judgements of teachers and agents of selection (ibid.:352).

In his later, encyclopedic work on French culture (1984:85–92), Bourdieu conceives of this phenomenon in terms of the operation of two markets, the sites of which are the family and the school respectively. In both of these sites the competencies deemed relevant are constituted by usage, and are simultaneously 'priced' – that is, made into capital. How you acquire the 'high-value' competencies, Bourdieu argues, is at least as important as (and in France perhaps more important than) the competencies themselves, and constitutes a separate form of capital in its own right. When consuming cultural products (such as art, literature, films) the value of the products chosen is partly determined by the value of the chooser, which in turn is largely determined through the manner of choosing. The manner of choosing, he argues, which constitutes the highest form of cultural capital can be acquired only from the family:

> What is learnt through immersion in a world in which legitimate culture is as natural as the air one breathes is a sense of the legitimate choice so sure of itself that it convinces by the sheer manner of the performance, like a successful bluff (1984:91–2).

This point is elaborated further, specifically in relation to art, in Chapter 6. In all of this, the basic 'commodities' which constitute the educational 'capital' at the end of the process are the qualifications and certificates which constitute the fifth level of the maintenance of inequality.

> By awarding allegedly impartial qualifications (which are also largely accepted as such) for socially conditioned aptitudes which it treats as unequal 'gifts', it [the school] transforms *de facto* inequalities into *de jure* ones and *economic and social* differences into *distinctions of quality*, and legitimates the transmission of the cultural heritage [the élite habitus]. In doing so, it is performing a confidence trick. Apart from enabling the élite to justify being what it is, the *ideology of giftedness*, the cornerstone of the whole educational and social system, helps to enclose the underprivileged classes in the roles which society has given them by making them see as natural inability things which are only a result of an inferior social status, and by persuading them that they owe their social fate . . . to their individual nature and their lack of gifts. (1974:42).[6]

This power to dominate the disadvantaged groups, Bourdieu came to call *symbolic power* ('the power to constitute the given by stating it', 1977a:117; see also 1977:165), and the exercise of it, *symbolic violence* ('the power to impose . . . instruments of knowledge and (*sic*) expression of social reality . . . which are arbitrary (but unrecognised as such)' 1977a:115). This power to impose the principles of the construction of reality – in particular, social reality – is seen as a major dimension of political power (1977:165). (This point is taken up and elaborated in a more general way in the next chapter.)

Where the fit between the objective structures and internalised structures is strong, then

> the established cosmological and political order is perceived not as arbitrary, i.e. as one possible order among others, but as a self-evident and natural order which goes without saying and therefore goes unquestioned, the agents' aspirations have the same limits as the objective conditions of which they are the product (1977:166).

However, the fit is never absolute, and a considerable and increasing number of children from underprivileged homes do 'make it' through the school system. One of the consequences of this widening base to the educational pyramid is the process of devaluation that has occurred with the certificates passed out by the schools. As 'everybody' gets qualified, he argues, selection and recruiting agents shift to other criteria, such as presentation, ease, style and so on, all favouring the product of the dominant elite habitus. These 'other' selection criteria then are part of the symbolic capital utilised by the dominant fractions of society to ensure the reproduction of their domination (1977:171–97; 1979c; and see Chapter 1 for an extended discussion of capital).

The possession of such symbolic capital enhances the 'productivity' of the educational capital gained from certificates and qualifications.

> the rate of return on educational capital is a function of the economic and social capital that can be devoted to exploiting it. (Bourdieu and Passeron 1979:79)

And further:

> the habitus inculcated by upper class families gives rise to practices which, even if they are without selfish motives . . . are extremely profitable to the extent that they make possible the acquisition of the maximum yield of academic qualifications whenever recruitment or advancement is based upon co-optation or on such diffuse and total criteria as 'the right presentation', 'general culture' etc. (1973b:98; see also 1984:85–92).

In this way, Bourdieu argues, in societies where the hereditary transmission of power and privilege is now frowned upon, the education system provides an avenue by contributing to the reproduction of the system of class relations, but concealing the fact that it does (1973b:72).[7] Thus educational capital (in the form of qualifications) is not enough in a society such as France. In order to convert it into social and economic capital, the individual must also be the possessor of an appropriate amount of symbolic capital, derivable only from the habitus of the dominant elite, which can only be legitimately acquired from the family. This leads Bourdieu to a consideration of what he calls the 'populist illusion', that is:

> the demand that the parallel cultures of the disadvantaged classes should be given the status of the culture taught by the school system (Bourdieu and Passeron 1979:72).

Bourdieu argues that there is more to mass school culture than a class habitus – it must conform to material conditions and levels of technology, as well as be seen to be in the 'best' interests of all. In addition, he claims that some aspects of school culture ('fluency of speech and writing and the very multiplicity of abilities', ibid.) are characteristic of all societies based on school learning.[8]

INTELLECTUAL HISTORY AND HABITUS

Bourdieu is also interested in exploring the relationship between schooling and the intellectual life in an historical context. In 'Systems of Education and Systems of Thought' (1967) he sets himself the question: Does school culture and thought replace the role of religion in socialisation for people in cultures with schools? He combines this with an examination of the way a common experience of schooling makes communication possible. 'The school', he claims, 'is the fundamental factor in the cultural consensus in as far as it represents the sharing of a common sense which is the prerequisite for communication' (1967:341). In non-school societies this function is fulfilled by religious institutions.

In a paradigmatic way people can be linked to their own period by their problem approach. Even though disagreements occur, outsiders can see (from an historical perspective) an implied basic concurrence – in their tacit agreement about what things are worth disagreeing about – 'the consensus in dissensus' (ibid.).[9]

> In all cases . . . the patterns informing the thought of a given period can be fully understood only by reference to the school system, which is alone capable of establishing them and developing them, through practice, as the habits of thought common to a whole generation (ibid.:342).

In an alternative exposition of this particular aspect of 'Intellectual Field' (1971), Bourdieu refers to these habits of thought as 'the Cultural unconscious' (pp. 180–85), and which subsequently becomes incorporated into the concept of *habitus*. It must be remembered of course that such influences can only directly bear on those who actually attend schools. However the divisions of school organisation are the principle of the forms of classification, which in turn are forms of (symbolic) domination (Honneth et al. 1985), hence the school's influence is diffused throughout the whole society – see Chapter 6 where this position is elaborated further in relation to art and aesthetics.

THE FIELD OF EDUCATION

To apply Bourdieu's most recent theoretical formulations to education does not necessitate repudiation of the earlier work, but a recasting of it. Education would now be seen as a field in a multidimensional social space through which individuals (or whole social groups) would trace a certain trajectory or path. The trajectory is a consequence of the positions held in related fields, which in turn is largely a consequence of the amount of capital held, relevant to the particular fields. As pointed out in Chapter 1, a field can be seen as a site of struggle over a particular form of capital. To take this idea further, some forms of capital (such as educational qualifications, family background) 'generalise' to a number of fields (even to some where they may have little utility) and can be used to maximise a position in such a related field, hence enhancing the trajectory. The major sites, Bourdieu has argued, for the acquisition of such generalisable forms of capital are the family and the schools. In his work on the French educational system, Bourdieu argues that the education site presupposes that of the family. That is to say, the struggle between the capital produced by these two sites is biased in favour of the family. The habitus of the dominant social and cultural fraction acts as a multiplier of educational capital, not just in the field of education but also in the related fields of jobs, community work, cultural consumption and so on. It is important to point out here that Bourdieu's instancing of his theoretical framework in relation to France, should not be taken as applicable to *all* societies, *all* educational systems. Change the society and naturally there will be a change in the contiguity and juxtaposition of fields, a change in the balance between family and school, between the kinds (and amount) of capital they produce, their generalisability, together with a whole host of other economic, social, political and cultural factors. Richard Nice emphasises this view in an interview (1985) and further makes the observation that Bourdieu (and French people generally) see education almost exclusively in terms of *training* and *selection*. There is no notion in his work of the individual, personal development implicit in the English-speaking world's understanding of the idea of education. Such a mechanistic view of education reflects in part, the field in French society where for virtually everything (job, status, mobility, power) paper qualifications are a necessary acquisition. The framework for analysis, however, while developing from his work in France (and Algeria) is generalisable to other countries, but requires active participation on the part of anyone who would wish to translate Bourdieu's model in terms of the social space of such other countries.

The problem of Bourdieu's writing on education being so closely tied to the highly centralised French system is very clearly spelt out by Archer (1984) in her critique of Bourdieu and Passeron's *Reproduction in Education, Society and Culture* (1977). It is this particular volume which in general is seen in the English speaking world as Bourdieu's *magnum opus* on education. The book itself was first published in French in 1970, hence is both a product and a culmination of his empirical work of the 1960s. It is our considerable loss, however, if we think that this is all Bourdieu has to offer the sociology of education.

Willis (1983), Giroux (1983) and Jenkins (1983) make the fundamental mistake of reading as *general theory*, what is in fact a *working out* in relation to the highly centralised French education system of a long-since reworked aspect of his method. Of course this 'working out' looks structurally-bound since that, as Archer (1984) points out, is the way the French system is – possibly the most highly bureaucratised and centralised system in the world (a Weberian paradise).[10] It is hardly surprising therefore that such a working out does not 'square' with the field of education familiar to those from much more decentralised systems. His method demands that empirical realities be faced in ethnographic detail – hence the charges that he is too exclusively French. But those who would invoke Bourdieu's method must put it up against the evidence of their own educational reality – reconstruct their own field and try to discern the precise forms of capital, and the kinds of strategies operative within it. Of those who dismiss Bourdieu because they don't recognise the French educational field, he says in an interview:

> They easily cross the borders, but with empty suitcases – they have nothing to declare. From the moment one really wants to understand the relations between the changes of the economy and the changes of the school system, it is necessary to go into details, and therefore into the details of a historic situation. But it is also under this condition that one works out concepts and methods that are susceptible to universal application, and also that one discovers very general mechanisms that are susceptible of being observed in the most different systems.
>
> (Schwibs 1985)

Hence there are two tasks in front of educationalists who would seek to use Bourdieu in relation to non-French school systems. First, it is necessary to catch up with Bourdieu theoretically, by seeing his work as a *method* of enquiry rather than a completed *theoretical* edifice; and second, to work out the method in relation to their own social space and the particular 'field' of education within it – Bourdieu's work on France cannot be taken as a substitute for this new empirical requirement. Nor should it be thought that a decentralised system is necessarily any less structurally bound than the French system. Power and control are likely to be exercised less directly, utilising contiguous fields, and hidden behind a much more opaque mask of ideology and rhetoric. Control, however, may be equally sustained.

EDUCATION, INEQUALITY AND THE REPRODUCTION DEBATE

The first part of this chapter has tried to show how power and control are exercised through schooling. For the remainder of the chapter attention will be turned to the broader issues of education and its role in the reproduction of inequality.

To recapitulate briefly, education is a field in which agents struggle for capital (credentials). But it is also related to other fields in the social space, and hence cannot be isolated for study from that social space and the relatively autonomous fields that surround it. Bourdieu's argument is that schools are artifacts of the dominant social and cultural fraction. Hence different groups have different relationships to schools, depending on their trajectory in relation to the dominant group. Traditionally, some groups have used the school system to reproduce their class position (various 'middle'-class fractions) while others have not (farmers, trades, 'working'-class groups). As education becomes increasingly widespread and available to all groups, other means are resorted to in order to perpetuate the 'distinctions' between such social groups. (The way this works in relation to class analysis is taken up in the next chapter.) The most obvious of these strategies in education is a resort to alternative private schooling, which can become a part of the dominant group habitus (as in England), and thus preserve an educational distinction through the acquisition of a certain symbolic capital (the ethos, style, modes of speech acquired at private schools), through a reconversion of economic capital, which ensures a place in the dominant group for the children. Hence private schooling becomes an extension of the family for the dominant group.[11] Other aspects of these 'distinctions' have been touched on above in the discussion of the five-level model of educational inequality, and in Chapter 1.

In addition to his work on fields and the social space, Bourdieu has also worked on developing his theory of practice, as outlined in Chapter 1. These theoretical developments, while causing considerable interest in the fields of anthropology and, increasingly, sociology, are virtually ignored by educationalists, by whom he is dismissed as a structurally deterministic, reproduction theorist. At the simplest level, portrayals of Bourdieu's work as merely reproductive can be represented as in Figure 4.2.

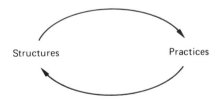

Structures   Practices

Figure 4.2   Simple reproductive model

In one of his major works, Bourdieu specifically rejects such a model as being of the 'objectivist' type, which fails to take *time* into account (1977:3). The addition of time to such objectivist formulations allows one to perceive the *dialectical* relations between objective structures and practices, thus providing a theoretical level which can account for change (including resistance). Further, Bourdieu uses a mediating concept (that of *habitus*) between objective structures and practice. At the very least then, his work should be represented as in Figure 4.3.

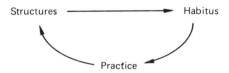

Figure 4.3 Minimal Bourdieu model

But of course this is not enough to parry the charges that the theory is merely reproductive. Two things need to be examined further: first the nature of *habitus* and its production and secondly the determinants of *practice*.

Both of these examinations have been undertaken in Chapter 1, where it is shown that practice cannot be reduced to either habitus or through habitus to objective structures, since historical circumstances play their part in its generation. Nor can it be reduced to specific historical circumstances or forces, since the perception of these social forces is filtered through the habitus. We are left with practice as a dialectical production, continually in the process of reformulation. The reformulation may be almost imperceptible in a slowly changing, traditional-type culture, or of major proportions in a revolutionary situation. The latter events would involve a disruption of the habitus-controlled perception of historical circumstances (the destruction of false consciousness, the overthrow of a ruling hegemony), and a refocusing on a new set of principles (a 'true' consciousness, a counter-hegemonic transformation).

The model now looks like Figure 4.4, always bearing in mind

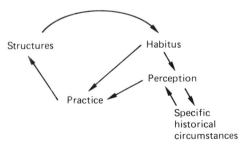

Figure 4.4 Reproduction and change

that the specific historical circumstances take on the attributes of structures in their turn.

This non-reductionist model of cultural practice, with a dynamic conception of habitus attached to strategy, with reflexivity and change built into it, and a clear dialectical link to the material world, does not appear to fit well with descriptions of Bourdieu's work by his educational critics. Giroux (1982) for example claims that a major gap in Bourdieu's theory is that it

> is a theory of reproduction that displays no faith in subordinate classes and groups, no hope in their ability or willingness to reinvent and reconstruct the conditions under which they live, work and learn.

On the contrary, as Nicholas Garnham and Raymond Williams point out (1980:211), it is the specification of 'the conditions under which reproduction does not take place leading to the more or less rapid transformation of the social formation' which is a part of the problem to which Bourdieu's *Outline of a Theory of Practice* is addressed.[12]

A careful reading of Bourdieu's ethnographic work adds a dimension not readily discernible from the earlier educational writing. It provides a foundation for a theory of practice which incorporates social change (see particularly the first paper in Bourdieu, 1979) and human agency (Bourdieu, 1977), as well as an examination of the structural limits within which they must work.

EDUCATION AS CULTURAL PRACTICE

As a form of cultural practice, education can be interpreted in terms of Bourdieu's more recent theoretical developments. It is clear that the school does function to reproduce social inequalities, but not in the mechanistic way of the early Bowles and Gintis (1976) model, which is the model that many associate with Bourdieu. The schools operate within the constraints of a particular habitus, but also react to changing external conditions (economic, technological and political). The perception of these conditions is filtered through the same habitus that is already established, often giving an air of unreality to the adaptations the schools make to changed external circumstances. For example, the reaction of many schools to rising levels of unemployment is to run courses on how to apply, to be interviewed, for a job – in Bourdieu's terms, to transmit the 'style' language and behaviour of the dominant habitus. The irony of this strategy is that it is the manifestation of this very habitus through the school system that has led to their 'failure' in the first place. What is preserved (although the form may change) in all of the reactions of schools to such changing external circumstances as unemployment is the continued dominance of the group whose habitus is embodied in the schools.

But the reproduction is not mechanical as in a photocopy. The cumulative tendency of such adaptations in times of economic 'down-turn' is for the schools to become more vocationally orientated. However, the reaction is not immediate, nor is it complete. There is a time-lag between structures and habitus, the source of which lies in the dialectic between changes in the production apparatus and changes in the education system (Bourdieu and Boltanski 1981:142). This lag (and the consequent discrepancies that will inevitably arise) has to be understood in terms of the present state and history of the relationship between the system of 'education' and the system of 'production'. In modern industrial states, this relationship is one in which the schools become the dominant agency 'for the production of producers' (ibid.). Bourdieu and Boltanski go on:

> But, because it fulfils not only functions of reproducing skilled labourpower (. . . technical reproduction), but also functions of reproducing the positions of the agents and their groups within the social structure (. . . social reproduction) – positions which are relatively independent of strictly technical capacity – the educational system *depends less directly on the demands of the production system than on the demands of reproducing the family group* (1981:142–3, their emphasis).

Furthermore, they argue that the education system organises itself in terms of the imperatives of its own reproduction. Each system (economy, family, education) obeys its own logic. The school has a relative autonomy (see Chapter 1) with respect to the economy, and its own tempo of evolution (ibid.). The main interplay between the systems of 'education' and 'production' is the conjunction between formal qualifications and jobs – the area in which the time-lag is perhaps the greatest, and which is most susceptible to the influence of the dominant habitus.

A point in the above passage from Bourdieu and Boltanski seems to me to provide the rebuttal for a criticism of Bourdieu in a paper by P. Willis (1983). In this reassessment of his *Learning to Labour* in the light of theories of both production and reproduction, Willis typifies Bourdieu's theory as in Figure 4.3 above – that is, as a cyclical sequence of: structures, which through symbolic violence produce habitus; which provides the dispositions toward practices; which reproduce the original structures (1983:118–19). Willis's major criticism (as that of Giroux) is that the theory does not allow for cultural production, specifically as it relates to the production of working-class cultural practices, and hence has nothing to say about a radical politics of education. Certainly Bourdieu rejects as an 'illusion' the idea that the culture of the disadvantaged is a sufficient basis for an educational programme (see above, p. 96), but this does not mean that he is uninvolved at the political level to broaden the accessibility of school programmes (see Fr. ed. 1989; Actes 1987, 1987a; 1985a; and note 14, Chapter 2). Nor can it be concluded that the theoretical model which Bourdieu has engendered is incapable of generating such an analysis. This analysis could well start with Bourdieu and Boltanski's statement that (see above): 'the educational system *depends less directly on the demands of the production system than on the demands of reproducing the family group.*'

Willis himself notes that 'Individual working class kids may succeed in education – never the whole class' (1983:129), which points to the need for a level of analysis less than 'the working class' (see also note 11). Bourdieu's theory would suggest that the reproduction of family groups is more significant than that of whole classes – which are doubtful entities anyway, except in name (see the discussion in Chapter 5 of this volume). It will be recalled that habitus itself is largely concerned with transmission within families. Willis's own analysis of 'the lads' should not be taken as an analysis of the working class. What of 'the ear'oles' who are equally from a working-class background? The reproduction of family habitus would seem to offer the possibility of a finer-grained analysis, and thus get us closer to knowing that which is not reproduced. It is what is not reproduced that is at once the engine of change and the arena for human agency. By using habitus as a generative principle, varying strategies can be explained in a way simple reproductive theories cannot match.

CONCLUSION

In this chapter I have outlined what Bourdieu has to say about education, and contended that educationalists who wish to invoke the work of Pierre Bourdieu in their arguments, are setting up a straw man if they rely only on his early work related to the French education system.

His theory of cultural practice develops the notion of reproduction to far higher levels than can be found in any of the specifically educational writing, and provides us with a unique methodological apparatus for a penetrating analysis of social inequalities and the part that schools play in their perpetuation.

NOTES

1. This chapter incorporates elements from two papers published previously: Harker, 1984, 1984a.
2. These dates are misleading and show the date of translation rather than their original publication date in French, the latest of which was 1970. The original sources of some of the ideas found in the books on education are to be found in the pages of *Actes de la recherche en sciences sociales*, and other journals – see, for example, Bourdieu 1967. In *Actes* the following show his continued interest in education: 1975/02:95–107 (with Luc Boltanski), 'Le titre et le poste: rapports entre le système de production et le système de reproduction'; 1975/3:68–93 (with Monique de St Martin), 'Les catégories de l'entendement professoral'; 1978/24:2–24, 'Classement, déclassement, reclassement'; 1981/39, 'Epreuve scolaire et consécration sociale. Les classes préparatoires aux Grandes écoles'; 1984/52–53:95–100, Le hit–parade des intellectuels français ou qui sera juge de la légitimité des juges?' A full issue was devoted to the issue of education and philosophy (47/48, Juin 1983), and educational matters are covered by Bourdieu and his colleagues in most issues. For other special issues devoted to education, see 1979/30 'L'Institution scolaire'; 1981/39 'Grandes et petites écoles'; 1982/42 'Classements scolaires et classement social'; 1987/69 'Pouvoirs d'école, I'; and 1987/70 'Pouvoirs d'école, II'. A well-known report written by Bourdieu for the Collège de France was issued to President Mitterrand in March 1985 (Bourdieu, 1985a). Further, Bourdieu and Monique de St Martin recently completed a report on transitions in the educational system, 'Structures objectives et représentations subjectives du champ des institutions d'enseignement supérieur', Juin 1986, Écoles des hautes études en sciences sociales. A large study of higher education, of which this report is a small part, has now been published (Bourdieu, Fr. ed. 1989).
3. This argument provides a parallel to that of Gramsci, who suggests that before even entering the classroom, a child from

> a traditionally intellectual family . . . has numerous advantages over his comrades, and is already in possession of attitudes learnt from

his family environment . . . . This is why many people think that the difficulty of study conceals some 'trick' which handicaps them – that is, when they do not simply believe that they are stupid by nature.

(Gramsci 1971:42–3)

Underprivileged people, Gramsci argues, see the children of the well-to-do 'complete, speedily and with apparent ease, work which costs their sons tears and blood' (ibid.). Further, Gramsci argues that the 'progressive' curriculum introduced into Italy in the 1920s 'presupposes that formal logic is something you already possess when you think, but does not explain how it is to be acquired, so that in practice it is assumed to be innate' (ibid.).

4. In addition to education, this proposition is explored in relation to language and linguistic exchanges (1977b); art and other aesthetic products (symbolic goods) (1968, 1971, 1980, 1980a, 1983); sport (1978); and to French society (1984).

5. This is borne out by research conducted in a New Zealand comprehensive high school into the subject option choices made by 298 Third Form pupils (Harker 1975). The pupils were assigned to one of four categories, depending on their father's occupation, and had the choice of four subject 'streams' – Latin, French, Bookkeeping or Modern (woodwork – metalwork for boys, typing/home science for girls). The results are shown in Table 1 for the group as a whole, and in Table 2 for all those pupils whose IQ scores fell between 95 and 105 – an average group. The striking retention of the pattern of option choice when controlling for academic aptitude fairly clearly indicates a different pattern of expectations on the part of the pupils and their families.

Table 4.1 Option choice by socio-economic group (percentages)

			OPTION	
	Latin	French	Bookkeeping	Modern
Professional	48	31	14	5
upper white collar	21	46	22	11
lower white collar	12	14	26	49
manual	3	8	25	64

Source Table 5, Harker, 1975.

Table 4.2 Option choice by socio-economic group of 'average' pupils – IQ scores between 95 and 105 (N)

			OPTION	
	Latin	French	Bookkeeping	Modern
Professional	-	3	2	1
upper white collar	1	7	7	3
lower white collar	-	6	8	12
manual	-	2	5	19

Source Table 6, Harker, 1975.

6. This same argument is explored in relation to unemployment in the context of Algeria (Bourdieu 1979:61–3).

7. Murphy's analysis of power (1982) is useful here, as he distinguishes between three types of power: power to command; power to constrain; and power to profit from. He argues that different social classes have varying amounts of power to profit from education systems, which may be totally unrelated to the powers to command or constrain the school system. Such a conception, Murphy argues, 'reveals the secret of the "misrecognition" of the underlying power relations upon which schooling is based, the secret of the misrecognition of scholastic hierarchies as hierarchies of innate ability, and therefore the secret of the school system's success as a mechanism for legitimating the transmission of inequalities' (Murphy 1982:193). The specification of these three types of power also allows a better understanding of the apparent contradiction between the autonomy of the school and its role in the 'reproduction and legitimation of the existing social class structure of society' (ibid.:194).

8. While deriving perhaps from his study of Panofsky there are some echoes of Gramsci who declined to idealise working-class culture or find in it material to form the basis of a curriculum (Gramsci 1971:33–40).

   For Gramsci, the inequality lay in the lack of access the 'subaltern' classes had to the traditional humanistic knowledge of the higher schools. Gramsci goes on to say that each social group has its own 'type' of school which perpetuates traditional functions (of super or subordination). Bourdieu expresses it in terms of differentiated schooling creating differentiated 'intellectual clans' (e.g. 'science' *vs* 'arts'). Common schooling, he goes on to argue, would have a unifying effect, thus helping to break down the pattern (1967:349). Similarly Gramsci sees the solution as:

   > a single type of formative school (primary–secondary) which would take the child up to the threshold of his choice of job, forming him during this time as a person capable of thinking, studying and ruling – or controlling those who rule (1971:40).

9. Further, these ideas are not new with Bourdieu. Durkheim also writes that 'education . . . exercises an irresistible influence on individuals' (1956:65). The schools, he claims, put their stamp on people which makes them of their age.

   > each society sets up a certain ideal of man, of what should be, as much from the intellectual point of view as the physical and moral; that this ideal is, to a degree, the same for all the citizens. . . . It is this ideal, at the same time one and various, that is the focus of education (ibid.:70).

Durkheim uses history to show the variability and compatibility of education with time and place. That is, there is no 'ideal' education, which must always operate under constraints ('ineluctable necessities' (ibid.:64)). For Durkheim education grows with, and is adapted to the other institutions in a society.

10. This may also account for Bourdieu's being seen as a Weberian or in a Weberian context by so many English speaking educationalists – Swartz (1977), Sharp (1980), Di Maggio (1982).

11. In an interview Bourdieu states that:

> The method of school reproduction is a method of statistical reproduction. What is reproduced is a relatively constant fraction of the class (in the logical sense of the word). But the determination of the individuals who will fail and of those who will be saved does not depend anymore on the family. Now the family is interested in specific individuals. If one says to the family: 'there will be 90% of them all together (who pass), but not a single one of your family will be among them', then that does not please the family at all. Therefore there is a contradiction between the specific interests of the family as a body and the collective interests of the class. As a result the real interests of the family, the interests of the parents who do not want to see their children fall below their level, the interests of the children who do not want to be brought down, who will undergo the failure with more or less rebellion according to their social origin, etc., will lead to extremely diverse and extraordinarily inventive strategies, which are seen to maintain the position.
>
> (Schwibs 1985)

12. For example, Bidet (1979:204) writes: 'It's precisely the displacement between *habitus* and situation, the irreducible novelty of the latter in relation to the successive conditions forged by *habitus* which, it would seem, establishes the dynamic principle of the model proposed.' Another anthropologist, M. Schiltz, interprets Bourdieu in the same way (1982:729): 'Practice, therefore, must be explained by habitus (its generative principle) on the one hand, and by irreducible novelty of historical situations on the other. So whether we are dealing with phenomena described as migration, revolution, or peasantisation, the practices associated with these phenomena are the product of the dialectical relationship between situations and habitus.'

5 Bourdieu's Class
Chris Wilkes

INTRODUCTION: CLASS, CLAIM AND COUNTERCLAIM

In Bourdieu's forms of analysis, class is fundamental to that side of his argument concerned with objective conditions. But his analysis of class does not depend on objective economic or indeed political criteria alone for its foundation, but on a broad-ranging account of class practices which includes food tastes, clothing, body dispositions, housing styles and forms of social choice in everyday life, as well as the more familiar categories of economy and polity. This extended exposition of class along a range of parameters does not dissolve class into a Weberian account of 'lifestyle' or reduce its power. Rather, it extends the force of class analysis, both in the *range* of its explanatory power, and in the *subtlety* of its classifications.

Bourdieu's work outflanks simple attempts at categorisation, which as pointed out in Chapters 1 and 2, is a process he finds both useless and contentious. Thus, while he is heavily influenced by Marxist thought, he has criticised the crude economism and structuralism of some Marxist work. Attempts at categorisation have been common, however. Garnham and Williams (1980) for example, have seen in his work the residuals of Marxism, and a useful reworking of old Marxist ideas. Rogers Brubaker (1985) has seen in Bourdieu a powerful example of a Weberian scholar at work in his lifestyle analysis. The origins of a writer's thought are often hard to establish, and this is especially true when sources are consciously used to generate complexity and to avoid the pitfalls of other approaches.

In Bourdieu's case, as we have seen in Chapter 2, there is a series of obvious contenders for the choice of 'main influence'. Certainly in a *positive* way, Lévi-Strauss (see Chapter 3), Durkheim and Wittgenstein (see especially Chapter 7) figure strongly, but perhaps much more importantly a series of approaches are significant as *negative* positions from which to break. As indicated in Chapter 1, the fundamental break in the area of class analysis is with various forms of structuralism, in particular with Althusser and his formalistic conception of social class. We need to explore this break in greater detail now. In a paper which establishes the framework of his method, Bourdieu begins:

> Construction of a theory of a social space presupposes a series of breaks with Marxist theory. First, a break with the tendency to privilege substances – here, the real groups, whose number, limits, members, etc., one claims to define – at the expense of relationships; and with the intellectualist illusion which leads one to consider the theoretical class, constructed by the sociologist, as a real class, an effectively mobilised group. Secondly, there has to be a break with the economism which leads one to reduce the social field, a multi-dimensional space, solely to the economic field, to the relations of economic production, which are thus constituted as coordinates of social position. Finally, there has to be a break with the objectivism which goes hand-in-hand with intellectualism and leads one to ignore the symbolic struggles of which the different fields are the site, where what is at stake is the very representation of the social world.
>
> (Bourdieu 1985:195)

In this way, using the familiar Parisian shorthand criticism of competing schools, Bourdieu distinguishes his own approach to class apart from the categorising tendencies of Althusser. The latter, concerned to establish the value of theory within the logic of Marxist science, clearly falls prey both to the privileging of theoretical categories, and by extension, to an overly-theoretical concern with class.[1] Fundamentalist conceptions of class determination predicated on economic domination, and, perhaps, at its limit, a conception of class which asserts the role of the 'economic in the last instance', are clearly also criticised.

Many of the arguments which Bourdieu's method comes to embrace have been an important part of the Anglo-Saxon literature in relation to class. Issues of structure and agency, of subjectivity and objectivity, of reflexive and non-reflexive methodology, of the consciousness of classes, and how to 'measure' them are each part of Bourdieu's approach to the issue, and are examined elsewhere in this volume. Thus the article by Marshall et al. (1985) critiquing structuralism, espouses a Weberian subjectivist class analysis, based on lifestyle in opposition to Wright's more structuralist and Marxist account. Both components of class analysis find echoes in Bourdieu's work. And an earlier debate between Payne and Payne (1983) on the one hand and Goldthorpe (1980) on the other, looks at the issue of mobility. Bourdieu's concern with individual and class trajectories finds a parallel here.

From the Anglo-Saxon perspective Nicos Poulantzas,[2] a relatively autonomous colleague of Althusser, is of particular importance in establishing strong arguments in the neo-Marxist literature on class, and this original work has been a major influence in some large-scale empirical studies of class. It is therefore informative to begin by comparing this recent work with Bourdieu's own counter-claim. Poulantzas proposes to turn Marx's original conception of class-in-itself and class-for-itself on its head, by postulating class as a *social relation* (not unlike Bourdieu) which is constituted in three domains of activity (fields in Bourdieu's terminology) – the economic, the political, the ideological, which then each constitute related dimensions of class. In the economic domain, social relations of production dominate. Within the political dimension, relations of subordination and domination in the workplace are important, while the ideological dimension distinguishes between mental and manual forms of labour, between the capacity to control, through 'expert and secret knowledge', and the incapacity to 'know' reflected in manual labour (Poulantzas 1968:14ff). Erik Wright, while critiquing Poulantzas in some detail (Wright 1978), used an extension of these categories on which to base large-scale comparative research on class.[3] Wright's own formulation seeks to relate dimensions of exploitation (economic relations), and domination (political relations) with a variety of measures of ideology, class biography, class community, class-related political activities and a series of demographic variables.

At first sight a series of homologies present themselves in the work of Wright and Bourdieu, which seem to make Bourdieu's attempted break with structuralism more apparent than real. As we noted above, Bourdieu's 'fields' find a similarity with Poulantzas' (and Wright's) domains. Each of these is distinct, and in Bourdieu's terms could be said to have its own types of capital, over which groups struggle. The homology can be further extended, when we remind ourselves that Wright, following Poulantzas, emphasises class as a *social relation*, much as Bourdieu seeks to emphasise social relationships at the expense of categories. His work is quite consciously distinct from such approaches, however, especially in its use of a unique method. But, his separation from structural Marxism does not constitute a 'clean break' with Marx. He argues:

It is clear that I could easily minimise the difference with Marx by, for example, tugging in my direction the notion of 'position in the relations of production' through one of the structuralist 'readings' which makes it possible to produce a Marx revamped for modern tastes and yet more Marxist than Marx, and so to combine the gratifications of belonging to the circle of believers with the profits of heretical distinction. But we are all so impregnated, whether we know it or not, whether we want it or not, with the problems which Marx has bequeathed to us, and with the false solutions he brought to them – class-in-itself and class-for-itself, working class and proletariat and so on – that one must not be afraid to 'twist the stick in the opposite direction'.

(Bourdieu 1985:195–6)

FIELDS, CAPITALS, CLASSES

In this chapter therefore, I want to argue that a parallelism such as that hypothesised above is misplaced, and that Bourdieu expresses his own view of class through a qualitatively different method. The elaboration of his methodological approach in relation to class occupies most of the remainder of the chapter.

In his approach to class, Bourdieu points precisely to the implications of the break with (Althusserian) structuralism:

More often than not, Marxism either summarily identifies constructed class with real class (in other words, as Marx complained about Hegel, it confuses the things of logic with the logic of things), or, when it does make the distinction, with the opposition between 'class-in-itself', defined in terms of a set of objective conditions, and 'class-for-itself', based on subjective factors, it describes the movement from one to the other (which is always celebrated as nothing less than an ontological promotion) in terms of a logic which is either totally deterministic or totally voluntarist. In the former case, the transition is seen as a logical, mechanical or organic necessity (the transformation of the proletariat from class-in-itself to class-for-itself is presented as an inevitable effect of time, of the 'maturing of the objective conditions'); in the latter case, it is seen as the effect of an 'awakening of consciousness' (prise de conscience) conceived as a 'taking cognizance' (prise de connaissance) of theory, performed under the enlightened guidance of the Party. In all classes, there is no mention of the mysterious alchemy whereby a 'group in struggle', a personalised collective, a historical agent assigning itself to its own ends, arises from the objective economic conditions (1985:199–200).

It is thus mistaken methodologically to objectify class as a theoretical category which depends entirely for its 'life' on objective conditions, nor is it acceptable to see class entirely as consciousness, a process of subjectivity entirely constructed at the levels of dispositions. At times, however, Bourdieu errs on both extremes of the arguments. In an interview, he comments on his objectivist conception of class in *Distinction*:

> My goal in *Distinction* was to show that these habitus connected to positions in social space, and that these habitus, these tastes, were unifying and generating principles. For this I needed an objectivist theory of class, as in class theory: I used class as an instrument to bring the occupants of adjacent positions together in social space . . . . And even in the discussion of the restrained criteria to construct the class like a logical class, like a theoretical class, in the most rigorously positivistic way: I always believed that class criteria play a role in the social space, and in the struggle over classifications, in which the condition of the construction of the classes are real, and mobilised groups are at stake.
>
> (Schwibs 1985:21)

In the same interview, he points to an example where he posited the subjectivist orientation to class:

> understanding class as a social construction could lead to a subjectivist deviation . . . the end of the first part of *Le sens pratique* was at the limit of the subjectivistic deviation [*but*] . . . there are objective bases to all judgements . . . . There is a real struggle of classes, a symbolic and individual struggle, or a collective struggle . . . (ibid.:23).

However, on each occasion when he either veers towards an objectivist account, as he does in *Distinction* (1984), or towards subjectivity, as in *Le sens pratique* (Fr. ed., 1980), his own assessment is given in terms of avoiding the problems of the 'limit at each end'. While his discussion may be a *post hoc* justification for a failure to meet his own standards in particular instances, his dialectical method, veering away from dogmatisms of extremes, is clearly revealed. It is a dialectic of the centre embracing the ambiguity of *both* extremes rather than the senselessness of neither.

His method, therefore, leads to a novel way of establishing a position on class:

> Classes (are) sets of agents who occupy similar positions and who, being placed in similar conditions and subjected to similar conditionings, have every likelihood of having similar dispositions and interests and therefore of producing similar practices and adopting similar stances. (However) This 'class on paper' has the theoretical existence which is that of theories . . . . It is not really a class, an actual class, in the sense of a group, a group mobilised for struggle; at most it might be called a probable class, inasmuch as it is a set of agents which will present fewer hindrances to efforts at mobilisation than any other set of agents. (1985:198).

The probability of actors engaging in class action is therefore inversely proportional to the distance between them, constructed in social space. But this simply increases the probability of class action: it does not necessitate it, as some Marxists then would argue:

> the probability of mobilisation into organised movements, equipped with an apparatus and spokesman etc. (precisely that which lead one to talk of a 'class') will be in inverse ratio to distance in this space (of social relationships). While the probability of assembling a set of agents, really or nominally – through the power of the delegate – rises when they are closer in social space and belong to a more restricted and therefore more homogeneous constructed class, alliance between those who are closest is never necessary . . . and alliance between those most distant from each other is never impossible (ibid.:198–9).

His solution to the problem as to what pushes agents to act is conjunctural – other events, such as the rise of nationalism, may effect the coalitions which takes place along unusual lines, or the intervention of leaders to 'name their constituents' in order to lead them, coupled with objective conditions ripe for political action (such as those of May 1968) provide the impetus which may cause the field of forces to alter its influence on agents. Classes thus seem to have the epistemological status of tendencies which depend on a series of factors, including conjunctural and voluntarist events, to determine whether they are actualised or not. Here, we see an interesting parallel in Bourdieu's work with the realist philosophy of Bhaskar and others.[4] Indeed, Sayer implies just such a connection in referring to the 'important advances made in the philosophy of social science by Giddens, Bhaskar and Bourdieu' (Sayer 1984:244).

Bourdieu gives this argument particular poignancy in a deliciously sharp critique of some members of the militant left: the point is nonetheless telling as to the conjunctural form of class action. Whether this action is 'real' or not may be perhaps resolved in the mind of the reader:

> A class exists insofar – and only insofar – as mandated representatives endowed with plena potestas agendi [the full power to act on behalf of] can be and feel authorised to speak *in its name* – in accordance with the question 'the party is the working class' or 'the working class is the party' a formula which reproduces the canonists' equation: 'The church is the pope (or the bishops), the pope is (or the bishops are) the church' – and so to make it exist as a real force within the political field.
>
> (Bourdieu 1985:217)

Again, in this uneasy dialectic between subjectivity and objectivity, Bourdieu now moves to the subjectivist end by arguing, if only to denigrate the voluntarist pretensions of the strident left, that it is in the naming of a class that a class is constituted. In this subjectivist parody, class and class action are taken to be a theatre, in which key vanguardist figures bring the play to life by asserting their right to 'name a class'.[5] On the other hand, in one of his earliest pieces of work, *Algeria 1960* (1979), he is willing to make the objectivist case more strongly:

> In Algeria, as in most developing countries, the most clear-cut division is that between the regular workers, manual or non-manual, and the mass of unemployed or intermittent workers, journeymen, labourers, or small traders . . . in fact, to each socio-economic position corresponds a system of practices and dispositions.
>
> (Bourdieu 1979:64)

Here too he is at his most determinist:

> We can take it as established that the sheer pressure of economic necessity is sufficient to impose forced submission . . . to the economic order imported by colonization; that it can bring about the collapse of the norms and mental schemes which traditionally

governed economic conduct; that it can also give rise to and sustain economic practices that are absurd both in terms of the spirit of the pre-capitalist economy and in terms of the logic of the capitalist economy.

(Bourdieu 1979:65)

These examples of class in its objectivist and subjectivist extremes give a clue to the overall dialectical quality of Bourdieu's methodological strategy. This dialectical conception of class is held together most satisfactorily in Bourdieu's discussion of class habitus and dispositions, to which we now turn.

CLASS HABITUS AND DISPOSITIONS

Distinction (1984) is a work dedicated to the examination of the genesis of social relationships. But it provides an example (as the reference to the Algerian work indicates), of how habitus is the link in the dialectic between objective and subjective components of class. In this section we concentrate on *Distinction*, and to a lesser extent, *Algeria 1960* to show how this methodological formula resolves itself in a series of concrete explanations.

Before we begin, it is worth making a further methodological point. Bourdieu has a formalistic insistence on presenting quantitative and statistical material to support what might be called structural generalisations – see the discussion in Chapter 3. But this evidence is rarely crucial; the qualitative material makes an intuitive appeal to the reader, and these qualitative analyses are piled one upon another, until the weight of intuitive evidence is overwhelming. Thus, the effect of the presentation of evidence is of a broad-based and heavily documented intuition.

Nowhere is this presentation of intuition more powerful than in *Distinction*, where the lifestyles of France's class structure are richly explored. In a section on food, which is one of many such descriptions, we find a typical display of the argument:

> The system of differences (between classes) becomes clearer when one looks more closely at the patterns of spending on food. In this respect the industrial and commercial employers differ markedly from the professionals, and a fortiori from the teachers, by virtue of the importance they give to cereal-based products (especially cakes and pastries), wine, meat preserves (foie gras,

etc.) and game, and their relatively low spending on meat, fresh fruit and vegetables. The teachers, whose food purchases are almost identically structured to those of office workers, spend more than all other fractions on bread, milk products, sugar, fruit preserves and non-alcoholic drinks, less on wine and spirits and distinctly less than the professions on expensive products such as meat – especially the most expensive meats, such as mutton and lamb – and fresh fruit and vegetables. The members of the professions are mainly distinguished by the high proportion of their spending which goes on expensive products, particularly meat (18.3 per cent of their food budget), and especially the most expensive meat (veal, lamb, mutton), fresh fruit and vegetables, fish and shellfish, cheese and aperitifs.

(Bourdieu 1984:184–5)

Bourdieu extends this analysis of food to an analysis of the 'body', a preoccupation of Foucault and others.[6] Bourdieu argues, again with intuitive appeal, that taste, and the production of a 'food lifestyle' is connected to social class, and the conception that each class has of its body, and in particular the social role that the body plays in the world. Thus, various forms of food are more clearly part of a 'male' or 'female', 'working class' or 'dominant class' world:

whereas the working classes are more attentive to the strength of the (male) body than its shape, and tend to go for products that are both cheap and nutritious, the professions prefer products that are tasty, health-giving, light and not fattening.

(Bourdieu 1984:190)

And:

At a deeper level, the whole body schema in particular the physical approach to the act of eating, governs the selection of certain foods . . . in the working classes, fish tends to be regarded as an unsuitable food for men, not only because it is a light food, insufficiently 'filling', which would only be cooked for health reasons . . . but also . . . it is one of the 'fiddly' things which a man's hands cannot cope with and which make him childlike . . . but above all, it is because fish has to be eaten in a way which totally contradicts the masculine way of eating, that is, with restraint, in small mouthfuls, chewed gently . . . (ibid.).

This leads to disparate conceptions of the body, which are systematically connected to the social roles that recreate habitus, which in turn implies a logic of self-presentation tending towards a class habitus of social function. Thus, the shape of the male working-class body, at least in a modal sense, is orchestrated through the eating of certain foods, the activity in certain kinds of sports which strengthen the body, the wearing of certain clothes which reflect masculinity, towards taking its place in production using just these skills. So, the relation between various forms of lifestyle and class practice at work has its links in the kind of manual work that the body is required to do. Failure to achieve that level of physical endeavour at work makes the individual marginal in the workplace. Lifestyle, however broadly conceived, on the one hand therefore, and social relations of production on the other hand, set limits one on another, which do not exclude the quiche-eating intellectual carpenter, or the fish-eating ditch-digger, but at least require that such individuals pay attention sufficiently to their bodies to enable them to take their place in the economic world. This makes a series of dispositions in relation to food, sport, clothes and entertainment, a matter of class choice, inferring one set of choices is more probable than another.

In this way, Bourdieu is equally able to offer an explanation of the middle classes. Workers, who use their bodies all day in their manually-based economic practice, have little use for such pretensions as jogging and health-fitness centres, which are largely (though not entirely of course) the preserve of the middle classes. To the extent that they do enter such a field, the working class are concerned to spend their efforts on weightlifting and activities directed towards strength, both fields in which manual dominance can be asserted. The middle class, however, is not concerned to produce a *large* strong body, but a slim, athletic and fit body, a body more suited to a world in which economic practice is constituted more strongly by the presentation of self, and the invocation of mental, rather than manual capacities. Thus, the middle class seeks sports which do not bring the body into crude physical struggle (such as rugby league, or boxing) and which allow the dignity of the individual to be maintained. Individualist sports (golf, squash, tennis, riding) are favoured because a certain kind of style and restraint is possible:

> a sport is in a sense predisposed for bourgeois use when the use of the body it requires in no way offends the sense of the high dignity of the person, which rules out, for example, flinging the body into the rough and tumble . . . . Ever concerned to impose

the indisputable image of his own authority, his dignity or his distinction, the bourgeois treats his body as an end, makes his body a sign of its own ease.

(Bourdieu 1984:218)

Bourdieu continues a longstanding interest in social taste in his detailed account of how class and art might be articulated – Chapter 6 addresses this aspect in detail. The argument, both a very general approach deriving from his method, and a specific approach concentrating on art, generates the view that the economic and cultural are deeply interpenetrated: at the heart of the economy is culture. Thus he comments:

The field of production, which clearly could not function if it could not count on already existing tastes, more or less strong propensities to consume more or less clearly defined goods, enables taste to be realized by offering it, at each moment, the universe of cultural goods as a system of stylistic possibilities from which it can select the system of stylistic features constituting a life-style . . . tastes actually realised depend on the state of the system of goods offered; every change in the system of goods induces a change in tastes.

(Bourdieu 1984:230–31)

Cultural and artistic interests are thus created to form products which people require according to their class conditioning. People choose to like artistic objects, therefore, because these objects fit their position, and these objects are offered through a series of appropriate institutions which provide the services (e.g. left and right bank shops in Paris). The distinction is precisely shown in the case of theatre:

Boulevard theatre, which offers tried and tested shows (adaptations of foreign plays, revivals of boulevard 'classics' etc.), written to reliable formulae and performed by consecrated actors, and which caters to a middle-aged, 'bourgeois' audience that is disposed to pay high prices, is opposed in every respect to experimental theatre, which attracts a young, 'intellectual' audience to relatively inexpensive shows that flout ethical and aesthetic conventions.

(Bourdieu 1984:234)

Bourdieu's actual objectivation of class is ambivalent, a point to which we will return in the conclusion. This ambivalence is reflected through *Distinction*, where he veers from a simple occupationally-based set of classifications, as he does in his survey material (see Appendix 3 in particular) towards a relational theory of class, as he does in three chapters (op. cit.) which deal in turn with the dispositions of the dominant, petit bourgeois and working classes expressly.

In his use of three broad qualitative categories (the *sense of distinction* for the upper class, *cultural goodwill* for the middle class, *the choice of the necessary* for the working class), Bourdieu is able to make clear and unambiguous connections between class and broad dispositions. Thus:

> the dominant class constitutes a relatively autonomous space whose structure is defined by the distribution of economic and cultural capital among its members, each class fraction being characterized by a certain configuration of this distribution to which there corresponds a certain lifestyle, through the mediation of the habitus;
>
> (Bourdieu 1984:260)

This habitus can be constituted in a certain way:

> Those who occupy the temporally dominant position within the dominant class are in fact placed in a contradictory situation, which inclines them to maintain an ambivalent relationship with cultural goods and those who produce them. Castigated . . . for philistine materialism . . . they have to invoke the very terms used against them by the intellectuals and artists.
>
> (Bourdieu 1984:316)

The purpose of his argument is to explain precisely how it is that the dominant class comes to have a 'sense of distinction'. Those comfortable among the bourgeois through long tradition, hold to traditional cooking, antique furniture and conventional highbrow music (ibid.:265). While his argument is far more complex than this simple (and too crudely reflective) account suggests, in particular in the way that his discussion of class fractions is expressed, what distinguishes *this* class is a habitus of legitimately established domination, a way of relating to the world, which, while ambiguous and variant across fractions of its structure, consistently alerts society to the structure of structured, authoritative power. Dominant fractions are thus able to own objects of unique and valued quality. And while their style may not always guarantee a high ranking in the 'disinterested' stakes of taste, their appropriation and patronage of cultural practices secures for them a position in relation to culture which tends to support their class reproduction – it is a limit beyond which they are unlikely to fall.

For the middling classes, the project of the struggle is different. Not for these people the firm view, held against intellectual fashion, if necessary. Here, class habitus is more likely to assume the tone of compliance and agreement, so as not to interfere with the authoritative tastes of the dominators to whose position they may aspire, and so as to distinguish them from the working class, from whom certain cultural civility saves them:

> Cultural goodwill is . . . cultural docility (the choice of well-bred friends, a taste for 'educational' or 'instructive' entertainments), often combined with a sense of unworthiness . . . commensurate with the respect that is accorded. The petit bourgeois is filled with *reverence* for culture . . .
>
> (Ibid.:321)

Hoping for acceptance and respectability, the petit bourgeois acknowledges respect for culture, but has no knowledge of it, and is thus the likely vehicle for many a cultural blunder. While cultural stupidity has few or no consequences for those in the dominant class, for the middle class such stupidity expresses a genuine incompetence, and a suggestion that their cultural place is forever outside the circles of those who 'know'. Educational capital, in particular, is important to the upwardly mobile middle classes, must be 'got right', and must take on a value as a determining class characteristic which it cannot have for those in dominant classes (Bourdieu 1984:331ff.). To elaborate on the discussion in Chapter 4, sacrifice, duty, attention to over-conformity identify this class, with those who have some economic capital (small shopkeepers) putting their well-focused efforts towards thrift and saving, whereas those with some cultural capital concentrate their efforts and energies on education. The bourgeois sense of ease and belonging is contrasted with petit-bourgeois lack of ease, overconventionalism and over-conformity.

His chapter on the working class is entitled 'The Choice of the Necessary' (ibid.:372ff.) but it would be quite false, in line with his general methodological procedure, to account for working-class habitus by some straightforward argument about economic constraint. His argument opposes such a view immediately. Having a million (ibid.:374) does not make one a millionaire; rather, this is the very definition of a parvenu. In the same line of argument, Bourdieu proposes that envy of aristocratic parties or jewellery for example, is really envy of money, rather than envy of the party or the purchase of an expensive diamond, which seem an obvious waste of money (op. cit.). The argument then can offer an explanation about the working-class prize-winners of large lotteries or an English football pool, who keep the job and the lifestyle they endured before the windfall. Most crucially as evidence for his argument, Bourdieu asserts that the same income associated with people of two different classes leads to different expenditures. Manual workers favoured by an increase in pay thus spend the same proportion of their income on food, and do not qualitatively alter their eating habits, even when the economic pressure to eat the cheapest food is released. On the other hand, junior executives, while eating plain food when necessity drives, qualitatively change their eating preferences as they move into the senior executive level:

> as one moves from the 30,000–50,000 francs income bracket into the higher bracket, the food purchases of senior executives do not change in at all the same way as those of manual workers. Though expenditure on food increases in both cases . . . the items which expand are, by order of importance, for senior execu- tives . . . aperitifs, restaurant meals, non-alcoholic drinks, lamb, cakes and pastries, beef, fresh fruit, fish and shellfish, cheese; and for manual workers: pork, aperitifs, rabbit, fresh fruit, dried vegetables, bread, fresh vegetables.
>
> (Bourdieu 1984:376)

Thus, within the working class, a virtue, or more broadly, a class habitus is established out of necessity which outgrows and transcends that necessity. Houses are constructed for convenience, rather than for taste. Television usage, arguably less influenced by economic pressures, does not fail to express quite distinct tastes, the working class indicating a preference for realistic and practical programmes, while the bourgeois show a disposition towards the disinterestedness of 'cultural' programming. Working men are forbidden every preten- sion (ibid.:382); bourgeois men cultivate pretension:

> Manual workers in general rather more often watch sport and circuses on TV, whereas junior executives and clerical workers much more often watch scientific, historical or literary programmes . . . . Out of very similar incomes, the manual wor-

kers spend more on food and less on everything concerned with personal appearance . . . the men's spending on clothes is 85.6 per cent, and the women's 83.7 per cent, of the corresponding amounts among clerical workers. They buy the same clothes more cheaply . . . and, above all, different clothes: on the one hand, leather or imitation leather jackets and lumber jackets (for cold, early-morning travel by scooter), boiler-suits, dungarees and overalls; on the other hand, overcoats (symbols of petit bourgeois respectability), blouses, aprons, sports jackets and blazers.

(Bourdieu 1984:394)

Taste, which might relate to a vast number of personal attributes, from cutting one's hair in a certain way to the sort of car which an individual buys, has relations with the division of labour, not in an unambiguous way, but mediated and moderated by social choice. Class is thus to be seen both as an act of social construction, as well as a product of the objectivist division of labour. This conception of class habitus provides a predisposition towards what can be called a social practice of class, a practice which has limits established to it, which are limits set by the division of labour. Class and class habitus must therefore be analysed in terms of the broad method being used in the general strategy. Class habitus creates meaning which allows participants of a social class to 'know the value' of certain practices and certain objects in a field, thus either acting towards a reproduction of the habitus of class, or its transgression. Agents are thus capable of knowing the implications of their class cultural practices, and of being able to modify them and struggle to change their value. These practices are thus historically constituted categories of meaning which orchestrate practice, both beyond the will of the individual and subject to that will.

Elements of class habitus are frequently oppositional, just as the division of labour between classes can be conceived oppositionally (ibid.:469). The intellectualism of certain of the middle classes can be opposed to the 'realism' of the working class, and the 'vulgarism' of the bourgeoisie. And, as Bourdieu is frequently saying, the ranking of intellectual values in one class finds its *obverse* in another class. What is witty, incisive and subtle to the intellectual middle class is considered, in the logic of this view, pretentious, teacherly and pompous by the bourgeois social order. Accordingly, social class must be considered a process of learning and relearning of classifications, codes and procedures which orchestrate social exchanges, including marriage, education, cuisine, art and culture, and which embody qualitative divisions in the social relations of production:

> The fact that, in their relationship to the dominant classes, the dominated classes attribute to themselves strength in the sense of labour power and fighting strength – physical strength and also strength of character, courage, manliness – does not prevent the dominant groups from similarly conceiving the relationship in terms of the scheme strong/weak; but they reduce the strength which the dominated (or the young, or women) ascribe to themselves brute strength, passion and instinct, a blind, unpredictable force of nature, the unreasoning violence of desire, and they attribute to themselves spiritual and intellectual strength, a self-control that predisposes them to control others; a strength of soul or spirit which allows them to conceive their relationship to the dominated – the 'masses', women, the young – as that of the soul to the body, understanding to sensibility, culture to nature.
>
> (Bourdieu 1984:479)

This account is a far more subtle presentation of class analysis than we find in *Algeria 1960* (Bourdieu 1979). Here in somewhat different empirical circumstances, Bourdieu is willing to make much closer connections between the over-riding imperatives of the economy and the way social practices are conducted. In a vivid description the difference is clear:

> Sometimes I work one day, sometimes four days, sometimes I'm out of work for a whole month. I have debts of almost 5000 francs. I borrow on one side to repay on the other, that's the way it's always been. I've got no trade, no qualifications, how do you expect me to live? I work as a labourer, I carry water, I carry stones on building sites . . . if only I could get a job! You see I've been got by the throat. When I'm not labouring, I go into town and I work as a porter in the market. I borrow left and right . . . I leave home at five in the morning and off I go. I look and look. Sometimes I come back at midday or one o'clock and I've still found nothing . . . my earnings are like my work. Never regular, never certain. What can I do? I earn about 10 000 francs a month on average. I'd do anything to earn my family a living. (Casual labourer, Constantine.)
>
> (Bourdieu 1979:66)

The job in which this informant is engaged is, as Bourdieu says, looking for a job. Here the dispositions of every waking hour are tied closely to existence and material work, and the dialectic between economy and practice is very close. Several conclusions derive from the comparison of 'class' in *Distinction* and 'class' in *Algeria 1960*. One can *not* conclude there is some simple development of ideas from one work to the other. Indeed it is the *conjunctural* nature of class which is evident – the account of the sub-proletariate in Algeria is clearly a different proposition, not just in content, but in terms of the form and shape of capitals involved, than the account of the working class in *Distinction*. Most crucially, the *mediation* between economy and culture is consistently more complex as the analysis moves from sub-proletariate to bourgeoisie because the question of social difference hinged on the possibility of *hiding* (diverting, disguising, treating as irrelevant) those matters of mundane economic survival. Further, no new account could be provided of Algeria given Bourdieu's method, even if his ideas had changed over time without further conjunctural analysis:

> Rereading this text (*Algeria 1960*) written more than a decade ago, I more than once felt the wish to refine and systematize the analyses, by investing in them all that subsequent work has yielded (particularly *Outline of a Theory of Practice*). But conscious of the futility of all forms of 'theoretical labour' that are not accompanied by empirical work on the things themselves (which would mean in this case a return to fieldwork which is not possible at present) I have refrained from doing it.
>
> (Bourdieu 1979:viii)

Finally, these accounts tell us that in its essence, social class is characterised as a *social practice* in Bourdieu, not as a category or as a lifestyle, nor even as a set of dispositions, but an activity in which categorisation, structures, dispositions and social choice combine.

CLASS TRAJECTORY

Before we conclude this chapter, we must review one refinement which adds an important twist to the way Bourdieu conceptualises class. Bourdieu uses the idea of class trajectory in two distinct connections to explain two related problems. Thus, he speaks of the trajectory of the social class (more generally of class fractions) to refer to their motion within the class structure: whether, as a group, they are on an upward or downward trajectory. This conception is then used to explain changes in the occupational or class structure through historical time. He also uses the term class trajectory to refer to the individual progress of a class agent through a life history – this is used to explain why certain *fractions* of social classes may veer towards the *tastes of another* class – perhaps because their origins, or their pretensions for the future, lie in the direction of this other class.

Classes and class fractions come and go: this implies the impossibility of simple class reproduction, and acts as an antidote to those who criticise his 'reproductionism':

> Nor is it accidental that the oldest classes or class fractions are also the classes in decline, such as farmers and industrial and commercial proprietors; most of the young people originating from these classes can only escape collective decline by reconverting into the expanding occupations.
>
> (1984:108)

The field of economic production, as of cultural production, experiences transformation in which, during long historical processes, there is a movement in the shape of class structure. This logically implies the obsolescence of certain bases for distinction and the emergence of new forms. The shifting forms of capital thus constitute new sites of struggle, new class fractions.

But the concept of the individual trajectory is perhaps even more important for Bourdieu than the idea of a collective trajectory, because it is here he attempts to refine his account of class habitus to the level of class fraction by reference to individual trajectory. As we pointed out in Chapter 1, it is possible to tell the children of the old bourgeoisie from those who have recently arrived by their 'approach':

> (cultural capital) opposes those individuals whose families have long been members of the bourgeoisie to those who have recently entered it, the parvenus: those who have the supreme privilege, seniority in privilege, who acquired their cultural capital by early, daily contact with rare, 'distinguished' things, people, places and shows, to those who owe their capital to an acquisitive effort directed by the educational system or guided by the serendipity of

the autodidact, and whose relationship to it is more serious, more severe, often more tense.

(Ibid.:265)

The first part of this process of cultural reproduction is, as Chapter 4 indicated more fully, to be found in the practices of education, in the credentialling and non-credentialling of the grade inflation, and the capacity to cash in education for economic capital, as well as in the family, which is central to the reproduction of class habitus. In the reproduction of the petite bourgeoisie, this form of reproduction of class habitus has a special importance:

> In limiting his family, often to an only son, on whom all hopes and efforts are concentrated, the petit bourgeois is simply obeying the system of constraints implied in his ambition . . . . The petit bourgeois is a proletarian who makes himself small to become bourgeois.

(Bourdieu 1984:337–8)

Family can thus be constituted as the connection between class trajectory and individual trajectory, thus supporting the claim made in the previous chapter that the family, and the strategies of family reproduction, should be units of study for class analysis. What Bourdieu is suggesting therefore, is that the class habitus of those born into the dominant class is like a second nature, a view of the world (and a position in it) which they accept with ease, grace and informality: for those newly arrived, the cultural capital is something to work at, to continually strive for: in short, parvenus show *some* of the dis-ease of the petite bourgeoisie from where they came. Thus one must conceive of classes as having dominant and dominated fractions, with dominated fractions having higher proportions of parvenus than dominant fractions. With changes in the economic structure, however, the dominant classes have to alter the quality of the capital they possess in order that their position can be maintained:

> as a result in changes in the economic structures, and chiefly through its use of the Paris Institut des Sciences Politiques, situated at the bottom of the specifically academic hierarchy of the 'Schools of Power', the Parisian *grande bourgeoisie* has reappropriated, perhaps more completely than ever, the commanding positions in the economy and the civil service . . .

(Ibid.:297).

As we have already seen, the urge for an upward class trajectory is an especially powerful component of the petit bourgeois class habitus. This need for ascendancy is traditionally concentrated in particular individuals who carry the investment of their class (ibid.:331). Hence the slope of the class trajectory of the rising petite bourgeoisie implies an aspiration for a lifestyle which speaks of a world better than they have. Various class fractions are thus led to involve themselves with various capitals:

> fractions richest in economic capital . . . concentrate their efforts . . . on saving . . . the fractions richest in cultural capital . . . mainly make use of the educational system (both exhibit) cultural goodwill and financial prudence, seriousness and hard work (ibid.:333, 337).

These fractions of the class, on the basis of differing compositions of capital which they have in their trajectory thus exhibit variant aesthetic dispositions. On the one hand, the intellectual fraction is able to cite a number of works of classical music, recall visits to the Louvre, and art museums; on the other side, while those with economic capital exhibit little or no knowledge of art, an interest in light, rather than heavy, opera, and no concern with aesthetic esoterica.

Devotion to culture is *most* keenly expressed by those who are *parvenus* to the petite bourgeoisie, newly arrived from the working class. They have jobs which are assured – their fraction of the petit bourgeois class is on an ascendant trajectory. They distinguish themselves (ibid.:351) from the declining fractions of the same class. Reactionary pessimism of the declining class fraction is to be contrasted with the moderate reformist leanings of the upward fraction (ibid.:350).

The slope of trajectory is thus also important in explaining political preference. Those with a future pursue political affiliations to dominant, reformist political movements; those in a decline turn to reactionary politics in order to prevent their economic capital from dissipating:

> A class or class fraction is in decline, and therefore turned towards the past, when it is no longer able to reproduce itself (ibid.:455).

This leads to a powerful conclusion. While people may thus be located in similar social space, we may be able to read variant class habitus by reference to the notion of class trajectory; that is, by reference to the history of the individual, and of the group.

Individual and collective class trajectory are thus closely bound together. The decline in a given class fraction means that, while some members of that fraction stay on a horizontal trajectory through luck, hard work, or caprice, the movement of the class fraction *changes the shape and composition of capital in the field*, thus devaluing the efforts of the individual trajectory. The only 'structural' salvation therefore is a reconversion of one kind of capital into another.

> the group . . . of small craftsmen and small shopkeepers, most of whose fathers were also small craftsmen or small shopkeepers, and who, for lack of the economic and especially the cultural capital they would need in order to attempt a reconversion, are condemned to carry on at all costs at the head of particularly threatened small businesses . . . which will not outlive them . . . is distinguished by systematically retrograde choices from the rest of the fraction, which contains a fair proportion of modern craftsmen (electricians, mechanics, etc.), possessing (degrees) . . . who, especially when young and Parisian, are very close to the technicians in their ethical and aesthetic and no doubt their political, choices.
>
> (Bourdieu 1984:350)

CONCLUSION

This chapter has reviewed a series of breaks which Bourdieu makes with a largely Marxist tradition of class analysis, a tradition which privileges substances at the expense of relationship, which stays at the level of 'theoretical class' on paper without recourse to the empirical, and which does not distinguish between the 'is' and the 'ought' of class. Marxists believe it is enough, Bourdieu claims, for them to 'name' a class, in order for that class to come into being.

In its place, Bourdieu uses his method of generative structuralism to conceive of the social space as a series of fields, in which capitals exist, and are struggled for by agents. Class is then argued to be constituted by those people in proximity in these social spaces. In his most objectivist mood, he says this about class:

> Social class is not defined as a property . . . nor by a collection of properties . . . nor even by a chain of properties . . . but by the structure of relations between all the pertinent properties which

gives its specific value to each of them and to the effects they exert on practices (ibid.:106).

Thus there is no simple reading of dispositions from class here; rather, an ambiguous objectification of class, sometimes as occupational group, but much more often, centred on the fundamental and qualitative distinction between bourgeois, petits-bourgeois and workers. Round these three pegs Bourdieu weaves an elaborate thread of habitus, and it is through ceaseless examples of the habitus, in its many elements – in its artistic components, in eating habits, in the dispositions of the body, in theatre-visiting (or not theatre-visiting), in a concern for music or no concern, in the political attitudes, the cars they drive, the men and women they marry, the sort of living rooms they construct – in all these ways, the lives of classes are drawn.

These ambiguities are made more complex and infinitely more powerful as a form of explanation with the use of the concept of trajectory, both of a class and of an individual, to account for the variations which fractions in a class may exhibit in their practice and in their dispositions.

In the last analysis, one might be tempted to argue, though, that Bourdieu leans rather heavily on a *political* account of class, with continual reference to the dominant and the dominated, as if the exertion of power finally accounted for the hierarchy. In a closer analysis one is forced to the view that the *volumes and composition of capitals* in *crucial* fields are what constitute class; the reconversion (or its impossibility) of economic into cultural capital (or vice versa) determines both the trajectory of classes, and the hopes individuals have in scaling the ladder. As in his other theoretical innovations, Bourdieu constitutes class as a *social practice* which only a dialectical method that ignores fake dichotomies between structure/agency, objective/subjective, class-in-itself/class-for-itself, economy/culture, can ever fully explain.

NOTES

1. For his most detailed critique of Althusser, see Bourdieu's article, Actes 1975c. For his most recent exposition on class, see 1987c, in which

Bourdieu reworks many of the arguments found in (1985), 'Social space and the genesis of groups'.

2. See Jessop (1985) for discussion of the relationship between Poulantzas and Althusser.

3. See Wright (1985). The work is especially important for Wright's autocritique in relation to the politicism of his own class theory.

4. See Bhaskar (1975; 1979), but also Ian Craib (1984), who spends some time on realist development, Sayer (1984) and Johnson et al. (1984). Again, an ambiguity emerges, for it is argued by Craib, for example, that 'Bhaskar's work . . . owes much to the debates stimulated by Althusser' (Craib 1984:124). Thus the arch-enemy is implicated in a parallel epistemology, if only at second-hand.

5. Argument on political representation is also to be found in earlier work. See, for example, Actes 1981 and Actes 1984b. See also the extensive and most interesting article by Patrick Champagne 'La manifestation: la production de l'événement politique' in *Actes* 52/3, 1984, pp. 19–41. Indeed, several issues of *Actes* have been devoted to political matters, including the double issue (no. 52/53) noted above, as well as two issues expressly related to political representation (the double issue (36/37) for February–March 1981 and no. 38, May 1981). It is important to stress that this reading of 'Bourdieu's class' could be taken to indicate a highly subjectivist analysis of class, indicating that classes could be said to exist only in the mind of the vanguardist believer. However, there is little doubt that this interpretation is highly ironic, directed at leftist posturing in a form of political satire, rather than being offered as a new dimension of class analysis.

6. The widespread interest in 'body' as problematic also has a history in Bourdieu's own work. See especially *Esquisse d'une théorie de la pratique, précédé de trois études d'ethnologie kabyle*, (Fr. ed. 1972); Bourdieu (with L. Boltanski and P. Maldidier) 1971; and Actes 1977a. Bourdieu had even earlier planned to undertake doctoral work with Canguilhem on the problem of trying to establish a physiological basis for the explanation of emotion, which would provide an empirical basis for some of Merleau-Ponty's ideas in phenomenology. This work was never completed, as Bourdieu's studies took him in other directions.

6 Making Distinctions: The Eye of the Beholder
John Codd

INTRODUCTION

Pierre Bourdieu's theoretical and empirical analyses of the art world constitute a substantial component of his published work spanning more than two decades (Bourdieu 1968, 1971, 1980, 1980a, 1983, 1984, 1985f, 1987d, 1988b). His central interest in the formation and reproduction of symbolic practices has drawn him inevitably towards the intellectual fields of art and literature, traditionally neglected areas for sociological study. As with other fields discussed in this book, Bourdieu has used the fields of art and literature to demonstrate that the cultural practices which constitute the production, distribution and consumption of symbolic goods are comprehensible within a theory of practice which admits neither transcendental/idealist categories of individual agency, nor deterministic explanations drawn from formal structuralism.[1] By analysing the literary and artistic fields in relational terms, he has been able to understand and demonstrate further the homologies between symbolic and economic production. Moreover, by the constant application of his own powerful explanatory metaphors, he has revealed the extant relations between aesthetic dispositions of individual agents and the objective systems of social differentiations within which acts of artistic creation and appreciation necessarily take place. He has shown that the attitudes which individuals assume towards works of art are manifestations of more pervasive dispositions from which all other attitudes of taste are derived. These dispositions are engendered by a social logic which relates the aesthetic choices (distinctions) made by individuals to the more general strategies of struggle by which groups maintain their social positions – see Chapter 1 for a discussion of general strategies of struggle.

In the Introduction to his major work, *Distinction*, Bourdieu (1984:6) defines his project as 'the science of taste and of cultural consumption.' His method is based on ethnography rather than argumentation.[2] Instead of engaging with the discourses of philosophical aesthetics or art criticism, he has grounded his theoretical claims in a series of empirical studies of the French art world.[3] Using observational and survey data collected over many years, he has attempted to reveal that regularities of taste within lifestyles are produced by social regularities which always have the potential to generate effects of cultural demarcation or *distinction*. For Bourdieu, this notion of *distinction*, with its connotations of both difference and superiority, is the theoretical key with which to unlock a social critique of aesthetic judgement. He takes the position that the making of aesthetic distinctions cannot have *a priori* validity because they are cultural practices engendered by the same general dispositions (habitus) as eating preferences, dress styles, sporting interests and other facets of day-to-day culture.[4] Thus, aesthetic distinctions identify different positions in social space so that:

> Social subjects, classified by their classifications, distinguish themselves by the distinctions they make, between the beautiful and the ugly, the distinguished and the vulgar, in which their position in the objective classifications is expressed or betrayed. (loc. cit.)

Bourdieu's thesis has continuity with his work in other fields: the systems of classification which structure aesthetic perception and judgements of taste are based upon differences in the cultural practices of various groups or classes. This leads him to a total rejection of idealist aesthetics as the viable ground for 'pure' judgement. Indeed, the discourse of high aesthetics itself, he declares, is constituted by arbitrary practices of distinction, by acts of cultural consecration, which legitimate social differences. He states his position thus:

> The science of taste and of cultural consumption begins with a transgression that is in no way aesthetic: it has to abolish the sacred frontier which makes legitimate culture a separate universe, in order to discover the intelligible relations which unite apparently incommensurable 'choices', such as preferences in music and food, painting and sport, literature and hairstyle. This barbarous reintegration of aesthetic consumption into the world of ordinary consumption abolishes the opposition, which has been the basis of high aesthetics since Kant, between the 'taste of sense' and the 'taste of reflection', and between facile pleasure, pleasure reduced to a pleasure of the senses, and pure pleasure, pleasure purified

of pleasure, which is predisposed to become a symbol of moral excellence and a measure of the capacity for sublimation which defines the truly human man. The culture which results from this magical division is sacred. Cultural consecration does indeed confer on the objects, persons and situations it touches, a sort of ontological promotion akin to a transubstantiation. (loc. cit.)

This rejection of all theories which confer transcendental or essential meaning upon works of art is consistent with Bourdieu's more fundamental rejection of all idealist dualisms (mind/body, agency/-structure, language/speech) and allows him to develop his own unique conception of art in terms of his generic concepts of habitus, cultural capital and social field.

This chapter presents an outline of the dialectical growth of Bourdieu's central concepts and attempts to show the emergence within his work of a theoretical position delineated by a critique of prevalent idealist and materialist accounts of art appreciation and creativity. The essential elements of this critique can be recognised in his early writings, but its penetrating force is the result of a convergence of his ethnographic method with his method of theoretical analysis. Such a convergence first becomes apparent in *Outline of a Theory of Practice* (1977) and reaches its culmination in *Distinction* (1984).[5] This chapter, therefore, traces the development of Bourdieu's sociology of art through the evolution of his method. Beginning with his earliest insights concerning the nature of artistic perception, the following discussion examines the gradual formation of his unique theoretical account of aesthetic judgement.

THE SOCIAL CONSTRUCTION OF ART PERCEPTION

Bourdieu's fundamental insight concerning the nature of artistic perception is that it necessarily entails an act of cultural decoding, an act of conscious or unconscious deciphering made possible by a cultural code which may or may not be consistent with the cultural code within which the perceived work was produced. Artistic competency can become symbolic capital, in Bourdieu's sense, because the meaning of an art work is socially constructed and exists as such only for those who have appropriated the means to decipher it. He gained this insight from his early studies of Panofsky (Bourdieu, Fr. ed. 1967) who had distinguished between different levels of iconographic meaning arising from different conditions of iconological interpretation.[6] According to Panofsky, the difference between the uninitiated perception of a naive beholder and the iconological interpretation of a discerning beholder, is dependent upon differences in the internalised codes with which each is able to decipher the object of artistic perception. But these codes are not generally recognised as constituting the conditions under which it is possible to experience the work of art as a work of art. Misunderstanding resulting from a misrecognition of the codes themselves produces 'the illusion of immediate comprehension' which in turn 'leads to an illusory comprehension based on a mistaken code' (Bourdieu, 1968:590). This mistaken code conveys the ideology of the 'fresh eye', which sustains the belief that art appreciation can be a spontaneous response to the intrinsic features of the art work. Thus the innocent eye of the uninitiated does not then know that it lacks the culturally consecrated perception of the educated. Not only does this effectively legitimate some codes while denigrating others, but

> In the absence of perception that the works are coded, and coded in another code, one unconsciously applies the code which is good for everyday perception, for the deciphering of familiar objects, to works in a foreign tradition: there is no perception which does not involve an unconscious code and it is essential to dismiss the myth of the 'fresh eye', considered as a virtue granted to artlessness and innocence (loc. cit.).

The difference between more and less sophisticated beholders is a difference in categories of perception. What the naive beholder recognises only as a flower or a battle, the educated beholder can interpret as symbol or myth. Bourdieu (ibid.:592) quotes Panofsky's comment that 'the naive "beholder" differs from the art historian in that the latter is conscious of the situation.' The 'situation' here refers to the social, historical and artistic context within which the work of art was produced, including the intentions (stated or inferred) of the artist, as well as the context in which the work is appreciated. A work of art (like any cultural object) is neither the expression of a subjective meaning nor the embodiment of an objective meaning but rather, it is an artefact which 'may disclose significations at different levels according to the deciphering stencil applied to it'. (loc.cit.)

According to Panofsky (1955), the primary level of apprehension relates the image to our immediate sensations or experiences (when a peach is described as velvety or lace as misty; when colours are spoken of as harsh or gay). The secondary level of interpretation, however, requires 'appropriately characterizing concepts' which relate to stylistic features of the work (its formal qualities) and thematic content (images and symbols). Within this secondary level, a further distinction is made between what he calls *conventional* meaning (e.g. recognising that the content of a picture represents 'The Last Supper') and *intrinsic* meaning (in which not only the images but also the methods of composition are treated as cultural symbols belonging to a particular age, a nation or a class). Whereas at the primary level the apprehension of an art work is confined to 'demonstrative concepts' (shape, size, colour), at the secondary level the apprehension of meaning 'presupposes a familiarity with specific themes or concepts which can only be transmitted through literary sources' (Bourdieu 1968:592) and which contextualise the art work so that its phenomenal meaning is embedded within other levels of meaning. Whether in any particular act of appreciation the object is perceived at the primary or the secondary level will depend upon whether the appropriate code has been mastered.

It is from Panofsky then, that Bourdieu takes the initial outline of his conception of art perception as a socially constructed system of categories. It is from Panofsky also that he draws his first formulation of the thesis that such systems of thought constitute cultural regularities within the dispositions of individuals which generate structural homologies in different areas of thought and action, and which may be termed 'the cultivated habitus'. Panofsky (1955) had written about the relationship between Gothic art and scholasticism and Bourdieu summarises his account as follows;

What the architects of the Gothic cathedrals unwittingly borrowed from the schoolmen was a *principium importans ordinem ad actum* or a *modus operandi*, i.e. a 'peculiar method of procedure which must have been the first thing to impress itself upon the mind of the layman whenever it came in touch with that of the schoolman'. Thus, for example, the principle of clarification (*manifestatio*), a scheme of literary presentation discovered by Scholasticism, which requires the author to make plain and explicit (*manifestare*) the arrangement and logic of his argument – we should say his plan – also governs the action of the architect and the sculptor, as we can see by comparing the Last Judgement on the tympanum of Autun Cathedral with the treatment of the same theme at Paris and Amiens where, despite a greater wealth of motifs, consummate clarity also prevails through the effect of symmetry and correspondence. If this is so, it is because the cathedral-builders were subject to the constant influence – to the habit-forming force – of Scholasticism, which, from about 1130–40 to about 1270, 'held a veritable monopoly of education' over an area of roughly 100 miles around Paris.

(Bourdieu 1971b:193)

Panofsky's brilliant insight, according to Bourdieu, is to provide a convincing explanation for 'the structural homologies that he finds between such different areas of intellectual activity as architecture and philosophical thought' (ibid.:194). It is an explanation, Bourdieu notes, which goes beyond the idealism of such notions as a 'unitarian vision of the world' or a 'spirit of the times'. As was pointed out in Chapter 4, such a view recognises the role of the school in the formation of a cultivated habitus which engenders not only specific competences but also the manner of exercising them. By developing this explanation specifically in relation to the formation of artistic perception, Bourdieu begins to make an important break with the long tradition of idealist aesthetics. It is a break, however, which is not complete until he succeeds in escaping from a form of idealism that is deeply enshrined in language itself.

In his earliest attempts to explicate the meaning of habitus, Bourdieu (1971b:192–3) construes it as 'a set of basic, deeply interiorized master-patterns' constituting a *cultural unconscious* which 'may govern and regulate mental processes without being consciously apprehended and controlled' (loc. cit.). He quotes Mauss, who had written about the principles or categories which are always present in language, but which cannot be submitted to examination and which exist 'in the form of habits governing consciousness, which are themselves unconscious' (Bourdieu 1971:181). Bourdieu adds that 'our common apprehension of the world is also founded on principles not open to examination and unconscious categories of thought which constantly threaten to insinuate themselves into the scientific vision' (loc. cit.). Hence, these unconscious categories or principles were defined as neither apprehended nor apprehensible, while at the same time they were said to structure and determine what *can* be apprehended. Construed in such terms, the ontological status of the habitus could only remain mysterious, if not mystical. Moreover, the very notion of a cultural unconscious comprising

principles not open to examination presupposes a dualism of mind
and body, a Cartesian legacy to which the post-Saussurean linguistic
structuralists had given a new prominence.[7]

It is not surprising, perhaps, that in an early formulation of his
theory of art perception, Bourdieu explicitly accepts a version of
linguistic structuralism when he asserts that:

> The repeated perception of works of a certain style encourages
> the unconscious interiorization of the rules which govern the pro-
> duction of these works. Like rules of grammar, these rules are not
> apprehended as such, and are still less explicitly formulated and
> formulatable . . . .
>
>   (Bourdieu 1968:601)

Here, acts of perception, like speech acts, are taken to be the outward manifestations and variable instances of an internal system of
abstract rules. But these are the very same structuralist propositions
that Bourdieu is later to reject – see Chapter 1. Significantly, therefore, as he subsequently uses and develops the concept of habitus,
he abandons this linguistic analogy with its attendant problem of
accounting for the nature of the relationship between these unconscious rules (hypostatised as mentalistic master-patterns or blue-
prints) and particular practices or acts of perception.

In *Outline of a Theory of Practice* (1977) Bourdieu makes more
frequent use of the word 'disposition' to imply a more precise
ontology for both structure and habitus. Thus, the habitus has *now*
become 'systems of durable, transposable *dispositions*' (1977:72). As
pointed out in Chapter 3, Bourdieu explicitly rejects the implication
that the habitus is some kind of 'ghost in the machine' determining
what is possible by some mysterious mentalistic mechanism. He
defines it as a generative principle which is *another name for* the
structural limits observable in practice itself. It is, in a physical sense,
nothing more than the inscription upon or inculcation within the
individual of the historically formed material conditions of the group
or class to which that individual belongs. Bourdieu's explanation is
as follows:

> Because the dispositions durably inculcated by objective conditions
> (which science apprehends through statistical regularities as the
> probabilities objectively attached to a group or class) engender
> aspirations and practices objectively compatible with those objec-
> tive requirements, the most improbable practices are excluded,

either totally without examination, as *unthinkable*, or at the cost of the *double negation* which inclines agents to make a virtue of necessity, that is, to refuse what is anyway refused and to love the inevitable (1977:77).

The habitus of a group or class exists in the dispositions (capacities, tendencies, abilities to recognise and to act) of individuals such that these dispositions are an embodiment within each individual of objective regularities, relations and structures that pre-exist the individual and have been socially constituted within the material conditions of existence pertaining to the group or class. Thus, individuals are disposed to recognise and to act in particular ways, which is also to act with meaningful intentions, and therefore to *choose* what each will do. Dispositions are neither mechanistic causes nor voluntarist impulses. They enable us to recognise the possibilities for action and at the same time prevent us from recognising other possibilities. Taken together, they constitute the habitus which is 'the durably installed generative principle of regulated improvisations' (1977:78). Thus, the habitus both generates practices and limits their possibilities. In Bourdieu's words, it

> produces practices which tend to reproduce the regularities immanent in the objective conditions of the production of their generative principle, while adjusting to the demands inscribed as objective potentialities in the situation, as defined by the cognitive and motivating structures making up the habitus (loc. cit.).

It is significant that for Bourdieu the habitus is no longer a master-plan located in the cultural unconscious, but a principle immanent in practice itself which is both generative (of perceptions and practice) and structuring (that is, defining limits upon what is conceivable as perception and as practice). With this powerful concept, Bourdieu can account for the genesis of aesthetic judgement without recourse to mystical notions of aesthetic meaning and without positing the existence of any universal properties of the human mind. The final denunciation of structuralist dualism is made in the following paragraph of *Outline*:

> Just as the opposition of language to speech as mere execution or even as a preconstructed object masks the opposition between the objective relations of the language and the dispositions making up linguistic competence, so the opposition between the structure and the individual against whom the structure has to be won and

endlessly rewon stands in the way of construction of the dialectical relationship between the structure and the dispositions making up the habitus (ibid.:84).

At this point, the ontological status of both structure and habitus loses much of its prior ambiguity. Bourdieu now asserts the materiality of that status with a stronger conviction. The practice of each individual is taken to be an embodiment of a collective history of practice. This means that the system of dispositions (habitus) which structures the practice of the individual is no more than a homologous variant of the systems of dispositions which have structured the practice of all the other individuals who have belonged to the same group or class throughout its history. In the process of social learning that is the genesis of practice, schemes of perception, conception and action common to all members of the same group or class are able to pass from practice to practice (i.e. from adult to child) without going through discourse or consciousness. Both structure and habitus, therefore, exist in what Bourdieu calls *bodily hexis*, which is 'political mythology realised, *embodied*, turned into a permanent disposition, a durable manner of standing, speaking, and thereby of *feeling* and *thinking*' (ibid.:93).

Bourdieu's account of knowledge as the embodiment of social structures is given its strongest formulation in *Distinction* (1984). Here, he argues that all knowledge of the social world is a structuring activity which intervenes between 'conditions of existence' and 'practices or representations'. He adds that

> the principle of this structuring activity is not, as an intellectualist and anti-genetic idealism would have it, a system of universal forms and categories but a system of internalized, embodied schemes which, having been constituted in the course of collective history, are acquired in the course of individual history and function in their *practical* state, *for practice* (and not for the sake of pure knowledge).
>
> (Bourdieu 1984:467)

The break with idealism is complete, but it has not resulted in a vulgar form of economism or a mechanistic materialism. Bourdieu's negation of all forms of idealism which separate knowledge from human practice or which posit a system of universal forms and categories, is not achieved by the advocacy of a reductionist materialism. He does not simply conflate knowledge and practice, but rather relates knowledge to practice through the classificatory schemes which both generate and structure all acts of perception and cognition.

The cognitive structures which social agents implement in their practical knowledge of the social world are internalized, 'embodied' social structures. The practical knowledge of the social world that is presupposed by 'reasonable' behaviour within it implements classificatory schemes (or 'forms of classification', 'mental structures', or 'symbolic forms' – apart from their connotations, these expressions are virtually interchangeable), historical schemes of perception and appreciation which are the product of the objective division into classes (age groups, genders, social classes) and which function below the level of consciousness and discourse. Being the product of the incorporation of the fundamental structures of a society, these principles of division are common to all the agents of the society and make possible the production of a common, meaningful world, a common-sense world (ibid.:468).

Similarly, aesthetic distinctions, artistic perceptions and judgements of taste, implement classificatory schemes (codes) incorporating conceptual oppositions homologous to the oppositions that constitute the social world. For example, the opposition between heavy and light (as in heavy music/light music) serves to distinguish bourgeois from popular tastes. Likewise, the oppositions between high (sublime, elevated, pure) and low (vulgar, low, modest), fine (refined, elegant) and coarse (heavy, fat, crude, brutal), light and heavy, free and forced, right and left, are homologous, Bourdieu suggests, to the oppositions constituting the field of social classes (bourgeois, popular; dominant, dominated). Thus, the social construction of artistic perception is enshrined in the very language through which it is conveyed and is embodied in the aesthetic dispositions of individuals. Bourdieu's theory has always been coherent but, finally, it is his ethnographic method which provides the evidence of these homologies.

THE GENESIS AND FORMATION OF THE AESTHETIC DISPOSITION

From his earliest published work on the appreciation of art, Bourdieu has argued consistently that aesthetic judgements are deciphering operations that involve misrecognised or denied social relationships. In *Distinction*, which is the culmination of twenty years' work on the sociology of taste, he demonstrates that all judgements of taste, including the aesthetic, are governed by the habitus which is acquired in a class-specific way. By analysing artistic perception and knowledge as forms of cultural capital, Bourdieu illustrates precisely how judgements of aesthetic taste contribute to the consecration of the social order. Thus, the recognition of 'good form' or 'pure taste', which Bourdieu calls 'The Sense of Distinction', is nothing more than the realisation in a cultivated (and educated) habitus of the aesthetics which distinguish the lifestyles of the ruling classes. Conversely, the working-class aesthetic (which derives its significance only from its opposition to the cultivated aesthetic – that is, by its emphasis on function rather than form) is a dominated aesthetic, which he calls 'The Choice of the Necessary'. Between these social polarities, he identifies what he calls the 'cultural goodwill' of the petite bourgeoisie which bears many of the outward trappings of refined taste but lacks the tacit knowledge and taken-for-granted subtleties that give to legitimate culture the sense of distinction. Cultural goodwill, therefore, which takes different forms depending on the degree of familiarity with legitimate culture, is often characterised by 'mistaken identifications and false recognitions which betray the gap between acknowledgement and knowledge' (Bourdieu 1984:323).

The sense of distinction, which is the hallmark of legitimate culture, is a form of cultural capital that is transmitted both by the family and by the school. Just as money derives its value from its convertibility into productive power, so cultural knowledge derives its value from its potential to generate acts of cultural distinction or demarcation. Thus the basis of aesthetic taste is to be found in a principle of social closure whereby groups try to improve their accumulation of cultural capital by excluding other groups.[8] This principle is manifested in the strategies of acquisition and exclusion by which groups try to improve or maintain their appropriation of certain economic or symbolic goods. While the middle classes are liberated to a degree from the 'necessary taste' of the lower classes, they find themselves caught in a struggle against the stylistic exclusiveness of the dominating classes. For working-class people, however, the principle that guides all the choices of their daily existence is one that derives from the conditions of economic necessity.[9] Rejecting the specifically aesthetic intentions of art for art's sake, they are inclined towards a pragmatic, functionalist 'aesthetic' which makes a virtue of necessity. This is the basis of class identity, according to Bourdieu, and is described in the following way:

> Necessity imposes a taste for necessity which implies a form of adaptation to and consequently acceptance of the necessary, a resignation to the inevitable, a deep-seated disposition which is in no way incompatible with a revolutionary intention, although it confers on it a modality which is not that of intellectual or artistic revolts. Social class is not defined solely by a position in the relations of production, but by the class habitus which is 'normally' (i.e., with a high statistical probability) associated with that position (ibid.:372).

Bourdieu's empirical research reveals regularities in judgements of taste amongst classes or class fractions which can be readily identified in terms of the social relationships between such judgements and the artistic legitimacy that can be fully recognised only by those possessing the cultivated habitus. The illusion upon which this artistic legitimacy depends is, in large part, the belief that the 'pure gaze' is the only appropriate aesthetic attitude with which to behold works of art. This implies a disinterested, detached, indifferent disposition towards the object of aesthetic appraisal which asserts the absolute primacy of form over function. Whereas the ordinary attitude towards the world subordinates form to function, or describes as 'beautiful' only those objects which have immediate appeal to the senses, the 'pure gaze' defines itself by introducing a deliberate distance between 'first-degree' perception and recognition or interpretation. The object is not what it seems to be, the way it appears to the innocent eye, but it is *recognised* as belonging to a category of cultural objects known in terms of general knowledge or by direct acquaintance.[10] As noted earlier, Bourdieu suggests that education can have a major influence upon the formation of what he calls 'the generalizing tendency of the cultivated disposition' (ibid.:23). He elaborates on this in relation to art, contending that:

> The generalizing tendency is inscribed in the very principle of the disposition to *recognize* legitimate works, a propensity and capacity to recognize their legitimacy and perceive them as worthy of admiration in themselves, which is inseparable from the capacity to recognize in them something already known, i.e., the stylistic traits appropriate to characterize them in their singularity ('It's a

Rembrandt', or even 'It's the *Helmeted Man*') or as members of a class of works ('It's Impressionist'). This explains why the propensity and capacity to accumulate 'gratuitous' knowledge, such as the names of film directors, are more closely and exclusively linked to educational capital than is mere cinema-going, which is more dependent on income, place of residence and age (ibid.:26).

The illusion of artistic legitimacy is nowhere more graphically evidenced than in the discourse used to convey a formal artistic education. The purpose of art education is to produce the aesthetic disposition through the inculcation of an intellectual capacity to perform operations of deciphering. Because it requires an explicit enunciation and systematisation of the practical principles of artistic judgement, this form of institutionalised learning produces a degree of scholastic knowledge about art and art works which constitutes a set of 'conventional norms governing the relation to the work of art in a certain historical and social situation and also to the beholder's capacity to conform to those norms, i.e., his artistic training' (ibid.:40–41).

The 'pure gaze' of the aesthetic disposition, which implies a break with popular taste, with the ordinary attitude towards the world, is at the same time a social break because of the way it is acquired. This explains the hostility of the working-class attitude towards *formal* refinement or experimentation within artistic media. Such hostility is more obvious in photography and cinema than in theatre or painting because the former have less artistic legitimacy. Thus,

A certain 'aesthetic', which maintains that a photograph is justified by the object photographed or by the possible use of the photographic image, is being brought into play when manual workers almost invariably reject photography for photography's sake (e.g., the photo of pebbles) as useless, perverse or bourgeois: 'A waste of film', 'They must have film to throw away', 'I tell you, there are some people who don't know what to do with their time', 'Haven't they got anything better to do with their time than photograph things like that?' 'That's bourgeois photography' (ibid.:40–41).

The working-class people who make these statements are unable to appreciate art for art's sake because they lack the detachment of the pure gaze. The temporal urgencies and material constraints of their daily lives constantly incline them towards a popular 'aesthetic' which makes them denounce the conspicuous formality of abstract art and reject the gratuity and futility of specifically aesthetic intentions.

Thus the photograph of a dead soldier provokes judgements which, whether positive or negative, are always responses to the reality of the thing represented or to the functions the representation could serve, the horror of war or the denunciation of the horrors of war which the photographer is supposed to produce simply by showing that horror (ibid.:41).

Such judgements issue from a disposition that is engendered by conditions of necessity and urgency, in which aesthetic considerations are subordinated to a moral imperative. Unlike the aesthetic disposition, which is constituted in conditions of *ease*, the habitus of working-class people prevents them from adopting a disinterested, detached or distant attitude towards either the world or their own experience. It is not merely the lack of artistic knowledge which prevents appreciation, but the absence of a disposition which can be produced only within a set of social conditions that have been relatively freed from the constraints of economic necessity.

The aesthetic disposition then, is formed in social conditions which always contain implicitly-shared perceptual codes, those of the *doxa*, the totality of pre-reflexive categories and tacit understanding which is never questioned or made explicit because it never becomes the subject of discourse – see Chapter 1, note 13. These codes, embodied in the habitus, produce an aptitude for perceiving and deciphering specifically stylistic aesthetic qualities. They also enable the development of artistic competences and at the same time shape the manner of applying them.

Once the cultivated habitus is formed, it is possible for specifically artistic competence to be acquired either by formal education or simply by continued exposure to works of art and regular acquaintance with the art world. Bourdieu holds that 'schooling provides the linguistic tools and the references which enable aesthetic experience to be expressed and to be constituted by being expressed' (ibid.:53). The preconditions for this to occur, however, include a degree of freedom from economic necessity and from the practical urgencies of daily existence.

Thus, the aesthetic disposition is one dimension of a distant, self-assured relation to the world and to others which presupposes objective assurance and distance. It is one manifestation of the system of dispositions produced by the social conditionings associated with a particular class of conditions of existence when they take the paradoxical form of the greatest freedom conceivable, at a given moment, with respect to the constraints of economic necessity. But it is also a distinctive expression of a privileged position in social space whose distinctive value is objectively established in its relationship to expressions generated from different conditions (ibid.:56).

For those who have this privileged social position with its leisurely conditions of existence and for whom the appropriate social conditions have engendered the system of dispositions constituting the cultivated habitus, education in the arts provides specific capacities for the symbolic consumption of art works. But it is important to recognise that such educational capital remains less important than social origin in determining basic differences in artistic competence among classes or class fractions.

While considerable artistic knowledge and specific competences can be developed through education, Bourdieu maintains that the aesthetic disposition cannot be acquired through institutionalised learning because it presupposes a tacit dimension of taken-for-granted awareness gained through repeated contact with legitimate culture and cultured people. The academic knowledge of art provided by the school system can make available conceptual schemes (e.g. 'classical'/'romantic') for the analysis and classification of art works, but it cannot provide the special competence of the 'connoisseur', which can only come from a deep-seated and prolonged familiarity with works. The social origin and conditions which produce the cultivated habitus, also engender 'a practical mastery which, like an art of thinking or an art of living, cannot be transmitted solely by precept or prescription' (ibid.:66).

The educational system makes available and transmits a discourse which constitutes an instrument of both communication and symbolic power. It enables aesthetic preferences to be rationalised so that taste can be legitimated by talk.[11] Thus:

By providing the means of expression which enable practical preferences to be brought to the level of quasi-systematic discourse and to be consciously organized around explicit principles, the educational system makes possible a (more or less adequate) symbolic mastery of the practical principles of taste. As grammar does for linguistic competence, it rationalizes the 'sense of beauty', in those who already have it, giving them the means of referring to principles (of harmony or rhetoric, for example), precepts, formulae, instead of relying on improvisation; it substitutes the intentional quasi-systematicity of the 'aesthetic-in-itself' produced by the practical principles of taste (ibid.:67).

Those who benefit most from this rational teaching of art are the scholars and intellectuals who comprise the dominated fraction of the dominating class. Their educational capital provides a substitute for the direct experience and spontaneity of taste which is believed to be a 'natural gift' in those who already possess the cultivated habitus. In contrast to the 'natural' recognition, or 'immaculate perception' of the 'true' aesthete, an academic art education makes possible an appreciation of art which draws upon concepts and rules. This produces an intellectual love of art which is often scorned by those who possess the gift of 'true vision' – a specific instance of the effect of schooling described in Chapter 4. For those who derive their aesthetic disposition entirely from their social origin and carry the cultural pedigree of the dominant class, the appreciation of art has all the intuitive qualities of a mystical union. For the dominated fraction, however, who depend upon rules and concepts to legitimate their taste, art appreciation sometimes becomes 'affected', 'bookish' or 'studied'. This distinction can be observed when scholarly art criticism is placed alongside the elegantly mystical modes of aesthetic discourse which serve the social function of giving plausibility to the ideology of natural taste. As an example of the latter, Bourdieu cites the following passage from a 'high culture' magazine:

> Ignorant or initiated, we are each of us disarmed before that mystery, the masterpiece. Uncertainly searching the canvas, we await the moment of grace when the artist's message will come to us. The silent clamour of Rembrandt, the infinite gentleness of Vermeer, no culture will make these things comprehensible to us if we have not restored the calm, created the expectation, prepared within ourselves the void that is propitious to emotion.
> (*Réalités*, March 1960 in Bourdieu 1984:568, n.63)

The tendency for such mystical discourse on works of art to exhibit an inevitable sense of arbitrariness and inexhaustibility of meaning diminishes the suitability of the school as an agency for the transmission of this specific form of cultural capital. Because a rationally constituted art education depends upon explicit principles, precepts and codifiable knowledge, the school is less effective than the family in fostering the competence to engage in mystical aesthetic discourse.

The language of art, therefore, is important to Bourdieu not for what it says about the intrinsic nature of art, but rather for the specific social effects that it has in producing distinctions within the dominant class, especially amongst those who occupy particular positions within the aesthetic field. The remaining part of the present discussion provides an outline of Bourdieu's critique of this field.

CRITIQUE OF THE AESTHETIC FIELD

Within the field of art criticism and philosophical aesthetics, Bourdieu's position stands in strong opposition to a long tradition of discourse about art and the art world which is deeply imbued with the 'intellectualist and anti-genetic idealism' that he so strongly rejects (Bourdieu 1984:467). It is a discourse, according to Bourdieu, which is forgetful of the historical conditions of its own production and which fails to take account of the social divisions and practices which necessarily precede it. Judgements of 'pure' taste which assume the 'illusion of universality' *produce* social differences which are mis-recognised as being aesthetic distinctions. For Bourdieu, this social amnesia which has sustained the whole field of philosophical aesthetics, is epitomised in Kant's *Critique of Pure Judgement*. With more than a little invective, he comments as follows:

> Totally ahistorical, like all philosophical thought that is worthy of the name (every *philosophia* worth its salt is *perennis*) – perfectly ethnocentric, since it takes for its sole datum the lived experience of a *homo aestheticus* who is none other than the subject of aesthetic discourse constituted as the universal subject of aesthetic experience – Kant's analysis of the judgement of taste finds its real basis in a set of aesthetic principles which are the universalization of the dispositions associated with a particular social and economic condition (ibid.:493).

The Kantian 'aesthetic' stands in diametric opposition to the popular 'aesthetic'. It insists upon the absolute primacy of form over function, whereas the popular 'aesthetic' implies the subordination of form to function. By distinguishing between 'that which pleases' and 'that which gratifies', Kant produces an aesthetic discourse in which the 'pure' taste of reflection is elevated to a position of superiority over the mere pleasure of the senses. But it thereby legitimates an aesthetic code, Bourdieu argues, which has within it a denied social relationship.

This pure aesthetic is indeed the rationalization of an ethos: pure pleasure, pleasure totally purified of all sensuous or sensible interest, perfectly free of all social or fashionable interest, as remote from concupiscence as it is from conspicuous consumption, is opposed as much to the refined, altruistic enjoyment of the courtier as it is to the crude, animal enjoyment of the people (ibid.:493).

Philosophical aesthetics, therefore, marks itself off not only from the popular 'aesthetic' of the working class, but also from the ethos of the petite bourgeoisie with its enjoyment of the *facile*, the 'charming'. It is only with an aesthetic distancing, the 'detachment of the pure gaze', that a work of art can be perceived with *pure* pleasure – pleasure that is 'predisposed to become a symbol of moral excellence, and the work of art a test of ethical superiority, an indisputable measure of the capacity for sublimation which defines the truly human man' (ibid.:491). Thus, the aesthetic point of view defines a social superiority which is misrecognised as being in the nature of the art work itself. It is the aesthetic point of view, Bourdieu holds, that creates the aesthetic object while simultaneously proclaiming the social position of the beholder.

Here we can discern the most radical features of Bourdieu's critique of the field of aesthetics. He shifts the focus of concern from the work of art *per se* to the aesthetic disposition from which it demands to be appreciated.

Any legitimate work tends in fact to impose the norms of its own perception and tacitly defines as the only legitimate mode of perception the one which brings into play a certain disposition and a certain competence. Recognizing this fact does not mean constituting a particular mode of perception as an essence, thereby falling into the illusion which is the basis of recognition of artistic legitimacy. It does mean taking note of the fact that all agents, whether they like it or not, whether or not they have the means of conforming to them, find themselves objectively measured by those norms (ibid.:28–9).

From his earliest work, Bourdieu has been steadfast in his denial that the appreciation of art is a 'natural' human experience. He has always insisted that art works are symbolic assets which exist as such only for those agents who have the means to appropriate them. Such means are acquired by achieving a degree of artistic competence which is *nothing more than* a degree of complexity or subtlety within the agent's system of cognitive classification. In one of his earliest papers on art perception, Bourdieu illustrates this as follows:

> For anyone familiar only with the principle of division into Romanesque art and Gothic art, all Gothic cathedrals fall into the same class and, for that reason, remain *indistinct*, whereas greater competence makes it possible to perceive differences between the styles of the 'early', 'middle', and 'late' periods, or even to recognize, within each of these styles, the works of a school or even of an architect.
>
> (Bourdieu 1968:596)

It is this kind of cognitive mastery, according to Bourdieu, which makes the appreciation of art possible and which gives the means for the specific appropriation of art works. Having the perceptual/cognitive capacity to classify provides necessary conditions for experiencing aesthetic gratification or for enabling art works to be valued in themselves.[12] Bourdieu points out that:

> Since the work of art only exists as such to the extent that it is perceived, or in other words deciphered, it goes without saying that the satisfactions attached to this perception – whether it be a matter of purely aesthetic enjoyment or of more indirect gratification, such as the *effect of distinction* – are only accessible to those who are disposed to appropriate them because they *attribute a value to them*, it being understood that they can do this only if they have the means to appropriate them.
>
> (Bourdieu 1968:601)

Also within the same paper, he critiques what he calls the *charismatic ideology* which defines aesthetic competence as a 'gift of nature' and is silent concerning the social prerequisites for the appropriation of culture. For Bourdieu, it is 'a self-seeking silence because it is what makes it possible to legitimatize a social privilege by pretending that it is a gift of nature' (ibid.:608).

While he has not departed from this basic position, Bourdieu's later work shows more precisely how this form of misrecognition is reproduced within the field of aesthetic discourse.

Every essentialist analysis of the aesthetic disposition, the only socially accepted 'right' way of approaching the objects socially designated as works of art, that is, as both demanding and deserving to be approached with a specifically aesthetic intention capable of recognizing and constituting them as works of art, is bound to fail. Refusing to take account of the collective and individual genesis of this product of history which must be endlessly 'reproduced' by education, it is unable to reconstruct its sole raison d'être, that is, the historical reason which underlies the arbitrary necessity of the institution.

(Bourdieu 1984:29)

The illusion of artistic legitimacy cannot be recognised for what it is while artistic competence is taken to be a 'gift of nature' (charismatic ideology) or while the meaning of art works is attributed to the intentions of the artist (essentialist analysis). Bourdieu's project demonstrates that the illusion results from a pervasive misrecognition of the reality that every act of artistic perception is located within a social field and that every work of art exists as such only to the extent that it is perceived by socially-situated agents. Thus it is a project which from the outset has necessitated an unequivocal negation of all idealist conceptions of art.[13] Bourdieu establishes this negation, not by engaging in philosophical aesthetic discourse, but by constructing and describing the social field in which such discourse is enacted and by showing ethnographically that field to be a theatre of symbolic struggles within the dominating class itself.

Constructing the field of aesthetics as an object of sociological analysis requires and makes possible a radical break with essentialist modes of thought which focus upon the 'genius' of the individual artist and the 'pure gaze' of the individual beholder. The illusion that a work of art is the expression of creative intentions is sustained by the charismatic ideology which explicitly proclaims the virtues of individual agency while implicitly denying the necessity of structural relations between social positions 'that are both occupied and manipulated by social agents, which may be isolated individuals, groups or institutions' (Bourdieu 1983:312).

Not only does the charismatic ideology encourage the glorification of 'great men', perceived as being unique creative individuals, but it produces a discourse in which 'expression' is taken to be the primary defining feature of art works. Before anything can qualify as art, it must necessarily be the expression of an emotion or intended meaning (Collingwood 1938:109). Thus, expressionist theories of art are couched in a discourse which construes the act of appreciation as a quest for the artist's intention.

Some expressionist theories hold that works of art express symbolic meanings of which the artist may not be consciously aware. Herbert Read (1943), for instance, accepts the Jungian theory that art is the expression of universal mythic content emanating from the deep sub-strata of the collective unconscious mind. These universal psychic symbols, originating in the primordial past, are implicit in all artistic expression, altering their forms but never their contents. Such theories often reach into the realms of mysticism where the work of art is comprehended as a symbol for some 'greater reality'. Cassirer (1961) seems to be suggesting this with his notion that symbolic forms embody a kind of intuitive knowledge. This is a form of expressionism that has become widely accepted through the work of Suzanne Langer (1953), a philosopher of art who has been strongly influenced by Cassirer.

The artist, according to Langer, knows in a non-logical, intuitive way the nature of emotions and can therefore create forms that will enable the true expression of these emotions. An artwork, therefore, is essentially 'objectified feeling' and its appreciation is no more than the intuitive knowledge of the feeling that it expresses. She says of music, for instance, that it 'expresses primarily the composer's *knowledge of human feeling*' and that the feelings revealed in music 'are presented directly to our understanding, that we may grasp, realise, comprehend these feelings, without pretending to have them or imputing them to anyone else' (Langer 1957:222). This occurs because 'there are certain aspects of the so-called "inner-life" – physical or mental – which have formal properties similar to those of music – patterns of motion and rest, of tension and release, of agreement and disagreement, preparation, fulfilment, excitation, sudden change, etc.' (ibid.:228).

Langer's theory of art presupposes an idealist essentialism which, in Bourdieu's terms, is also an implicit refusal to recognise that artistic practice is socially situated practice. He argues, following Panofsky, that the perception of artistic form is always mediated by socially constructed aesthetic codes. Bourdieu has consistently denounced theories which proclaim the superior reality of art and the autonomous genius of the artist. In an early paper, he quotes the painter Kandinsky, who said, 'That is beautiful which corresponds to an inner necessity.' Bourdieu then comments that:

The declaration of the automony of the creative intention leads to a morality of conviction which tends to judge works of art by the purity of the artist's intention and which can end in a kind of terrorism of taste when the artist, in the name of his conviction, demands unconditional recognition of his work.

(Bourdieu 1971:165)

Bourdieu's central concern is with the political functions of symbolic practices. There is no place here for Romantic notions of artistic creation or celebratory pronouncements about 'great' works. Within Bourdieu's sociology of art, the artist is a cultural producer occupying a position within a particular social field.[14] Likewise, every art work is a cultural product situated at a conjuncture of economic, social and historical conditions, any of which may change with the course of time.

Thus the sociology of intellectual and artistic creation must take as its object the creative project as a meeting point and an adjustment between determinism and a determination. That is, if it is to go beyond the opposition between an internal aesthetic theory, obliged to treat a work as if it were a self-contained system with its own reasons and *raison d'être*, itself defining the coherent principles and norms necessary for its interpretation, and an external aesthetic theory which at the cost often of detrimentally diminishing the work, attempts to relate it to the economic, social and cultural conditions of artistic creation (ibid.:185).

It is not a question, according to Bourdieu, of giving priority to either agency or structure, or of settling disputes about voluntarism and determinism. The object of analysis for a sociology of art is the social field, whether of the artist or the spectator, and the struggles for power, both economic and symbolic, which always accompany acts of creation and appreciation. The precise nature of the field as a field of strategies and struggles (see Chapter 1), indicates the nature of Bourdieu's break with structuralist analyses of art which relegate all considerations of 'artist-as-creator' to the realm of bourgeois ideology. Within Bourdieu's sociology of the aesthetic field, the artist/author occupies a *social* position no less significant than that of the beholder/reader, such that the actions of each are limited and mediated by the conditions of their artistic practice.

Some structuralists have insisted upon a complete negation of the concept of creative agency (authorship) within analyses of art and

literature. Roland Barthes, for instance, argues with reference to
literature that 'a text is not a line of words releasing a single "theological" meaning (the "message" of the Author-God) but a multidimensional space in which a variety of writings, none of them
original, blend and clash' (1977:146). Bourdieu would agree with
this critique of the charismatic view of the artist as a fixed origin of
meaning but he would not go as far as Barthes who also asserts that
'a text's unity lies not in its origin but in its destination . . . the birth
of the reader must be at the cost of the death of the Author'
(ibid.:148). Bourdieu does not banish the artists altogether from the
aesthetic field but he does accept the ideological effects of an exclu-
sive preoccupation with their artistic intentions and personal life
histories. He has maintained from his earliest work that aesthetic
codes, embodied in the aesthetic disposition, mediate between the
conditions of artistic production and the conditions of artistic reception. Moreover, this mediation occurs at a cognitive level, so that:

> Like painting, perception of painting is a mental thing, at least
> when it conforms to the norms of perception immanent in the
> work of art or, in other words, when the aesthetic intention of the
> beholder is identified with the objective intention of the work
> (which must not be identified with the artist's intention).
>
> (Bourdieu 1968:594)

But, just as the objective intention of the work of art is not to be
identified with the subjective intention of the artist, neither is it to
be identified with an intrinsic, self-limiting, self-regulating formal
structure. Every work is a cultural object situated within a field of
social forces, which effectively limits the range of possible meanings
and therefore the possible positions (stances) that can be taken in
relation to it. Nevertheless, no work is assigned permanently to a
particular field, even by its maker, and the field in which it is situated
at a given time not only determines its meaning, but also its value.
This is particularly evident for collaborative arts, such as theatre,
cinema and television, but even where artistic production is more
readily attributed to an 'individual', as in paintings or poetry, there
is always a field of other agents, either preceding the 'creative' act
(e.g. teachers, patrons, contemporary artists) or mediating between
production and reception (e.g. critics, publishers, art dealers and
entrepreneurs). Thus, as with practices in other fields, Bourdieu
refuses to polarise structure and agency in his construction of the field
of artistic practice. With this field construct (discussed in Chapter 1)

he is able to show how artistic practices result from choices that are always made within structured limits. Thus:

Every position-taking is defined in relation to the *space of possibles* which is objectively realized as a *problematic* in the form of the actual or potential position-taking corresponding to the different positions; and it receives its distinctive *value* from its negative relationship with the coexistent position-takings to which it is objectively related and which determine it by delimiting it. It follows from this, for example, that a *prise de position* changes, even when it remains identical, whenever there is change in the universe of options that are simultaneously offered for producers and consumers to choose from. The meaning of a work (artistic, literary, philosophical, etc.) changes automatically with each change in the field within which it is situated for the spectator or reader.

(Bourdieu 1983:313)

Bourdieu illustrates this by reference to the effect of the 'so-called classic works, which change constantly as the universe of coexistent works changes' (loc. cit.). Further illustrations could be found in John Berger's *Ways of Seeing* (1972) where he shows how the art of the past has been influenced by the rise of capitalism and the advent of technology. Berger's essay, which was presented as a BBC television series, traces the history of European oil-painting between 1500 and 1900, illustrating the ways in which changing attitudes towards property and exchange produced a particular way of seeing the world. This way of seeing found its symbolic form in images which presented objects as commodities, celebrating their materiality and exchangeability. What are now the acknowledged masterpieces of this tradition, the works of painters like Rembrandt, Vermeer, Poussin, Chardin, Goya and Turner, became exceptional not because they were exemplars of the tradition, but because they stood in opposition to it. Their uniqueness, and subsequently their 'greatness', was derived initially from their antagonism to the thousands of paintings which were typical of the tradition. However, since the invention of the camera and the technology of reproduction, these 'exceptional' images have become commonplace and are now seen as constituting a tradition which has retrospectively replaced the very tradition to which they were originally opposed. The change has occurred, not in the images themselves, but in the aesthetic field within which they are situated. Thus, the social conditions of the present can transform the art of the past. Another illustration of this is provided by Bourdieu in his analysis of the ways in which aesthetic value is *produced* by dealers, art critics and publishers through acts of consecration which may take the form of 'discovery', 'revival' or 're-reading' (Bourdieu, 1980a:263).

CONCLUSION

Consistent with the general method outlined in Chapter 1, Bourdieu defines the literary and artistic field in terms of the positions, power relations and struggles of different agents and groups. This enables the specific economy of artistic practices to be understood without recourse to either 'the charismatic image or artistic activity as pure, disinterested creation by an isolated artist' or 'the reductionist vision' which claims to explain artistic production in terms of class or group interests. (Bourdieu, 1983:316).

Bourdieu's interest in aesthetics has a very long history, and remains at the centre of his current concerns. Among his most recent projects is an attempt to explore the genesis of the contemporary French aesthetic field, by establishing the crucial changes that were made in that field, most notably by Flaubert and by Manet. The shape of contemporary intellectual discourse can thus be considered to be, in part, a product of a field which they helped constitute.[15]

Bourdieu's method is one which follows directly from the particular way in which he defines the object of enquiry, as the following statement points out:

> Given that works of art exist as symbolic objects only if they are known and recognized, i.e. socially instituted as works of art and received by spectators capable of knowing and recognizing them as such, the sociology of art and literature has to take as its object not only the material production but also the symbolic production of the work, i.e. the production of the value of the work, or, which amounts to the same thing, of belief in the value of the work. It therefore has to consider as contributing to production not only the direct producers of the work in its materiality (artist, writer, etc.) but also the producers of the meaning and value of the work – critics, publishers, gallery directors, and the whole set of agents whose combined efforts produce consumers capable of

knowing and recognizing the work of art as such, in particular teachers (but also families, etc.).

(Bourdieu, 1983:318–19)

Thus, it can be seen why Bourdieu is less concerned with the nature of art *per se* and more with the social conditions in which works of art acquire meaning and value, that is with the whole field of symbolic production, which includes not only the conditions of production of a set of objects socially constituted as works of art, but also with the genesis and formation of the aesthetic disposition in individual agents. For it is the aesthetic disposition, Bourdieu maintains, which gives agents the capacity to make aesthetic distinctions, which are necessarily also social distinctions, making it possible for them to apprehend and appreciate the set of objects that have been culturally consecrated as works of art.

NOTES

1. Although Bourdieu's work marks a significant departure from the two dominant French aesthetic traditions of existentialism and structuralism, it can be seen also as a synthesis of these two traditions. By always grounding his analyses in the world of practice, he avoids the limitations of both idealist and materialist accounts of art. He recognizes the interdependence of the symbolic and the economic without resorting to the social determinism of traditional Marxist theories.
2. His project is sociological rather than philosophical and his discourse embodies this particular scientific interest. He does not collapse one discourse into another by reducing the problems of 'beauty' or 'aesthetic value' to the same ontological level as the social and political. Rather, he develops a discourse in which all the practices associated with the art world, including the discourses of philosophical aesthetics and art criticism, can be understood in social scientific terms as forms of cultural production.
3. In the Preface to the English language edition of *Distinction*, Bourdieu acknowledges that his empirical work inevitably reflects the specificity of the French intellectual field but his use of the comparative method, he believes, enables him 'to enter into the singularity of an object without renouncing the ambition of drawing out universal propositions' (Bourdieu 1984:xi).
4. Bourdieu is aware that such a position could be described as 'barbarous' because it 'transgresses one of the fundamental taboos of the intellectual world, in relating intellectual products and producers to their social conditions of existence' (1984:xiii).

5. Of course, earlier French books, as well as several articles are also crucial. See especially *Un art moyen, essai sur les usages sociaux de la photographie*, with L. Boltanski, R. Castel and J. C. Chamboredon (Paris: Minuit, 1965); 'Le Paysan et la photographie', with M. C. Bourdieu, *Revue Française de Sociologie*, 2, 1965, 164–74; 'La Musée et son public', *L'Information d'Histoire de l'Art*, 3, 1965, 120–22; *L'amour de l'art, les musées d'art européens et leur public*, with A. Darbel and D. Schnapper (Paris: Minuit, 1966); 'Eléments d'une théorie sociologique de la perception artistique', *Revue Internationale des Sciences Sociales*, 20(4), 1968, 640–64 (for a translation of which see Bourdieu, 1968); 'Sociologie de la perception esthétique', in *Les Sciences humaines et l'oeuvre d'art* (Brussels: La Connaissance, 1969, 161–76 and 251–4; 'Disposition esthétique et compétence artistique', *Les Temps Modernes*, 295, 1345–78; 'L'invention de la vie d'artiste', *Actes*, 2, 1975, 67–94; 'Anatomie du goût', with M. de St Martin, *Actes*, 5, 1976, 2–112; 'Titres et quartiers de noblesse culturelle. Elements d'une critique sociale de jugement esthétique', with M. de St Martin, *Ethnologie Française*, 8 (2/3), 1978, 107–44; 'Des goûts artistiques et des classes sociales', with D. Eribon, *Libération*, 3(4), 1979, 12–13; and 'Pour une sociologie de la perception', with Y. Delsaut, *Actes*, 40, 1981, 3–9; 'Le marché des biens symboliques', *L'Année sociologique*, 22, 1971, 49–126; 'La production de la croyance', *Actes*, 13, 1977, 3–43.

6. Iconography refers to acts of making images (encoding), whereas iconology refers to acts of interpretation (decoding).

7. Structuralism, as a pervasive intellectual movement, was at its peak in Bourdieu's formative years. The movement, led by Lévi-Strauss (1958), had rediscovered the work of Ferdinand de Saussure (1916) and by the late 1960s had embraced most disciplines (cf. Ehrmann 1970; Robey 1973).

8. Cultural or symbolic capital is acquired, Bourdieu argues, through cumulative acts of distinction which are the products of internalised social structures. Thus:

> Distinctions, as symbolic transfigurations of de facto differences and, more generally, ranks, orders, grades, and all other symbolic hierarchies, are the product of the application of schemes of construction which, like (for example) the pairs of adjectives used to utter most social judgements, are the product of the internalization of the structures to which they are applied; and the most absolute recognition of legitimacy is nothing other than the apprehension of the everyday world as self-evident which results from the quasi-perfect coincidence of objective structures and embodied structures.
>
> (Bourdieu 1985:204)

9. Bourdieu refuses to romanticise working-class culture by searching for its 'heart' or essence. In his terms, class is defined not by culture, but by position and habitus. Hence, working-class culture is constituted of practices which have a relational opposition to bourgeois practices.

10. There are strong parallels here with the work of Gombrich (1960), which Bourdieu himself has noted (1980).
11. It can be argued (Codd 1982) that the education of artistic appreciation involves an initiation into a particular logic and language of interpretation which makes the justification of aesthetic judgements possible. Bourdieu's position, however, goes much further by claiming that such language always conveys a legitimation of social power.
12. The theory that art appreciation is a form of cognitive appraisal has some obvious links with Wittgenstein's notion of 'seeing as'. (Casey, 1966; Scruton, 1974; Best, 1980; Codd, 1982).
13. The well-established tradition of idealist aesthetics includes such names as Santayana (1896), Croce (1922), DuCasse (1929), Collingwood (1938), Read (1943), Langer (1953, 1957) and Cassirer (1961).
14. Janet Wolff (1981:27) cites the historical evidence which shows that 'the conception of the artist as unique and gifted individual is an historically specific one, and that it dates from the rise of the merchant classes in Italy and France, and from the rise of humanist ideas in philosophy and religious thought'.
15. This work, which is not yet published in full, promises to be Bourdieu's most ambitious theoretical and empirical task to date – but see Bourdieu 1987d and 1988b.

7 Language, Truth and Power: Bourdieu's *Ministerium*[1]
Ivan Snook

INTRODUCTION

Bourdieu holds that language is part of the way of life of a social group and serves essentially practical ends. In this he stands opposed to 'the intellectualist philosophy which makes language an object of understanding rather than an instrument of action' (1977b:645). The origin of Bourdieu's view lies in the European philosophical tradition which, since Kant, has been concerned more with human activity than with human theorising. In this chapter, then, Bourdieu's position will be discussed within this European tradition and contrasted with the 'intellectualist' tradition so familiar to philosophers in the Anglo-Saxon world, the broad outlines of which will first be sketched in.

Since the beginning of critical reflection there has been a well-recognised connection between language and truth, and a clear, though largely unrecognised, connection between language and power. Near the beginning of Western philosophical thought, Plato developed an elaborate theory about the relationship between language and reality. The function of language was to mirror the world of Forms and when it did so, the knowledge captured was true. His educational theory rested on this: learning consists in progressively coming to terms with the Reality revealed by language. Ultimately, a chosen few come to grasp reality as it really is, to apprehend the Form of the Good, the ultimate source of intelligibility and value. These people alone are fit to exercise power over the lives of others.

The view that it is possible for language to mirror reality has held sway for many centuries and has consistently functioned as a justification of political power: witch-doctors, gurus, prophets, judges, priests, physicians and scientists have claimed rights over others on the basis of their superior grasp of the truth. In time, however, the dominance of this position came under attack. The

160

Nominalists undermined the existence of universals, locating them in language rather than in reality, and later a compromise was sought in the suggestion that the mind forms universals by abstracting from the characteristics of individuals. Thus it came to be held that universals exist only in the mind (Kolenda 1973:77). Locke elaborated this position and Berkeley took it to its extreme, arguing that mind, not reality, is basic and human thought is the source of all knowledge. Berkeley anticipated the twentieth century by recognising that language has functions other than describing reality but the issue of language was not to the fore among the British empiricists. The task of loosening the Platonic grip fell to the continental 'existentialists' and American pragmatists, who focused attention on human activity and began an attack on what Anscombe calls the 'incorrigibly contemplative conception of knowledge' (quoted in Bernstein 1972:57).

While this 'contemplative' conception is still prevalent and perhaps still dominant in contemporary British philosophy, Bourdieu, like many sociologists in the European tradition, has a totally different conception of the nature of knowledge and the place of language in it. The remainder of this paper will develop Bourdieu's position by relating it to its antecedents and particularly to the work of Nietzsche and Wittgenstein, who have been strongly influential on the development of his ideas.[2]

NIETZSCHE

For Nietzsche, whom Bourdieu frequently acknowledges, knowledge is not a body of theoretical information about the world but 'an instrument, designed in accordance with and limited to the satisfaction of human needs' (Hollingdale 1973:131). Our knowledge is essentially a matter of practice which is motivated by our needs and desires and not by some impartial search for truth. Indeed, for Nietzsche, there is no truth or knowledge in the traditional sense. The notion that some of our beliefs are true has to be replaced by the idea that some of our beliefs have survival-value:

> Truth is that sort of error without which a particular class of living creatures could not live.
>
> (quoted in Solomon 1972:113)

and again,

What is truth? Perhaps a kind of belief that has become a condition of life?

(Nietzsche 1967:289)

Humans, then, strive to satisfy their needs. To do so they construct ways of viewing the world which are expressed in language, and hence language is necessary for any thought whatever. But it is a functional thing, a form of acting. Its aim is not to contemplate the way things really are. Philosophical ideas, thought by many to capture truth, grow out of an evolving tradition shaped and expressed by the languages used to reveal them:

> Owing to the unconscious domination and guidance of similar grammatical functions . . . everything is prepared at the outset for a similar development and succession of philosophical systems; just as the way seems barred against certain other possibilities of world interpretation.

(Nietzsche 1927:402)

According to Nietzsche, the dominance of language has blighted thought, for we have confused its function: philosophers have tried to squeeze living wisdom out of 'concept-mummies' (Nietzsche 1954:479). In a provocative passage, however, Nietzsche makes it clear that in the last analysis there is no escape from the tyranny of language. As humans we must use and develop language for it is itself one of our basic needs, a practice we cannot do without. It is, as he puts it, 'a primary form of life' (1927:422). Human beings are involved in living and this makes certain demands on us. Language is one such demand and in its turn it too makes demands on us: our ontology, our metaphysics, our philosophy derive from (or 'mirror') our language. And our language is a praxis. Here we have the first and significant strand in Bourdieu's reconstruction of language and the social world.

Nietzsche has another contribution to make to Bourdieu. It is the centrality of power or, as Nietzsche put it, 'the will to power'. It is this which explains the belief systems and moral codes we have and it is this alone which can justify them. This will to power is initially a psychological theory. In common with the animals, humans have a drive to conquer others. In humans, however, this is thwarted by social life and becomes turned inwards:

> All instincts which do not discharge themselves outwardly *turn*

inwards – this is what I call the *Verinnerlichung* of man: thus it was that man first developed what he afterwards called his 'soul'.
(Nietzsche in Hollingdale 1973:117)

Henceforth humans must struggle to overcome these negative inner forces. The 'superman' (or 'overman') doctrine develops this into a social theory, for this person overcomes not only himself but others as well. In the end he overcomes human nature. He is master of his fate, can use all his talents fully, enhance his creative potentials and achieve personally-chosen and difficult goals. The sole purpose of history is to produce such persons. They take life by the throat and thereby create the values the rest of us must live by. As Nietzsche himself says:

The noble type of man feels *himself* to be the determiner of values, he does not need to be approved of, he judges 'what harms me is harmful in itself'. . . . He *creates values*.
(Ibid.:145, italics in the original)

The will to power has progressed from a psychological theory to a social theory and finally to an ethical theory: morality expresses the will to power. This is true even of the Christian 'slave morality' which Nietzsche despises because it consists in a blatant will to power masked by the denial of the will to power. Powerful, self-controlled, leaders deserve no criticism and need no defending. They are the standards by which the rest are to be judged. In the last analysis, power determines value.

Nietzsche's basic position is clearly revealed when he attacks the priests who have acquired power by a warped language which they use to turn decent human values into the conterfeit, mealy-mouthed 'virtues' of Christianity:

The concepts 'beyond', 'Last Judgement', 'immortality of the soul' and 'soul' itself are instruments of torture, systems of cruelties by virtue of which the priest became master, remained master.
(Nietzsche 1954:612)

Small wonder then that Bourdieu cites Nietzsche as one of the few philosophers (Marx and Pascal are others) to perceive 'the science of language as pragmatic sociology' (Bourdieu, Fr. ed. 1982:165) for he set out to discover within the formal properties of language the effects of the social conditions of their production and their circulation (loc. cit.).

Of course Bourdieu in no way subscribes to the voluntarist and individualist conception of power for which Nietzsche is renowned. Bourdieu focuses on the social and structural dimensions of power and on the ability of a person to gain power by speaking for and representing a group. This he calls the *ministerium*, which will be discussed later in this chapter.

WITTGENSTEIN

Wittgenstein took up the idea of language as a practical activity and further elaborated its function within a social form of life. In his *Philosophical Investigations* he recanted on his earlier work and rejected the Platonic tradition concerning the nature of language. It had been assumed that language aims at mirroring reality and that words gain their meaning by naming objects in the world: the word *block* stands for the physical object it names. Meaning is a function of words, and it is words which name. Wittgenstein turns all this on its head by stressing language as communication. He sets out a series of communications between a builder and his apprentice. Initially there are only the two people and four categories of objects: blocks, pillars, slabs, beams. The builder needs these objects in a certain order and the apprentice's task is to pass them to him. Four words are used: *block*, *pillar*, *slab*, *beam*. The builder calls out a word and the apprentice brings him the object he has learned to bring at that call. The story is gradually extended so that the two men are operating a language with a richer vocabulary containing pronouns, connectives and adjectives (Wittgenstein 1974:3e–5e).

He thus argues that the basic notion of meaning arises because words are used in certain activities by people: it is persons who 'mean'. Thus by *block* the builder means 'bring me that object there'. The builder is not stating facts or describing states of affairs: he is issuing commands. The apprentice is not understanding propositions or absorbing information: he is obeying his master. From this derives Wittgenstein's notion of a language game, which is central to his philosophy and may have been significant in the development of some of Bourdieu's key ideas. Yet it is an obscure notion in Wittgenstein and its elusiveness is instructive. Conceived in one way, the language game is simply a set of verbal moves: language, though rooted in activity, is an autonomous practice. Many of those who use the idea still see language as an autonomous symbolic system divorced from its origin and point. The other interpretation is that 'the game' is all of a piece: it includes the reciting of the words and the performance of the required actions (the apprentice brings the blocks). Here the focus is on the game as an activity, something that people do:

> The child does not learn that there are books, a chair etc., but learns to fetch books, set himself on a chair, etc.
>
> (Wittgenstein in Brand 1979:110)

It is this interpretation which is crucial for Bourdieu's account: language includes both the words and the actions with which they are woven.

What then constitute the boundaries of language games? Again, Wittgenstein is less than clear. At one level the entire system of human communication can be seen as *the* language game. At another, there are limitless varieties of language games. David Bloor argues that progress can be made only if language games are seen as social institutions (1983:41). Wittgenstein himself seemed to forge this link by his mysterious talk of 'forms of life' which define what we can sensibly say:

> Why can't my right hand give my left hand money? My right hand can put it into my left hand. My right hand can write a deed of gift and my left hand a receipt. But *the further practical consequences would not be those of a gift.* [italics mine] (1974:94e)

Here we find an important aspect of Wittgenstein's thought. What is the answer to his opening question? The temptation of the linguistic philosopher who believes he is following Wittgenstein is to say 'that just isn't how we use the word "gift".' A more accurate answer is that such an activity would have no point: the 'game' could not be continued, because the left hand could not do anything with the gift (and so on). There is, therefore, no form of life in which this kind of 'gift-giving' would make sense. Making sense is a social act and this 'act' does not qualify.

This helps to explicate Wittgenstein's notion of a rule. In contrast to those who saw grammatical rules as ensuring the agreement of words with things, he stressed the central role of interpersonal agreement. Anyone can point to a red object and call it 'green'. What distinguishes the correct rule-followers is that they agree with the members of some community. Rules are a social matter and are revealed in action: they are not conscious signs in the heads of an individual.

The question then arises as to the relationship between language games and truth. If 'forms of life' serve essentially pragmatic ends, is there any connection between them and the world in which we live? Wittgenstein's answer as organised by Brand seems to be as follows (Brand 1979:123–46).

1. Language games as closed systems of understanding belong to *the* language game, the everyday language of adults. 'The language of the grown-up is that of a nebulous mass of language, his mother tongue, surrounded by discrete and more or less clear-cut language games, the technical languages.'
2. Speaking is not an autonomous activity but part of the praxis of life. 'The word "language-game" is supposed to emphasize here that the speaking of a language is part of an activity, or of a form of life.'
3. The language game . . . does not itself have a ground. 'You must consider that the language game, so to speak, is something unforeseen. I mean, it is not grounded. Not reasonable (or unreasonable).'
4. There are rules which can never be spoken at all, which only lie in the shadow, and these are fundamental, because they are found apart from all doubt, in that they are never put into question.
5. We are tempted to call language arbitrary. 'Grammatical rules first determine the meaning (they constitute it), are therefore responsible to no meaning and are to this extent arbitrary.'
6. But 'why do I not call the rules of cooking arbitrary? . . . Because I consider the concept "cooking" as defined by the goal of cooking but not, on the contrary, the concept of "language" by the goal of language'.
7. Reality is not arbitrary. If things were other than they in fact are, our normal language games would lose their point. 'The procedure of putting a lump of cheese on a balance . . . would lose its point if it frequently happened for such lumps to suddenly grow or shrink for no obvious reason.'
8. Agreement, nevertheless, is crucially connected with language. 'Outside of language there is no agreement. And without agreement there is no language.'
9. But agreement is not arbitrary. By experience we learn to judge

in a certain way. 'You have to consider the praxis of language, then you will see it.'

At the conclusion of his book, Bloor (1983) argues that 'conservative' philosophers such as Winch have misinterpreted Wittgenstein's social significance and the 'true heirs' to the subject that used to be called 'philosophy' are the 'sociologists of knowledge'. Those who would enter into that inheritance must take literally the claim that meaning is use and see what it entails. This use will involve the whole culture. The stream of life in a language-game involves the whole, turbulent, cross-cutting stream of interests that we come across among people (ibid.:183).

Bloor, writing in the 1980s, does not mention Bourdieu (or Nietzsche) but I want to suggest that Bourdieu is very centrally an heir to Wittgenstein's legacy in that he fully endorses the idea of language as a practice and profitably extends the notion that it is rooted in social groups.

BOURDIEU

As early as the 1950s, when he was writing up his Algerian studies, Bourdieu was developing a position on language. Writing of the Kabyle's elaborate code of honour he said:

> The system of honour values is enacted rather than thought, and the grammar of honour can inform actions without having to be formulated. Thus, when they spontaneously apprehend a particular line of conduct as degrading or ridiculous, the Kabyles are in the same position as someone who notices a language mistake without being able to state the syntactic system that has been violated.
>
> (1979:128)

Here we notice that Bourdieu has set out a view of language with four features which suggest links with Nietzsche and Wittgenstein:

1. There is, first of all, the emphasis on practice. A system of values is usually viewed as a deductive system able to be described in logical terms. 'Day-to-day' values are deduced by a process of reasoning from a general set of fundamental principles or basic values. Bourdieu, however, sees the Kabyle system of honour as a system of actions in which people participate fully without

knowing exactly what they participate in: they are agents and actors, not believers or observers.

2. Like the honour system, language is a praxis. He speaks of a 'grammar of honour' and likens it to the (more literal) grammar of a language. Neither is a set of descriptive generalisations or rules from which particular sets of behaviour or particular sentences are derived logically. In both cases some activity is prior and the 'grammar' is a set of rules for accomplishing the aim of the activity. Here is a very clear account of a form of life – a generalised way of acting in which language finds its place without becoming divorced from the point of the form of life. Similarly, there is at least the intimation of a socially-rooted language game (including, but not consisting of, words spoken), with its own purpose and its own regularities ('rules').

3. In both cases there are rules (in the sense of regularities, accessible in principle to a certain kind of observer) but in each case the rules are not consciously present. The participant (and the 'observer' insofar as they are a true participant) can recognise a social or linguistic mistake without being able to state the rule being broken. This is clear enough in a social practice: one joins in and 'picks up' the moves, knowing 'intuitively' what to do next and being 'subconsciously' aware of what dare not be done. Similarly, as Wittgenstein tried to show, the fluent users of a language know how to speak and can recognise a *faux pas* without being able to state the rules or cite the rule being broken.[3]

Saussure had distinguished *la langue* (language) from *la parole* (speech), the latter being the practical application of the former. Similarly, Chomsky talks of 'competence' and 'performance', the former involving sets of skills or pieces of knowledge, the latter requiring the relating of these to a concrete situation. Bourdieu, however, rejects such a dichotomy.

Interestingly, Chomsky himself has noted the connection between language and social custom. Beginning with language, Chomsky draws a parallel:

Another analogue to the case of language, perhaps, is our comprehension of the social structures in which we live. We have all sorts of tacit and complex knowledge concerning our relations to other people.

(Chomsky 1979:69)

4. It follows, of course, that the social situation, or social practice, is central. To learn that a form of behaviour is wrong is to learn how to apply terms such as 'noble', 'degrading' or 'worthwhile'. There are not two activities, that of appraising in terms of social rules and that of attaching appropriate words in terms of linguistic rules. There are no rules, social or linguistic, apart from a group of people with plans and projects. Like Wittgenstein, Bourdieu reconciles the two: a form of life involves a group of people involved in some activity; their language is part of that activity; it is a 'game' played by the group for its communal ends. Its standards come from the group and from the aim of the group. Neither language nor life is a mystery.

The idea that language is a social practice was foreshadowed by Nietzsche and elaborated by Wittgenstein. Both, however, had blind spots. Nietzsche recognised language as a social activity but located power in individual *psyches* rather than social groups. Wittgenstein realised the place of language in 'forms of life' but tended to see language games as *mental* activities and forms of life as static social modes in which language games secure their meaning and grounding. What is needed is a way of combining Nietzsche's tantalising view of power with Wittgenstein's seminal notion of a 'form of life'. Power must acquire sociological significance and forms of life must be firmly rooted in the material world.

Whatever Bourdieu may have thought about these matters in the 1950s, his later works indicate that he has faced the basic issues and elaborated his views to account for the challenges thrown up – see Bourdieu 1989. To his earlier analyses he has added two significant notions:

(1) the idea of language as part of the 'economic';
(2) his account of symbolic violence.

LANGUAGE AS AN ECONOMY

Other chapters have shown that a unifying idea in Bourdieu is 'the economic' extended beyond both the 'ordinary-language' and the Marxist sense. On this account, the field of language also involves symbolic goods which, like material goods, are exchanged:

> The linguistic exchange is also an economic exchange which is established in a symbolic balance of power between a producer

endowed with linguistic capital, and a consumer (or a market), and which is calculated to procure a certain material or symbolic profit (1982:59–60).

So it is that language is part of a social style and is in principle no different from a person's dress, material belongings, or artistic taste, as described in other chapters. Each of these are possessions which count in the cut-and-thrust of life and each is of use to the possessor as they struggle to secure their share of goods against the claims of others.

There are times, for example, when a knowledge of Latin (useless, we might say, in itself), constitutes valuable capital. Without it, other skills or competencies are of little value (even if they are very useful). The possessor, however, is in a good position: the knowledge can be used like money to buy a position in the civil service. To defend Latin in the modern school system, argues Bourdieu, is to defend a threatened form of capital. Despite efforts to suggest that it has intrinsic value, it cannot be defended without defending its 'market' (1977b:651). When the 'market' is gone, all that remains is an examination system which looks as if it still depends on the commercial value of the devalued product.

As should be clear from reading Chapters 4 and 6, it is one of the functions of schools to integrate young people into the same 'linguistic community'. 'A language', argues Bourdieu (ibid.:652), 'is worth what those who speak it are worth.' At one and the same time people learn 'the language' (i.e. the words, grammar, forms of expression, etc.) and the 'game' in which there are winners and losers. It is interesting to note here that in Wittgenstein's account of language games, there is no suggestion of winners and losers: the game analogy cannot be taken that far. Bourdieu, however, concentrates on the sense of games in which 'beating others' is crucial – see the discussion of strategies in Chapter 1. This, he believes, is closer to real life where the same people control both the rules of language and the rules of power:

> When one language dominates the market, it becomes the norm against which the prices of the other modes of expression, and with them the values of the various competencies, are defined. The language of grammarians is an artefact, but, being universally imposed by the agencies of linguistic coercion, it has a social efficacy in as much as it functions as the norm, through which is exerted the domination of those groups which have both the means

of imposing it as legitimate and the monopoly of the means of appropriating it (1977b:652).

SYMBOLIC POWER

This brings us close to the central role of power in Bourdieu's theory of language. Here, it seems to me, 'existential' Nietzsche corrects 'linguistic' Wittgenstein. For Wittgenstein's 'forms of life', however social in intent, were never given sociological dress and hence have tended to remain as idealist constructions of marginal relevance to social science. By taking hold of Nietzsche's view of power, Bourdieu provides material grounding and sociological significance for Wittgenstein's 'language games' and 'forms of life'.

This he does by extending and elaborating the idea of speech-acts. Wittgenstein, Austin, Searle and other 'linguistic' philosophers recognised that some forms of a language can be construed primarily as human acts; thus 'I promise to give you $100', 'I take you for my wife', 'I bet you . . . ', etc., are not just pieces of speech but constitute actions of promising, marrying, placing a wager, etc. Such speech-acts Austin called performative utterances and his theory involves the ideas of 'illocutionary force' and 'perlocutionary force'. He argued that utterances have:

(1) 'a meaning' in a language;
(2) an 'illocutionary force' i.e. what a speaker *does* in speaking: 'the door is open' may entail 'shut the door'; and
(3) a 'perlocutionary force', or the effects of speaking. The hearer may get angry with the speaker rather than comply with his implicit command.

Bourdieu extends this idea and locates it securely in the material world. Thus he criticises those philosophers who, following Austin,

> search in the words themselves for the 'illocutionary force' which they catch a glimpse of from time to time in performatives.
>
> (1982:132)

Here, it must be said, Bourdieu is careless in suggesting that Austin and his followers locate 'illocutionary force' and 'perlocutionary force' in language.[4] They take pains to argue that the social situation is crucial in determining the 'meaning' of utterances – this point is taken up again in Chapter 9. Where Bourdieu does seem to go beyond the philosophers is when he sees language as an instrument of domination. For him, Austin's 'performative utterances' are merely examples of the nature of language as a whole.

> The question of performative utterances becomes clear if it is seen as a particular case of the effects of symbolic domination which is present in every linguistic exchange (1982:68).

Linguistic 'signs' are not merely symbols to be understood in some intellectual sense. They are cultural symbols (like sceptre, wig, or vestments) which require that the user be believed or obeyed (ibid.:60). Language is part of an activity in which some people dominate others. Just as those with financial capital hold sway over those without it, so those with linguistic capital control those with limited resources. For it is language which defines a group and gives someone (a spokesperson) authority within the group and power to speak for the group. It is here, according to Bourdieu, that philosophers like Austin go astray. For they seek to understand language apart from the people who use it. To search in language for the source of its power

> is to forget that authority comes to a language from outside it as is shown in a concrete way by the *skeptron* which, (according to Homer) was handed to the orator as he rose to make a speech (1982:105).

Language, then, has to be authorised. This normally means that a person is given authority to speak (or utter performatives). Of course both Wittgenstein and Austin recognise this but where they view it as a neutral context of language, Bourdieu sees the power component as central. Status, style, mode of address are one and the same: they indicate that a certain person is to be believed, obeyed, or respected. This marks an important (though controversial) break with the linguistic tradition which assumed that while 'performative utterances' depend for their efficacy on some fact about the hearers, descriptive utterances require only truth conditions. Bourdieu puts all language into the 'relativistic' mould: descriptive claims, no less than others, require an acceptance of the authority of the utterer. Some people have secured (Bourdieu sometimes says 'usurped') 'the right' to speak and this gives them power over the rest. We will return to this point in Chapter 9.

The intimate connection between language and other forms of power is brought out when Bourdieu discusses the position of those who do not fully possess the habitus, those who are not fully part of the social space, those whose trajectory is different from that of others. They are like 'a valet who speaks the language of the gentleman' or 'the ward orderly that of the doctor' (1977b:653): they do not properly belong in the language game. They are recognised for what they are even if they have mastered the 'language', for

> What speaks is not the utterance, the language, but the whole social person. (loc. cit.)

This explains why in a particular social setting some seem to be able to speak confidently, plausibly and with a large degree of acceptance while others are 'out of their depth', their most cogent arguments ignored. What was shown in Chapter 4 to apply to education, and in Chapter 6 to art, also applies to language:

> Total, early, imperceptible learning, performed within the family from the earliest days of life and extended by a scholastic learning which presupposes and completes it, differs from belated, methodical learning not so much in the depth and durability of its effects – as the ideology of cultural 'veneer' would have it – as in the modality of the relationship to language and culture which it simultaneously tends to inculcate. It confers the self-certainty which acompanies the certainty of possessing cultural legitimacy, and the ease which is the touchstone of excellence; it produces the paradoxical relationship to culture made up of self-confidence amid (relative) ignorance and of casualness amid familiarity, which bourgeois families hand down to their offspring as if it were an heirloom (1984:66).

It is a matter of capital, investments, profit:

> Because competence is not reducible to the specifically linguistic capacity to generate a certain type of discourse but involves all the properties constituting the speaker's *social personality* . . . the same linguistic productions may obtain radically different profits depending on the transmitter.

> (1977b:654–5)

The spokespersons or ministers represent and speak for the group, but as is shown in Chapter 3, groups are mere abstractions until someone speaks for them and so brings them into existence. In a section uncannily reminiscent of Nietzsche, Bourdieu says:

> The charismatic leader manages to be for the group what he is for

himself, instead of being for himself, like those dominated in the symbolic struggle, what he is for others. He 'makes' the opinion which makes him; he constitutes himself as an absolute by a manipulation of symbolic power which is constitutive of his power since it enables him to produce and impose his own objectification (1984:208).

In these ways, Bourdieu takes seriously Nietzsche's insight into the relationship between language and reality. By language we create our world. But the 'we' is not just any old 'we' – it is those with the power to make their words stick. A dominant ethnic group, for example, can exercise power over the others because there is an objective relationship which the dominant language mirrors:

> What passes between two persons . . . owes its particular form to the objective relationship between the languages . . . that is to say between the groups who speak the languages (1982:61).

So it is that Bourdieu elaborates language into a theory of *ministerium* by which a representative (minister) represents a group and calls it into existence. He suggests that Nietzsche in criticising Christianity was really criticising the style of representative typical of Catholic Christianity. The priests claim to represent the community but, by taking to themselves the virtues, they control the masses while pretending to speak on their behalf. This he calls the *oracle effect*: by submerging himself in the group ('servant of the people', etc.), the minister becomes more significant than the group and acquires a special status from speaking for the group:

> In the limiting case of dominated groups, the symbolic act by which the spokesperson constitutes himself, the constitution of the 'movement', is at the same time the constitution of the group; the sign makes the thing signified, the signifier identifies himself with the thing signified, which would not exist without it, and which reduces itself to it. The signifier is not only that which expresses and represents the group signified; it is that which *signifies* its existence, which has the power to call the group which it signifies into visible existence by mobilising it. It is only this which can, under certain conditions, by using the power conferred on it by the act of delegation, mobilise the group to demonstrate. When he says, 'I am going to show you that I am the representative by presenting the people I represent to you' (it is the eternal debate over the number of demonstrators), the spokesperson demon-

strates his legitimacy by demonstrating the group who delegate him. This power to demonstrate the demonstrators is only made possible because, in a certain way, the spokesperson is the group which he demonstrates (1984a:59).

It is clear, therefore, that in Bourdieu's account of language there is a direct relationship between a language which authorises, the person who is authorised and the state of affairs authorised. There is no point in trying to locate temporal priority. The priest uses a language shared by the faithful in order to control them by making them feel guilty. He *uses* his language as a strategy to bring about guilt. Language is more than a form of words; it is the 'game' by which he calls forth guilt, promotes repentance, forgives the sinner, and the like. The priest engages in symbolic violence. The people must recognise that he speaks for them (this is true: hence a form of recognition) and to believe he is at their service (this is false: hence a form of misrecognition).

The mystery of ministry only acts on the condition that the minister disguises his usurpation and the *imperium* which it confers to him, by presenting himself as a simple minister. The person who fills the position of minister is only able to profit from the misappropriation of power if the misappropriation is disguised – this is the very definition of symbolic power. Symbolic power is a power which implies the recognition, that is to say the misrecognition, of the violence which is exercised through it. Thus the symbolic violence of a minister can only be exercised with this sort of complexity accorded to him, by those over whom the violence is exercised, encouraged by the denial that misrecognition produces (1984a:61).

In seeing language as an institutional practice as well as a social one, Bourdieu provides a solution to the problem the 'linguistic' philosophers did not solve or even pose: what is the connection between the linguistic categories and the institutional world in which people exercise control over others? Bourdieu may indeed make good a deficit not only in the linguistic philosophy but in all modern philosophies which locate conceptual change in the realm of ideas. Writing, for example, of Kuhn's influential account of progress in science, Bloor argues that the theory of scientific 'revolutions' is inadequate to explain 'paradigm' shifts:

His critics . . . have put their finger on a point where Kuhn is not being sufficiently sociological. A potential anomaly can only create a crisis and precipitate a revolution if somebody makes it so, hence the whole process depends on *the balance of power in the relevant group.*

(Bloor 1983:142, italics mine)

For this reason, Bourdieu argues, institutions and ideologies tend to choose nonentities as their ministers

simply because they have nothing with which to oppose the machine. This explains why both in the French Communist Party in the 50's and in China during the 'Cultural Revolution', the young served very well as symbolic warders, as guard dogs. Now what characterises the young, is not only the enthusiasm, the naivety, the beliefs, all that one associates without too much thought with youth; from the point of view of my model they are also those who have nothing; they are the beginners, they come into the field without capital. And from the point of view of the machine they are cannon fodder to fight the old guard who, beginning to have capital, whether through the Party, or through themselves, use this capital to contest the Party. The one who has nothing does not lay down conditions; he is so much less likely to oppose the machine which gives him so much, according to the measure of his unconditionality, and of his nothingness (1984a:68).

In this way, Bourdieu draws attention to familiar experiences including that of the mediocre academic who by adopting an ideological pose secures more attention than his slender scholastic achievements warrant. As Bourdieu puts it:

This or that intellectual of twenty-five could have, *ex officio*, by being delegated by the apparatus, some audiences (publics) that only the most celebrated intellectuals could attain in their own right as authors (loc. cit.).

Bourdieu has not solved all the issues concerning language – that would be asking too much. What he has done is to incorporate language into a social theory which stresses the actual strivings of human beings. He refuses to view language as an epiphenomenon to action or as a mental force behind action. Rather he views it as a particular kind of practice, complementing and competing with other important practices. It involves shared aims and strategies and a shared way of talking about these. As such, language is not the *parole* of individuals struggling to give vent to their *langue*: it is part and parcel of the way in which a human group actualises its hopes, plans, and ambitions. The model of language is not scientific description but daily communication, in which people are ordered, advised, and persuaded and in which they listen, obey, avert to, and get angry.

Finally, and most importantly, he sees power (symbolic violence) as central in language. He recognises that language is one of the ways by which humans control each other. This they do in a variety of ways but one way which Bourdieu highlights is by the creation of guilt:

> Paradoxically, those who are made nothing in order to become everything can reverse the terms of the relation and reproach those who remain merely themselves, who *only speak* for themselves, of being nothing, neither in fact nor in right (since they are incapable of self-sacrifice, etc.). It is this right of reprimanding, of being able to make someone feel guilty, which is one of the profits of the militant (ibid.:63).

If this seems a long way from language, it is only because Bourdieu has taken us a long way in language. No longer a theoretical body of propositions, laws and deductions, it has become an integral part of the battle to control others.[5]

CONCLUSION

We began with the 'intellectualist legend', which makes language a tool of understanding. Many theorists, among them Nietzsche and Wittgenstein, have urged us to focus on the active pragmatic aspects of language: by language, humans achieve their purposes. In place of language as individual expression, there is language as social action: it is the means by which a social group communicates and expresses the aims, needs and condition of its members. All this is, or should be, commonplace in the mid-twentieth century. But Bourdieu adds a further dimension. Language is to be seen as part of a group's way of life. It may involve words but it need not. Just as groups acquire their reality from being named, so individuals acquire power from being allowed to do the naming. A group exists when it is named; the namer is important when recognised as the representative (minister) of the group.

But what answer is there to the other question concerning the relationship between language and reality? The traditional picture placed power at the service of truth; is truth now utterly subservient to power? Bourdieu does not tackle this directly. Like Wittgenstein he could say that it is unlikely that the various practices would succeed unless they were 'true to life' or he might invoke Nietzsche and assert that

> What is needed is that something must be held to be true – not that something is true.
>
> (Quoted in Solomon 1972:113)

and that

> Truth is that sort of error without which a particular class of living creatures could not live (ibid.).

More accurately, we have to say that, as originally conceived, the question no longer exists. 'Does language correctly capture the way the world is?' depends on accepting the assumption that language tries to capture the world. This is what Bourdieu denies. Language is a human activity – like cooking or soldiering – and its success lies in its effects: 'the proof' of the pudding is in 'the eating'; the proof of the military strategy is in the battles won.

So, for Bourdieu (as for Nietzsche) power can be evaluated only in terms of its success. But, as Wittgenstein might have said, 'What does "success" mean here'? Success need not presume truth, but it does seem to presume value. And, as Nietzsche found, the justification of value is as problematic as the justification of truth.

NOTES

1. The author wishes to thank Dr Tom Bestor for helpful criticisms of an earlier draft. He is in no way responsible for any weaknesses in this version.
2. The brief account of Nietzsche and Wittgenstein is not meant to imply a conscious amalgamation of their themes in Bourdieu's work. Its implication, rather, is that while Bourdieu uses Wittgenstein for support, his interpretation is moderated by the Nietzschian stress on power which he has, perhaps unconsciously, absorbed. As a result, relating the themes of Nietzsche and Wittgenstein helps, I believe, to illuminate Bourdieu's notion of *ministerium*.

3. Bourdieu frequently acknowledges the importance of Wittgenstein's insights concerning the unconscious nature of linguistic rules. He believes that this point is crucial for sociology. Thus, he argues that sociologists must learn to recognise that while 'the unconscious is not a useful construct, it is important to recognise that a similar idea can be expressed by the phrase "the subjects use signs without realising it"'. In this way, he says, sociological language will gain in rigour and precision what it loses in magic and charm (1973:152).

4. Bourdieu's major analysis of Austin is to be found in Actes 1975d. For an analysis of the law as a symbolic struggle, see Actes 1986b; Bourdieu 1987.

5. On this particular point, a seminal article is to be found in Actes 1983. Here Bourdieu applies his general model of linguistic habitus to the question of popular speech in order to attack naive notions of what constitutes everyday discourse, and to show how 'the popular' can be misused politically.

8 Bourdieu on Bourdieu: Learning the Lesson of the *Leçon*
Ian Duncan

In 1982 Pierre Bourdieu took up the Chair of Sociology at the Collège de France, following the death of its incumbent, Raymond Aron. His inaugural lecture, *Leçon sur la leçon*,[1] which might be glossed as 'lecture on lecturing', is a meditation on his roles of inaugural lecturer and of professional sociologist, setting forth his understanding of the nature of his discipline, or science as he prefers to call it. For Bourdieu, as pointed out in Chapter 1, being a sociologist entails a strict reflexivity, for sociologists must treat themselves in the same way as they treat the objects of their research. The idea of reflexivity has been explored since the late 1970s by some anthropologists who are concerned to overcome the conventional separation between anthropologist and informant. Paul Rabinow writes

> Anthropology is an interpretive science. Its object of study, humanity encountered as Other, is on the same epistemological level as it is. Both the anthropologist and his informants live in a culturally mediated world, caught up in 'webs of signification' they themselves have spun. This is the ground of anthropology; there is no privileged position, no absolute perspective, and no valid way to eliminate consciousness from our activities or those of others (1977:151).

This position was being worked out through the experiences of fieldwork, where anthropologists were trying to shake themselves free from the idea of the informant as someone to be interviewed, observed, written about, as the main source of data. Rather, it was the anthropologist's own experience which became the primary datum for reflection, and the ethnographies or texts produced became interpretations of that experience.

Bourdieu's reflexivity arises, as we shall see, from a passionately presented conviction about the position of the sociologist as being as equally 'culturally mediated', i.e. historically situated, in particular, in the world of prestigious universities. The following is a presentation, largely in Bourdieu's own words, of his belief in the sociologist's critical self-analysis in order to become aware of the historically-conditioned nature both of his or her specific standpoint and of the means of acquiring knowledge. It is an argument which avoids the narcissistic self-absorption that might befall reflexive or interpretive anthropology, and yet shares its concern to recognise the full status of the people social scientists study.

Bourdieu begins by comparing an inaugural lecture with a rite of investiture, through which the new master 'is authorised to speak with authority . . . which . . . institutes his word as legitimate discourse, delivered by the proper quarter' (LL:5). This is achieved in a 'magical' fashion, by means of a silent and invisible exchange between the candidate and the scholars who, simply by being physically present, thereby acknowledge the universal acceptability of his 'parole', of what he says.

The inaugural lecture, Bourdieu says, is like a paradigm, whose message consists in seeing itself as a 'discourse which is itself reflected in the act of discourse' (ibid.), and thereby demonstrates a fundamental quality of sociology as he understands it: 'every proposition set forth by this science can and must apply to the subject who does the science [the sociologist]' (LL:5–6). Without this critical detachment the sociologist will, he says, be justifiably accused of being some kind of terrorist-inquisitor.

Like Dumont's *sannyasin*,[2] the sociologist has the almost ascetic duty of rending the ties that normally bind him to groups. Born of the people, parvenu among the elite, the sociologist may acquire that special insight associated with every kind of social displacement only by refusing to accept both the 'populist representation of the people, which deceives only those who create it, and the élitist representation of the élite, neatly made to deceive those who are in it and those who are not' (LL:6).

The sociologist finds his weapons against social determinism in the very discipline which brought them to light and thus to his conscience, in the sociology of sociology. 'Science, especially sociology, is [to be] used against, just as much as following, its own formation. Only history can extricate us from history. Therefore the social history of social science, insofar as it is seen as a science of unconscious acts, in the great tradition of epistemological history, with figures such as Georges Canguilhem and Michel Foucault, is one of

the most powerful tools for breaking out of history, from the hold
of the past surviving into the present, or from the present which,
like intellectual fashions, is already past the moment it appears'
(LL:6–7). Fundamental to this task of knowing the subject of knowledge, is the sociology of the education system and of the intellectual
world, which has been explored in Chapters 4 and 6. Bourdieu
reaffirms this as the most direct approach to uncovering those categories of thought lying below the level of conscious thought, which
delimit what is thinkable, which predetermine thought, and which
evoke the whole world of assumptions and presuppositions, the
biases education makes us accept and the gaps it makes us ignore,
'tracing out that magical circle of impoverished complacency in which
the schools of the élite wrap their chosen few' (LL:7).

This kind of awareness indicates how sociology has developed:
Durkheim could never have conceived of his social history of the
education system as a generative sociology of the categories teachers
and academics work with, even though he provided the tools to do
so. Similarly, a social history of the workers' movement and its
relationships with theoreticians could show us why those who profess
Marxism have never truly put Marx's thought, and especially the
uses that have been made of it, to the test of the sociology of
knowledge, which Marx himself originated. 'However,' he goes on,
in markedly passionate language, 'we may never have the confidence
that historical and sociological critique may completely prevent the
theological or terrorist use of canonical writings, but at least we can
expect it to bring the clearest and most resolute [minds] to break
out of their dogmatic slumber and put to work, to the test, in
scientific practice, those theories and concepts on which the magic
of exegesis, which is always being embarked upon anew, bestows
the false eternity of mausoleums' (LL:8).

Bourdieu explicitly dissociates himself from current anti-insti-
tutional fashions (*contra* Touraine). He is more concerned to avoid
the temptation of the 'sovereign vision', when sociologists become
like the kings of old, invested with the power to *regere fines* and
regere sacra, i.e. to regulate, control or rule over the temporal and
non-temporal, and claim the right to specify the boundaries between
classes, regions, nations, to decide whether social classes exist or
not, and whether a social class – proletariat, peasant, petit bourgeois
– or a geographical unity – Brittany, Corsica, Occitania – is a reality
or a fiction, assuming thereby the functions of the ancient *rex*.[3] Or
like the censor, in whom the power of the *constitution* is vested and

who is in charge of the categories of the social world, he is responsible for the technical procedure, the *census* or counting, of classifying citizens according to their fortune, of assigning them like a judge
to their rightful place in the hierarchy, in the public estimation.

Sociology must focus upon, instead of letting itself be overcome
by, 'the struggle for the monopoly of the legitimate representation
of the social world, the struggle over classification which is an aspect
of every class struggle – age classes, sexual classes or social classes'
(LL:9) (see also Bourdieu 1985:208). It is not possible to stand apart
from the process of classification, like some sort of mythical Master
of the Categories, although it is possible with zoological or biological
classification. But in anthropological classification the objects being
classified are the classifiers themselves.

Furthermore, there are always people who do not accept their
ranking. 'Indeed history shows that it is usually those who are dominated, who, almost always under the leadership of people claiming
the monopoly of power, people who are often themselves poorly
classified with respect to the dominant power – who try to break out
of the bondage of legitimate classification, and transform their vision
of the world by freeing themselves from those incorporated limits
which are the social categories of perception of the social world'
(LL:10).

Sociologists are no longer like divine spectators who alone know
the truth or, to put it simply, say what is correct. Rather, they strive
to speak the truth about those struggles whose stakes are the truth.
Thus, instead of deciding between those who affirm and those who
deny that a class or a region or whatever exists, a sociologist tries
to establish the specific logic behind their attempts, and to determine
the chances of the different sides.

This is Georges Duby's method (Duby 1980). Instead of unques-
tioningly accepting as a historian's tool the schema of the three
orders (also spoken of as the three estates of the realm – clergy,
nobility, workers–farmers) which is the classificatory system by which
history thinks of feudal society, he subjects the schema itself to
historical analysis. He shows that the idea of dividing up society in
this fashion is both the stake or prize and the product of the struggles
between the groups claiming the monopoly over the power of the
constitution, the knights and bishops, and itself contributed to producing that very reality in this form for us to think about.

Although the idea of struggle has already been introduced in his
lecture, Bourdieu now turns to what Wacquant indicates is his main

preoccupation, 'the nature and logic of symbolic domination, i.e. the wielding of symbolic power defined as the capacity to impose and inculcate means of understanding and structuring the world (symbolic systems) that contribute to the reproduction of the social order by representing economic and political power in a disguised, legitimate form that endows them with *taken-for-grantedness*' (Wacquant 1984). The criteria used by the sociologist in forming his understanding of the characteristics and opinions of the different social classes are themselves the product of 'the whole history of symbolic struggles whose stake is the existence and definition of classes and which have contributed in a very real sense to the making of those classes' (LL:11). Thus, past sociologies have produced a working class and led it to believe in itself as a revolutionary proletariat. Sociologists must be ready more and more to recognise the objects of their study as being the products of past social-scientific practice.

Sociological knowledge (the understanding of social laws such as that cultural capital attracts cultural capital, as for example in the way educational systems eliminate those children with the least cultural capital while adding to the capital of those with the most) has a liberating effect, Bourdieu believes, to the extent that it demonstrates how the laws and functions of the social mechanism depend for their efficacy on being disguised. This is the foundation of symbolic violence. 'This particular form of violence may be exercised only upon knowing subjects, but whose acts of knowledge, because they are impartial and mystified, conceal the tacit recognition of dominance which is implied in the misrecognition of the real foundations of dominance' (LL:13–14). Sociology is opposed to all those who rely upon the shadow of misrecognition to carry on their trade.

Fully consistent with the analysis of language outlined in Chapter 7, Bourdieu claims that it is absolutely necessary for the sociologist to repudiate all 'regál temptations' (recalling his discussion of the classical *rex*), particularly when dealing with scientific and intellectual life in general. As with language, he likens sociology to a game, with a stake, rules, conventions and investments, from which one may pretend to be disengaged, for the sake of theoretical distance, but in which one is nevertheless involved with the stakes and investments one puts in. Any claim therefore to be objective is bound to be false as long as it ignores or refuses to see the point of view on which it is based, and thus the game as a whole. It is possible thereby to see that the claims to objectivity of those engaged in the struggle are really symbolic strategies intended to impose the partial truth of one group, as the whole truth about objective relations between groups.

Struggle is characteristic of science, and the more science advances, 'the more participation in the scientific struggle pre-supposes the possession of important scientific capital' (LL:16). Scientific revolutions, therefore, are the concern of those who are scientifically the richest, not the most deprived. There are simple laws, Bourdieu states, which help us to understand how even prod-ucts which are relatively free from the social conditions of their production, such as scientific truths, arise nevertheless out of the historical circumstances of a particular social configuration, i.e. a social field. 'If there is a truth, it is that truth is the stake in the struggle; but this struggle will lead to truth only when it obeys the logic that one may overcome one's adversaries only by using the weapons of science against them' (ibid.). This is contrasted with those who play the game by allying themselves with external powers, replacing scientific critique by political denunciation. Bourdieu is very critical of those sociologists who step outside of their discipline and get caught up in the game of politicisation, who are always part of the scene, with an answer for everything, who 'spend their life putting themselves in a position where . . . science is overcome in advance' (LL:17). Social science must reject the pressures of legitim-ation and manipulation – for Bourdieu the moral force of sociology lies in the way it demonstrates the relationship between the actions or discourse of the scientist, artist or radical activist and the social conditions from which they arise, and the specific interests they serve, but not in order to encourage any kind of bitter, destructive or belittling stance which can be so beguiling to those who hold it. Rather the sociologist should try to develop some way of overcoming this attitude of superiority, of removing this 'terrorism of resentful feelings . . . [by] beginning with changing the desire for social revenge into a demand for compensatory equality' (LL:18).

The sociologist, like a monk, is one who attempts to stand outside society and observe it critically,[4] and yet cannot help but speak its language. Thus, Bourdieu declares, society reflects upon itself through the sociologist 'and through him all social agents can come to know a little better who they are and what they are doing. But to entrust him with this task is the last thing wanted by those who have thrown in their lot with misrecognition and denial, who are prepared to accept as scientific that discourse which does not speak of the social world or which speaks of it in a way that is not speaking of it' (LL:19).[5]

He speaks of the resistance shown to what sociology can reveal in terms of Freudian denial: 'The refusal to accept a traumatising reality being the measure of defended interests, one can understand the extreme violence of the reactions of the holders of cultural capital to those analyses which bring to light the conditions of production and reproduction denied to culture. People who set themselves up as examples of the unique and innate are made to discover the common and acquired. Knowledge of the self is truly a descent into Hell, as Kant puts it. Just as, in the myth of Er, the souls have to drink the water of the river Unmindfulness, which induces forgetfulness, before returning to earth to live the lives they themselves have chosen, men of culture owe their purest cultural enjoyments to a forgetting of the origins which lets them live their culture as if it were a gift of nature' (LL:19–20).[6] It is a defence psychoanalysis knows well, a form of false reasoning which believes it can accuse scientific objectivity of being banal and vulgar. 'The opponents of sociology have the right to ask if an activity which supposes and produces the negation of a collective denial can exist, but they have no right to question its scientific character . . . it is only the relative autonomy of the field of scientific production and the scientific interests which grow out of it that may authorise and support the appearance of a range of scientific products, mostly critical products, which appear before a demand for them exists' (LL:20).

In this lecture, which uses religious language so liberally, sociology takes on an almost mystical character. Bourdieu speaks on the one hand of 'the theological or terrorist utilisation of canonical scriptures' (LL:8), and on the other suggests that the sociologist, like the *yogi* tearing aside the veil of *maya*,

> reveals the *self-deception* [in English in the original], the lie which is collectively maintained and fostered and which, in every society, is at the foundation of the most sacred values, and thereby of the whole of social existence. With Marcel Mauss [sociology] teaches that 'society always pays itself in the false coin of its dreams'. This is to say that this iconoclastic science of aging societies can at least contribute to making us, even just a little, masters and possessors of social nature, by increasing our knowledge and understanding of the mechanisms which underlie all forms of fetishism: I am thinking of Raymond Aron, who so well exemplified this teaching,

of what he calls 'secular religion' – the State cult which is a cult of the State, with its civic festivals and ceremonies, national or nationalist myths, always predisposed to instigate or justify racist contempt or violence, and which is true not just of totalitarian States. And I think also of the cult of art and science which, in the name of substituted idols, may concur in the legitimation of a social order for one part founded on an unequal distribution of cultural capital. In any case, we can at least expect social science to hold back from the temptation of magic, that *hubris* of ignorance ignorant of itself which, debarred from any relationship with the natural world, survives in a relationship with the social world. The revenge of the real is ruthless upon ill-informed good wishes and utopian voluntarism: and the tragic destiny of political enterprises which made use of some presumptuous social science is there to remind us that the magical ambition of transforming the social world without understanding the motives for doing so, lays itself open to being replaced by another, rather more inhuman violence, the 'inert violence' of the mechanisms which pretentious ignorance has destroyed.

(LL:21–2)

This long quotation well illustrates what may be called the religious character of Bourdieu's vision. Language itself is seen as a mist, a veil always imposing itself between the seeker and the social world. Language, he says, expresses things more easily than relationships, states rather than processes. Thus, if we say of someone that he has power, or we ask who really holds power today, we are thinking of power as a substance, which may be held, preserved, transmitted, we are asking science to tell us 'who governs', we are assuming that power is located somewhere and asking if it comes from above – the common view – or from below. The illusion of 'thingness' and the illusion of persons are not opposed: they go together. There is thus a whole range of false problems arising from the opposition between individual–person, interiority, singularity on the one hand and society–thing, exteriority on the other. 'The ethico-political debates between those who give absolute value to the personal, the in-dividual, individualism, and those who give primacy to society, the social, socialism, can be set against a background of that never-ending theoretical debate between a nominalism which reduces social realities, groups or institutions to theoretical artifacts with no objective reality and a substantialist realism which reifies abstractions' (LL:23).[7]

These oppositions are so entrenched in ordinary thought that a massive, constantly renewed effort is required to supersede them, for it 'is easier to treat social facts as things or people than as relations' (ibid.), but Bourdieu sees the principle of historical action, that of the artist, scientist, ruler, worker or petty official, as lying, not in consciousness nor in things, but in a relationship, a 'relationship between two states of the social, that is between history objectified in things, in the form of institutions, and history incarnated in the body, the form of that system of lasting dispositions I call habitus. The body is in the social world, but the social world is in the body' (LL:24).[8]

As Wacquant indicates, it is not easy to grasp Bourdieu's 'conceptual artillery' without seeing how it may be worked out in a lengthy case study. Then one may achieve that

> decisive break with the ordinary view of the social world which determines the fact of replacing the naive relationships between individual and society by the constructed relationship between the two modes of existence of the social – habitus and the field, history as body and history as thing. Thus in order to constitute convincingly as a logical chronicle the chronology of the relationships between Monet, Degas and Pissaro, or Lenin, Trotsky, Stalin and Bukharin, or even Sartre, Merleau-Ponty and Camus, we would in effect need a sufficient knowledge of two causal, partially independent series, the one being the protagonists' social conditions of production or, more precisely, of their lasting dispositions, and the other the specific logic of each of the rival fields in which they engage these dispositions – artistic, political or intellectual, without forgetting, to be sure, the conjunctural or structural constraints bearing upon these relatively autonomous spaces.
>
> (LL:24–5)

By considering each of the universes as a field one is able 'to enter the most singular detail of their historical singularity' (LL:25), thereby revealing a 'particular case of the possible', as Bachelard puts it,[9] one configuration among many others of a structure of relationships. One must look for the pertinent relationships, which may at first be imperceptible, between realities which are directly visible, such as individual people with their own names, and collective persons, both designated and produced by the sign or acronym which constitutes them as jural beings.

Poincaré defined mathematics as 'the art of giving the same name to different things'. Similarly, sociology

> is the art of thinking of things which are different on the surface as similar in their structure and function, and of transferring that which has been established with respect to a constituted object, for example the religious field, to a range of new objects, the artistic field, the political field and so on.

> (LL:26)

This kind of theoretical induction, based upon the hypothesis of formal invariation within empirical variation, allows sociology to encompass a more and more extended range of objects with a more and more reduced number of concepts and hypotheses, like other sciences which, in Leibniz's phrase, 'become more concentrated the more they are extended'.

To elaborate a little further on the discussion begun in Chapter 3, thinking in terms of a field requires a conversion (in the religious sense) from the ordinary view of the social world which recognises only invisible entities, the individual, the group, relationships understood as intersubjective interactions; the idea of the field 'breaks with the realist representation which tends to minimise the influence of the *milieu* so that direct action becomes interaction. It is the structure of the relationships constituting the field which orders the form that visible relationships of interaction may take on, and the actual content of the experience which agents may have of it' (LL:27). Focusing on the space of relationships in which agents move implies a radical break with that philosophy of history which is implied by ordinary usage or by the language of half-scholars.

> There is no end to the list of errors and mystifications, the mystique, arising from the way words designating institutions or groups – the State, bourgeoisie, employers, church, family, school – may be constituted as subjects of propositions of the form 'the State decides' or 'the school eliminates' and, thereby, as historical subjects with the capacity to propose and achieve their own ends. These processes, whose meaning and end are not, properly speaking, thought of or posed by anybody at all . . . , thus turn out to be laid down in reference to an intention which is not so much that of a creator conceived of as a person but that of a group

or an institution functioning as the final cause which can justify everything without explaining anything. Using the famous analysis of Norbert Elias, it can be shown that this theologico-political vision does not even justify itself in that case which at first sight might best confirm it, namely the monarchical state which shows itself in the monarch himself – 'l'Etat, c'est moi'. . . . Court society operates as a gravitational field in which the holder of absolute power is himself engaged, even when his privileged position allows him to draw off in advance the greater part of the energy generated by the equilibrium of forces. The principle of perpetual motion activating the field is not to be found in some primordial unmoving mover – here 'le Roi Soleil' – but in the tensions which are the product of the structure making up the field (differences of rank between princes, dukes, marquises, etc.) and which work to reproduce that structure. It is found in the actions and reactions of the agents who, on pain of excluding themselves from the game, have no choice other than to struggle to keep or improve their position in the field, thereby burdening everyone else with those forces, often experienced as unbearable, which gave birth to the antagonistic coexistence.

(LL:27–8)

No matter how different the fields are, whether of court society, political parties, businesses or universities, they operate only through what agents invest in them, in the different senses of that word, what resources they bring to bear on them; even their rivalry and antagonism serve to preserve, or sometimes transform, the structure of the field.

What does one get out of the game? The game itself. The stakes Bourdieu sees as arising from the relationship between the game and the feel ('*sens*') for the game; what is valued is not outside this relationship but necessarily and absolutely within it. 'The motive, sometimes called the motivation, is not in the material or [even] symbolic end of the action, as a naïve finalism would put it, nor in the constraints of the field, which would be the mechanistic view. It is in the relationship between habitus and the field, which means that habitus helps to determine that which determines it' (LL:30–31). *Illusio*, that 'ontological complicity between habitus and the field' (LL:30), is an illusion only when the game is viewed from the outside, not recognising that investments in the game are well-founded illusions. 'Ultimately, through the games it offers, the social world obtains for agents something other and better than the apparent stakes, the manifest goal of action. The hunt stands for more than the prize – there is a profit in acting which is greater than the profits explicitly sought – salary, prize, recompense, trophies, title, office – and which consists in the fact of starting from indifference, of affirming oneself as an acting agent, involved in the game, engaged, living in a world inhabited by the world, oriented towards ends and endowed, objectively, and hence subjectively, with a social mission' (LL:31).

'Social functions are social fictions. And rites of institution make those whom they institute as king, knight, priest or professor (by forging his social image, fashioning the representation which he can and must give as a moral person, i.e. as plenipotentiary) a mandated spokesman for the group. But they also make him in another sense. By assigning him a name, a title, which defines, institutes, constitutes him, they summon him to become what he is, that is, what he ought to be; they enjoin him to fulfil his function, to take part in the game, in the fiction, to play the game, the function' (LL:31-2). Confucius was simply confirming the truth of rites of institution when he invoked the principle of 'justification of names', asking each person to conform to his function in society, to his social nature. Giving himself completely to his office and thereby to the body which conferred it upon him, the officeholder ensures the eternity of his office, pre-existing and surviving him.

Bourdieu's concluding paragraphs strike an explicitly Durkheimian tone. 'Destined for death, that end which cannot be taken as the end, man is a being with no reason for being. Society, society alone, bestows, in varying degrees, the justifications and reasons for living' (LL:32). 'Indeed, without going so far as to say, with Durkheim, "society is God", I would say "God is never other than society"' (LL:33). It is society which has the power to bless, to elevate people from facticity, contingency, absurdity, and to condemn to hell and damnation.

However, 'a clear vision of the truth behind all missions and consecrations does not condemn one to resignation or desertion. One can always enter the game without any illusions, by a conscious and deliberate resolution. . . . If those who have taken sides with the established order, whatever it may be, have little love for sociology, it is because it introduces a freedom with respect to the original act of consent ['adhésion primaire'] which makes even conformity acquire an air of heresy or irony' (LL:34).

There is in Bourdieu's style of writing, in the way he repeats but inverts phrases, and in his puns, that circular or spiral quality of the reflexivity he is presenting. For instance, the following:

> Such would doubtless have been the lesson of an inaugural lecture in sociology devoted to the sociology of the inaugural lecture. A speech which takes itself as its own subject draws attention less to what it is talking about, which could be replaced by any action, than to the process of referring to what one is actually doing, and to what distinguishes the process from the fact of simply doing what one does, of being, as we say, completely what one does.
>
> (LL:34–5)

Many who have been brought up in the tradition of Anglo–American social science often express their difficulties with French thought in terms of an impatience with the style of writing. On first reading Bourdieu seems as obscure as any other, but if it is understood that his style, like his work, is a meditation upon itself, that it must necessarily be turning back on itself, reflexive, then it can be seen to have its own appropriateness.

Bourdieu says that his reflexivity has an unusual, insolent quality. It disenchants, breaks the spell. 'Thus it introduces a distance which threatens to destroy . . . that belief in the institution which is the ordinary condition of its proper functioning' (LL:35). But his commitment to this perspective is reiterated in his conclusion:

> This freedom with respect to the institution is without doubt the only compliment worthy of an institution of freedom which is always committed to the defence of that freedom with respect to institutions which is the condition of all science, particularly a science of institutions. . . . The paradoxical activity which consists in using a position of authority to say, with authority, what it means to speak with authority, in order to teach a lesson, a lesson of freedom with respect to all lessons, would be simply inconsequential, if not self-destructive, if the very ambition to create a science of belief did not presuppose a belief in science. Nothing is less cynical, less Machiavellian in every way, than paradoxical statements which state or declare the very principle of the power they exercise. No genuine sociologist would take the risk of tearing down the thin veil of faith or bad faith which constitutes the spell of all the pieties of the institution, if he had no faith in the possibility and the necessity of universalising that freedom with

respect to the institution that sociology gives; if he did not believe in the liberating virtues of what is without doubt the least illegitimate of symbolic powers, science, especially when it takes the form of a science of symbolic powers, capable of restoring to the social subject mastery over the false transcendence that misrecognition never ceases to create and recreate.

(LL:35–6)

NOTES

1. Reference is made henceforth to the (Fr.ed.) 1982a edition of the lecture as 'LL'. The pagination of this edition, from which all translations are made for this paper, is different from the (Fr.ed.) 1982b edition reviewed by Wacquant (1984).
2. The *sannyasin* is the renunciant of Hindu religion who, unlike the world-despising gnostic, renounces not the physical world but the social world of his existing roles (member of a caste, father, son, husband or a family, etc.). However, this renunciation of inherited roles does not mean the renunciation of society. The renunciant 'although dead to society not merely has the right to speak but also is a sought-after spiritual teacher; his thought, which is a negation of caste, in this way filters back into the caste' (Dumont 1957:17). Bourdieu speaks of one's not being able to move into sociology without breaking the bonds and act of consent tying us to groups, without abjuring the beliefs which make us belong, without disowning all links of filiation and affiliation (LL:6). For an argument with some interesting parallels, see Bourdieu and St Martin (Actes 1982).
3. The same comparison between the *rex* and the politically ambitious sociologist is made in Bourdieu 1985, especially pages 208–10.
4. A contemporary Cistercian has argued that the monk, both by his physical separation from the world and, more importantly, by his renunciation of normal lifestyles and of social and class identities and rewards, is able to develop a more critical and insightful perspective on his society (Merton 1973).
5. This role for the sociologist as one who exposes neuroses in society is a precise parallel to the thinking of the Frankfurt School theorist Habermas (see Wilby 1979). In this view the sociologist is the psychoanalyst of society, seeking to 'free' society from its neuroses and allowing it to be liberated in much the same way that Bourdieu is here arguing for the liberating role of sociological practice. For Bourdieu's own comments on the Frankfurt School, see Honneth and Schwibs 1985.
6. The myth of Er occurs in Book X of Plato's *Republic*.
7. See Chapter 1 for a discussion of Bourdieu's handling of the structure/agency debate.

8. The last full-blooded Moriori, Tame Horomona Rehe, died in the Chatham Islands in 1933 (Simpson 1950:60–66). He had become so obese that a hole had to be knocked in the wall of his house for his body to be taken out. It was as if the death of his entire tribe was being expressed in the very immobility of his body.
9. See Chapter 3 for a brief discussion of Bachelard's influence on Bourdieu.

9 Conclusion: Critique
The Friday Morning Group

INTRODUCTION: THE CHALLENGE OF BOURDIEU

The major purpose of this chapter is to develop a full critique of Bourdieu's contribution, by reviewing the areas of criticisms which his work has already attracted and by suggesting an alternative theoretical position. We conclude by reviewing Bourdieu's new work in order to consider the directions his work is likely to follow in the future.

We begin with a consideration of selected themes within Bourdieu's work having particular relevance for the field of Anglo-American social science. Perhaps the most important reason why social scientists should consider Bourdieu's work is the transformation this interest would effect on their conception of the centrality of the problem of theory and practice in the social sciences. We hope that one of the results of the present volume will be to correct this imbalance.

Part of the problem lies in the fact that English-speakers expect a grand theory from continental theorists, whereas, as we have shown throughout this book, what Bourdieu offers is a method: a way of looking at societies; a way of asking questions. But it is not just a set of procedures employed in the process of acquiring knowledge of a given society, field or subject-matter. To define it in such a way would be to presuppose that social science merely consists of a body of knowledge or an array of alternative theories, some of which represent the nature of social reality better than others. This is a view of social science which Bourdieu would reject because it denies the social determinants of its theoretical practice. For him, as shown in Chapter 8, the basic requirement of a scientific sociology is that its theory and method are both interdependent and totally reflexive. Sociological discourse can and should be applied to its own field of cultural production. The sociologist, no less than any other intellectual agent, is involved in a struggle for symbolic capital.

In other words, what we have is a conception of sociology which recognises that it is itself constituted of cultural practices within a social field. It is a sociology in part intent not on finding out 'what is', but in questioning 'what is thought to be'. For Bourdieu, the practice of theory within the sociological field presents a continuing challenge to the dominant and 'legitimate' modes of representing and classifying the world.

As we have tried to show throughout this book, in such a method, social reality is neither material nor symbolic in its essence; it exists in the interrelationship between the two. The method seeks to avoid the subjective–objective polarisations of both phenomenology and structuralism, but one would have to recognise that this cannot be achieved simply by an eclectic method which welds the two approaches together. The task requires new conceptual tools with which to challenge the traditional oppositions that have been enshrined in language itself.

BOURDIEU AND THE FIELD OF FRENCH SOCIOLOGY

Bourdieu has been writing for over a generation now: his work must therefore be assessed in relation to the field of postwar French sociology. This is true in two specific ways. First it is true in the sense that other works provide the 'antidote', the opposite or mirror-image of Bourdieu's efforts, and the context in which he has specifically struggled to gain his own ascendant position. Clearly these other works cannot be separated out from the central preoccupations which inform Bourdieu's work. Indeed, it would be unthinkable to prepare an exegesis of Bourdieu's work without some account of the Parisian sociological field, since it is only in this field that his contribution fully makes sense as an intellectual intervention. Secondly, it makes sense to locate Bourdieu's work in a broader field in order to draw out some of the more enduring themes which both he and others make use of in their work. For example, the naive outsider might ask how the political theories of Foucault and of Bourdieu align – did Foucault's anti-state politics have an effect on Bourdieu's later work? An adequate answer would need to be discovered further back in French intellectual history, at least back to the sources of political and sociological reconstruction which derive from the period of the 1960s. In a certain way, both Foucault's and Bourdieu's political theory result from long engagements with the Marxism of the 1960s and 1970s. Indeed both strategies, in different ways, are formed, at least in part, in reaction to the over-strident dogmatism of Balibar, Althusser, Poulantzas and others.

They both attempted to sustain a radicalism which remains at some distance from Marxism, though they have produced somewhat different solutions to the same problems.

However, the field of French sociology is not readily amenable to any straightforward plotting of positions, capitals and fields. Lemert's book, *French Sociology* (1981a) is an example of such an attempt; it is not without its profound difficulties. In a recent interview, Dan Sperber commented (in response to the question 'Could you describe how you see the field of the social sciences in France today?'):

I do not see it very clearly. It is an extremely varied field which does not seem to have any general direction. In the sixties and seventies there was an impression, I think a mistaken one, that there were some main lines. I am thinking of structuralism, for example. But if you had taken stock of all that was being done within the social sciences in France at that time, it would not have been possible to fit everything that was being done under one conceptual scheme. Since the mid-seventies, there has not even been a slogan.

Within French academic institutions, there is considerable freedom for the researchers and academics to do whatever they want. Hence criteria of excellence and standards of expression are shared to only a moderate degree. Perhaps it is the case that in some other countries there are common aims and standards in the social sciences, but this is not really the case in France today. If there is a general point to be made with regard to the current situation, it pertains to a certain discontent with the general flashiness of the discourse of the sixties and early seventies. There is now a much greater concern for hard scholarship. One might add also that the French social sciences are now more international in orientation. Twenty years ago, a great many French scholars just did not use English. Today it is much more common for French social scientists to publish their work in English and American journals. French sociology is less parochial than it used to be.

Overall, there is a kind of vacuum, and one has the feeling that some way or another it will be filled in the near future. The French intellectual scene is unlikely to remain empty for too long.

(Sperber 1986:85)

If the field has a vacuum at its centre, it must therefore be set against the situation of an earlier generation, when the vacuum was filled by the great patrons of the academy, who bought their acolytes in return for favours – academic, occupational and otherwise. More than this, however, and perhaps more pertinent to the field Bourdieu now inhabits, is the intellectual status of the field in the era of post-structuralism and post-modernism. Sperber may well be right to point to an intellectual vacuum in Paris, but he may be proposing the wrong explanations for this state of affairs. Clearly enough, one can overstate the nature of intellectual fields by positing a dominance of certain positions, such as Giddens' (1979) arguments about the dominance of functionalism after the war. Such a tendency has led in some instances to devastating analytic mistakes, such as the propositions concerning the 'end of ideology' debate, an account of social theory propogated by Lipset, Bell and their co-workers during the 1960s. However, Sperber is right to cautiously assert the dominance of structuralism in an earlier era. But this 'structuralism' was a complex intellectual phenomenon itself, embracing Lévi-Strauss, Saussure, Chomsky, Althusser and others, and was thus hardly a monolith. Coupled with these structuralist tendencies, one must also point to the phenomenological revolution in social science, taking its lead in France from Merleau-Ponty and developing into a sociology of everyday life. Further, the feminist revolution played its part in critiquing the so-called functionalist orthodoxy, asking for liberation politics, reflexivity in social scientific practices and a transformation of the sociological agenda. Coupled with the Marxist challenge familiar to all students of the 1960s and 1970s, these new tendencies might well have offered orthodoxies themselves, but they did not last. By the mid-1970s (some would say earlier) the new revolutionary doctrines were losing their power, and newly-arriving students, searching out their intellectual idols, were confused to find a changed and decaying structuralism, a Marxism under attack from the so-called 'new philosophy' (Bernard-Henri Lévi, André Glucksman et al.), an ever-more dominant Foucault, intent on attacking the pretensions of Marxism to a formalistic and a universalistic science, as well as a feminist movement far more polyglot and dispersed than before.

These were some of the currents through which Bourdieu both absorbed influences, and against which he set himself up in opposition. Thus, the visitor to Paris in the mid-1980s certainly found many disclaimers from those in sociology as to the existence of schools. In feminist circles, for example, people would say the movement was in disarray, and then perhaps name writers who still had an influence (Kristeva was often mentioned). Marxism was discounted as a movement; people spoke of its almost complete absence as a central focus, though Godelier and others were still read. What emerged was a systematic lack of symmetry between social movements and social theory, which meant that the collective political hopes embedded in, and connected with social theory appeared to have faded, perhaps finding their last flourish around the work of Foucault. Thus instead of the political cohesiveness of previous years, the followers of social theory now appeared more closely directed towards their work, and less towards their politics.

Coupled with this (perhaps temporary) move away from social movements there was also a movement both inwards towards self-reflection and outwards towards foreign researchers. Functionalism (never dead, of course) was cautiously being rediscovered; American sociology in general was being slowly investigated; other alien beings (Norbert Elias, Habermas, Giddens) were being examined often for their possible use-value.

In this new environment, one could not therefore point easily to a series of distinct schools, set in the constellation of sociology for ever, but rather to a far more limited battle concerning several key figures, all well-known to those familiar with French sociology. Among the list of those who were still read and who mattered in this somewhat more limited way (e.g. Crozier, Touraine, Boudon, Foucault, Baudrillard, Morin) Bourdieu must be numbered.

But the seeming disintegration of fixed positions in the field must be connected to the underlying intellectual current associated with this disaggregation, the move to post-modernism (Bauman 1988). This apparently broad-based trend away from ethnocentrism, universalism and scientism in social theory has been associated with the gradual collapse in the unthinking acceptance of Western philosophical and intellectual thought by those outside the narrow centres of power. Whether this trend is entirely plausible, and whether it can be applied to French theory or not, it certainly resonates in the work of at least some of the major figures responsible for the changes to the new system of theoretical coordinates. In Derrida's deconstruction, we see a direct attack on the certainties of language, and a profound critique of meaning systems, which undercuts the position of many of those not only in linguistic theory, but also in certain branches of social philosophy and philosophy itself. Kristeva's self-conscious theoretical project was to set intellectual categories alight. In Foucault's work, we see a profound tendency towards historical relativism, and an assault on scientistic capacities to dominate. In all these movements, there is a sense of loss, a loss of the generalising principle which had coordinated both theories and researchers across political and empirical terrains in a previous era. In its place, post-modernism offers a plurality of cultures, a plurality of theories, newly-reconstructed foundations of legitimate discourses, a loss of faith in totalising politics, and a rejection of the entire modernist apparatus of culture, science and reason.

Bourdieu's own sociology places him in these currents, but he has always kept his intellectual distance from those around him. Many have compared his work with Derrida's deconstructionist project, but it is clear that Derrida's rapid sweeps of intellectual innovation are, for Bourdieu, insufficiently well-established in systematic studies to be the basis for any change of heart which would take him in this direction. Touraine, one of Bourdieu's principal antagonists in the struggle to gain the chair at the Collège, offers a political and theor-etical strategy too weighed down with voluntarist aspirations to gain support from Bourdieu. In Foucault's case, perhaps the possibility existed for a systematic collaboration. Foucault sponsored Bour-dieu's candidacy at the Collège; many of Foucault's arguments con-cerning symbolic systems, the state and forms of knowledge find some harmonies in Bourdieu's work. Further, both writers rejected the attempted Marxist takeover of radical thought, and both attempted to retain radicalism outside Marxism. However, here the symmetry ends, because it is clear that Foucault's brand of street politics did not find favour with Bourdieu, who felt such actions to be irresponsible in the sense that they furthered the cause of the theorist rather better than they did those who were oppressed. More than this, Bourdieu and Foucault must be distinguished along several other dimensions – Bourdieu's adherence to a theory of social class (however much modified) over and against Foucault's wholesale rejection; Foucault's self-conscious rejection (avoidance of) state power contrasted with Bourdieu's fascination with the categorising and limiting mechanisms by which the state 'acts to legitimate'; finally, Foucault's thorough celebration of relativism in contrast to a mediated form of universalism in Bourdieu's method.

Bourdieu rejects claims that he is universalistic, particularly in the specific forms of theoretical universalism associated with the 'great masters'. Indeed such claims would be faintly ridiculous in a world where a (universal) declaration concerning the end of 'Big Science' has been posted. Nonetheless, Bourdieu's method is trans-cultural and trans-historical at a certain level. Thus Bourdieu proposes empirical study in contextual settings to elaborate his methodology, to generate precise understandings of the practices of social life. In addition, the method is filled with (made up from) a complex set of theoretical concepts (habitus, field, strategy, struggle, capital) which are applied in a multitude of settings with surprising success. Not that this is some form of old-fashioned positivism, under another guise. It seems more likely that Bourdieu is using a philosophical strategy not unlike Bhaskar's (1979) transcendental realism, in which social systems can be seen to have three domains of reality – one associated with deep structures or tendencies in society (to which Bourdieu's method is directly addressed), another with 'experiments' conducted by researchers (Bourdieu in his reflexive mood), along with the experience of everyday life. Thus a universal method is tied to particularistic studies in a form of scientific reflexivity, which reveals social formations as having both singular and universal tendencies, both unique features as well as features which could have been ancipated.

Bourdieu is, therefore, a methodological universalist in a world inhabited by theoretical relativists. In this, of course lies both the distinguishing quality of his approach, and the possibility that he or someone with similar characteristics can 'fill the vacuum' which is said to inhabit the centre of sociology, and which calls out for universalism. Yet Bourdieu's own theory offers a counter-explanation here. Attempts to draw a field together around some quasi-universalistic theoretical proposal cannot succeed in a world in which the capitals at work are distinctly post-modernist and anarchic in character. Moreover, Bourdieu is profoundly pessimistic politically. The clarion call to action, which called the intellectual troops of a previous generation to action will not issue from Bourdieu's camp. Indeed, if Bourdieu's interests are to form a source of wide coalition in social theory, it may be necessary to consider the need for a dual transformation, both in the general dispositions of those who inhabit the field and who shape its capital and, at the same time, in the politics of disenchantment which is embedded in Bourdieu's method.

It is at this point that the greatest contrast can be made with Bourdieu's nearest equivalent in the English-speaking world – Anthony Giddens. Giddens does not include sociology and the sociologist as part of the social reality being studied; Giddens' theory of structuration does share commonalities with Bourdieu's generative structuralist method – the detailed conceptual apparatus is distinct, but the objective is much the same – to illuminate what Giddens calls the *duality of structure* (1981:19) and Bourdieu calls *double structuration* (Fr. ed. 1987:158). Indeed, both Bourdieu and Giddens are best classified as structuration theorists, rather than trying to squeeze them into pre-existing pigeon holes of the post-structuralist, neo-Marxist type. Structuration theory, in our opinion, covers for English-speaking readers what Bourdieu attempts to convey through the terms 'generative structuralism' or 'constructivist structuralism'. Thompson (1984:148–9) is of a similar view.

To the readers of this book who are familiar with the works of Giddens, many similarities will be obvious and we do not propose to catalogue them. Rather, we attempt an evaluation of the two rather different solutions to the double structuration problem.

The first point to make is that the way the two writers conceive of structure is quite different. For Giddens, structures are recursively organised sets of *rules* and *resources* which govern transformations (1982:35). These sets of rules and resources are organised into *institutions* (Giddens 1984:28–34). Whether transformation takes place or not is governed by a set of conditions which Giddens calls *structuration*, which mediates the contingent acts of agents to produce social systems. 'Structures', Giddens claims, 'are, in a logical sense, properties of social systems of collectivities, not of the situated activities of subjects' (ibid.). In our view, Giddens' conceptualisation of structure as *rules* and *resources* in *institutional* contexts oversimplifies the complex nature of social practices – an argument fully developed by Thompson (1984:148–72). It is also our view that Bourdieu's analysis, reflecting his continual involvement in fieldwork, better reflects the subtlety of social practices and does not abstract structure from the social practices of individual agents. Firstly, he achieves this by substituting the idea of *strategy* for that of *rule* (see Chapters 1 and 2) which breaks with the linguistic notion of grammatical rules implicit in Giddens' conception. People adopt strategies which are the result of other social practices; they do not follow rules. Second, Bourdieu's analysis of what Giddens calls *resources* is greatly facilitated by his insight into the different *forms* of capital, over which people struggle (see Chapter 1). This allows Bourdieu to construct a much more complex vision of *resource* than Giddens is able to provide. Thirdly, the rather static notion of *institution* in Giddens' work, is replaced in Bourdieu's work by the idea of *field*, as a dynamic field of forces and of positions. Positions in fields constitute one of the forms of capital over which agents struggle, and utilise various strategies to attain. This gives a dynamism to Bourdieu's conception of structure, which is not so readily apparent in Giddens' approach. For Bourdieu it is the agents who construct their social world and act to maintain or enhance their position in it. As a fieldworker, reflecting on his own experience, Bourdieu wants to work between empirical and theoretical practices. Giddens, with his theoreticist emphasis on rules (and resources) in institutional contexts, is working from the top down, privileging the reproduction of structures over what Bourdieu would see as the attempts by agents to reproduce their positions in fields of struggle.

A second point to make about the two solutions to the double structuration problem concerns the way the two writers conceive of agency. To be an agent one must have choices, and if structural constraints reduce an individual's options to one, then it is fairly clear that agency can no longer be invoked. Under such circumstances, Thompson (1984:169) argues, 'structure and agency no longer appear to be the complementary terms of a duality but the antagonistic poles of a dualism'. In this sense, agency presents a problem to both theorists, since neither admits any influences on agency that are exogenous to their model. Structure constrains (and enables) options but always within limits. Additionally there is a stratification of options available to individuals in social systems. Both theoretical systems allow some individuals more options than others, with some having no options at all. Giddens' answer is to make a distinction between 'options' and 'feasible options' such that an individual with only one feasible option is still an agent, as there is the possibility of taking an *un*feasible option. However, as Thompson points out (1984:169), this solution merely bypasses the problem rather than resolving it.

> Giddens manages to preserve the complementarity between structure and agency only by *defining* agency in such a way that any individual in any situation could *not* be an agent.

Similarly Bourdieu conceives of agency in such a way that everyone is an agent whether they like it or not. Agents occupy positions within fields which, as we have pointed out, effectively limit the range of actions or options. Neither the objective social structures (which limit the options) nor the dispositions of agents (which make a choice between options or strategies) are independent entities – one is embedded in the other – a double structuration.

> The history of the individual is never any more than a certain

specific case of the collective history of his group or class and, in consequence, the systems of individual dispositions are *structural variants* of the group or class habitus, systematically arranged even in the differences that separate them. . . . 'Personal' style, that is, the particular mark borne by all the products of a single habitus, practices or works, is simply a *deviation* itself regulated and sometimes even codified, in relation to the *style* of a period or a class . . . .

(Bourdieu 1977:86)

For Bourdieu then, agency is always confined to the constraints of the habitus which embodies the history of the group or class to which the agent belongs. It seems to us that neither Giddens nor Bourdieu successfully avoids some degree of social (or cultural) determinism in their accounts. For Bourdieu this shows up in a number of places. When an individual only has one option, 'making a virtue of necessity' does not resolve the fact that they are no longer an agent.

Bourdieu's chapter on the working class in *Distinction*, for example (1984:372–96), is distinctly not an argument about how limited the chances of the poor constrain, in some naive fashion, what choices exist for members of this class. Indeed this argument would *only* be possible if one form of capital was all that existed. Limits on economic capital do not by themselves constitute limits on all other forms of capital. To argue in this way, of course, would be to fall foul of an economic determinism, from which Bourdieu is at pains to distance himself. But class is not, of course, just relations of production either – it is also habitus. If habitus did not matter, then income would directly determine consumption, or, in a Marxist inflection, position in the relations of production would determine consumption. However, both habitus and objective conditions matter together, so choices are always possible. Thus it is that people in different class positions make different choices over how to spend similar increments in wages. What is necessary to each class may thus vary. It is nonetheless determined in the end, even if choices are different among different forms and compositions of capital, depending on the class location under consideration.

The choices are thus both more free and more constrained than we might imagine in Bourdieu's account. In the working class, *some* form of art is essential, not because economic necessity requires it to be so, but because it is an essential part of the life we call working-class. Art ought to be bought cheaply and it ought to be bought for effect. Nevertheless, it ought to be bought, for precisely the same reason that the haute bourgeoisie might (partly) 'acquire' art – to adorn the walls of the house. But Bourdieu argues, contrary to orthodox arguments, many other choices are also forced on agents in other classes. Taste is a central component to membership of the upper classes – parvenus take a long time to realise that certain 'wasteful' expenses are not at all choices but essential to achieving the membership they seek of the 'effortlessly superior' dominant order. Thus while economic necessity does not press down, symbolic necessity does. It is thus wholly ironic that Bourdieu's critics have sometimes attacked what they take to be a form of objective, economic determinism. If a case can be made for determinism in Bourdieu's work, it must be in the subjective realm of habitus, where choices for *all* classes (because of the complexity of all the forms of capital) are variously constrained.

Social practices, then, appear and disappear within the constraints of habitus and structure, since there is no other source for their generation. In a similar way, Bourdieu sometimes reduces the power of language to the institutional authority of the utterer (see Chapter 7). The authority of a person to speak is bestowed by position within a field. This ignores the rational force of an utterance that stands *outside* (or above) structural constraints. This point is elaborated by Thompson (1984:70) who argues that when one makes a statement or assertion, one is laying claim to some truth:

> This is a claim which can be criticized, which can be doubted or disputed by others, and which can withstand such criticism to the extent that it can be *supported by reasons* (*sic*). While what counts as 'reasons' may vary from one context to another and may even depend upon certain institutional factors, nevertheless the claim which calls for support by reasons is not reducible to the authority bestowed by an institution.

That Bourdieu's position on this matter has changed to some extent is indicated in his interview with Mahar (see Chapter 2) where he concedes that under some conditions 'there is some power to ideas'. These conditions must be exploited, otherwise 'the power structure is so terrible and so complete'. This implies an acknowledgement of the overly deterministic nature of his earlier formulations.

It seems to us that this rethinking by Bourdieu gives a clue to the way out of the reductionist impasse in structuration theories – the positing of exogenous concepts that allow for *pro*duction in ways not inevitably sanctioned by 'structured-in' and regulated alternatives. Until this occurs on a more systematic basis it is our view that neither the idea of structuration in Giddens, not the various constructs (habitus, capital and field) in Bourdieu succeed in wholly surmounting the structure–agency problem. Rather, they both disolve agency into the all-encompassing structures, which, however flexible, make no allowance for the unique, innovative options which must lie at the heart of a concept of agency which has any measure of autonomy from the structures. To deny such an autonomy is to beg the question of reductionism.

We are conscious of a certain irony here in that we are perfectly illustrating the operation of structural power. We are criticising a theory for stepping outside the structure of the field. How can the field be transformed unless such steps are taken? Perhaps Bourdieu constitutes such an exogenous source of transformation for Anglo-American social theory. We should attend to the details of the structure of the French intellectual tradition as represented by Bourdieu *because* it offers us a way out of some of the structural problems in the field.

Bourdieu's major contribution to cultural theory has been a synthesis of the economic and the symbolic orders. The key to this synthesis is symbolic power, which is not simply the misrecognition of material forms of power, but is a form of power with its own autonomous material force. The force of symbolic power, according to Bourdieu, exists not in the domain of ideas but within the domain of practice itself. Thus, economically-based relations of dependency and domination are manifested in hierarchised cultural practices which prevent the very recognition that such relations are economically based. In this way, the dominant culture establishes patterns of distinction or hierarchical classifications of meaning, and also legitimises those patterns and classifications by producing the linguistic practices which give them force. This is what Raymond Williams (1973:7) calls 'the selective tradition' (that which, within the terms of an effective dominant culture, is always taken to be 'the tradition', 'the significant past').

Because culture is defined in material terms, Bourdieu is able to avoid the problems of meaning associated with such notions as 'false consciousness' and 'ideology'. Culture is not inculcated as so much cognitive information (e.g. knowledge, values, beliefs), but rather, it is learned with the body and is incorporated into ways of doing things (e.g. standing, speaking, eating). The value of any cultural product is determined not by its meaningfulness nor by its usefulness, but by the social distinction embedded in such meaning or use. Bourdieu is interested in the effects of cultural products upon the social positions of the beholder or producer. Within his theoretical framework, speech and other communicative acts are vehicles of power. For example, he uses the metaphor of a cultural field or market to provide a way of describing discursive practices and relating them to the social and historical, or material conditions of their production and reception, as well as with the structured dispositions of individual agents. Bourdieu achieves a synthesis of the economic and the cultural by extending the use of the term 'economic' and its correlate 'capital' to include the exchange of anything of value. As we have pointed out, it becomes an extensive metaphor which embraces all aspects of social life. For example in Chapter 6, Codd showed that within the world of art the metaphor can even work in reverse – the cultural capital of the bohemian artist is achieved by an explicit rejection of the need for worldly goods.

Bourdieu joins those who reject both substantively and methodologically the identification of the economic with the ideological domain. Implicit in this view is the rejection of the notion of a dominant ideology, in favour of one of social fractions within a dominant group. His analysis of social structure has concentrated on these various social and cultural fractions, and the attempts that they make to maximise their strategic advantage. Two critical aspects of his methodology, the move from rules to strategy and the concept of capital, aid him in this analytic project.

The pervasiveness of the economic metaphor may be attributed to the closure of Bourdieu's conceptual system which makes it hard to turn out of the 'hermeneutic circle' of analysis, i.e. concepts/notions may appear to be so tied together as to make ready-made answers. This is how metaphor is often used in the Anglo-American tradition. For Bourdieu, however, the economic metaphor should be taken to be much more than comparative. The point is not simply to create an analogy between the cultural and the economic. The explanatory power of the metaphor derives from its interactive force, so that what is generally taken to be strictly economic practice is able to be understood as simply a particular case of a general theory of the economics of practice (cf. Bourdieu 1977:177). Moreover, we have tried to show how, by taking symbolic capital to be a special instance of economic capital, culture can have material force. Because culture is embodied (in language, action, style), objectified (in art works, buildings, books), and certified (in educational credentials), it can be exchanged, converted and reconverted to produce power and domination. We have illustrated this process in various ways throughout the book. The possessors of economic capital, for example, can maximise social capital for their offspring by purchasing private education in a system which rewards such education providentially. In a general sense, therefore, the 'owners' of cultural capital attempt to monopolise cultural production, or at least to monopolise the power to name that which counts as cultural production in the fields of art, literature and science. At the same time this group will attempt to maximise the importance of cultural capital in both symbolic and material ways, *vis-à-vis* other forms of capital. In other words, there is a strategy being implemented by the dominant class in a struggle which engages all social classes and fractions. The stakes at issue involve not only the legitimation values of the forms of capital involved, but their capacity for convertibility and value into the final prize of symbolic capital. In his studies of France, Bourdieu has concentrated on the specific form of these strategies between classes, concentrating on dominant strategies in particular. There are undoubtedly other strategies being pursued in other social classes, and while Bourdieu rejects the 'dominant ideology' thesis, he does seem to argue for a 'dominant cultural' thesis, even if his conception of 'culture' is far more complex and dynamic than the alternative conceptions. The content of this dominant culture is continuously changing, in response to the struggle for symbolic capital between the various fractions of the dominant group. Various ideologies are utilised in this struggle, but it is not the ideologies that endure, rather it is the continued political dominance of the dominant class. In short, what Bourdieu has offered, for better or worse, is a *general* theory of capital, which is not merely economic, or even predominantly so, but which extends the arguments of famous predecessors into a large variety of new fields.

Thus Bourdieu refuses to define symbolic capital as any less 'material' than any of the other forms of capital. It is simply economic capital misrecognised as such. Does symbolic capital then equate with power, or can it be exchanged for a kind of political capital? Bourdieu's conception of power is very complex, and its meaning in any single situation is often obscure. Of course, social life involves relationships, and relationships inevitably involve control of some by others – this requires power in a general sense, even in situations governed by 'automatic' etiquette. Bourdieu himself says:

the concessions of *politeness* always contain *political* concessions. The term *obsequium* . . . could be reserved to designate the public testimonies of recognition which every group expects of its members (1977:95).

Thus, to take a trivial example, a group of anonymous individuals boarding a bus require some subtle modes of control if any of them are to actually get on. Someone must go first, someone yield, if even this simple enterprise is to be successful. Bourdieu, however, wants to go beyond the somewhat trivial (though not always obvious) point that some people control others. He tries to show that the control mechanisms in a social group are not arbitrary or unpredictable: some people, or sub-groups *possess* more power than others. They define the field, determine its rules, shape the language in which it is discussed and prosper from their dominance, but always as a result of struggle with others. That they can succeed in exerting this power is as a result of a recognition of their symbolic capital by others. At this point, the person trained in the empiricist tradition of social science or used to Popperian demands for falsifiability, wants to ask whether this is a 'mere' tautology or a useful empirical hypothesis to be investigated field by field. Bourdieu will not accept the dichotomy in which the question is posed. At one level, the basic claim is tautological, reminding us that in any group some people's view of things will prevail but telling us nothing about the characteristics of such people. They are 'powerful' in the sense that their view has prevailed: they may or may not be powerful in any other sense. Bourdieu, however, *is* interested in the nature of the dominant groups and in the ways in which power is in general exercised. The economic analogy, already discussed, is part of this generalising process. Thus his ethnographic work, particularly in *Distinction* and *Homo Academicus*, is devoted to illuminating the nature of the power-relations in particular fields but also – via 'cultural capital' – drawing attention to the general 'class' characteristics of the dominant. The way out of the potential tautology is thus through the conjunctural analysis of power in specific ethnographic circumstances. General principles of politics are embodied in specific explanations of how power is constituted. The important question is not the naive one, 'Does power exist?' but rather, 'What are the shapes and forms of capitals in a particular political field, and what political relations can be discerned?'

Thus, we argue that Bourdieu's intellectual project, though still incomplete, is an important and original contribution to contemporary social thought. In the previous eight chapters we have attempted to introduce and clarify the conceptual structure and methodology, as well as illustrating the way they have been put to work in various fields. In the course of developing this conceptual structure, Bourdieu has undertaken empirical work in a number of disciplines. As the previous chapters indicate, this work spans education, sociology, anthropology, linguistics and philosophy. Such a broad intellectual target has attracted widespread interest, comment and criticisms, many of which have been discussed in the previous chapters. We will undertake a short review of the main critiques before detailing our own criticisms and moving on to indicate the areas of Bourdieu's current interests.

THE CRITIQUE OF BOURDIEU'S METHODOLOGY

A study of the secondary literature (which is now considerable, and growing daily) reveals many specific criticisms. Some of these criticisms, however, are less substantial than they appear; others are telling and enduring. For example most arise from reviews of single texts,[1] or reviews of single themes in his work.[2] While it is wholly understandable, given the limited translation of other materials into English, we hope to have displayed enough of Bourdieu's wide interests to put these views to rest. The partial analysis of his work in narrow specialties is the single most common source of criticism which he has attracted. This is particularly the case in the field of education, where English-speaking critics seem unaware of his detailed historical and ethnographic work. This sometimes places criticisms, which seem plausible when only 10 per cent of the work is considered, wholly out on a limb when the remaining 90 per cent comes into view.

Nonetheless placing these criticisms to one side in the face of Bourdieu's complete achievement, does not in any way remove the importance of other criticisms which remain. There appears to be five substantive areas of criticism.

Firstly, Bourdieu is sometimes characterised as presenting causal explanations which are tautological or circular definitional exercises.[3] These criticisms are frequently associated with charges of conceptual fluffery. In general these arguments look to the causal power of Bourdieu's theory, and suggest that he produces pseudo-explanations, and that such a closed theoretical system might blur real struggles between groups (Collins 1988).

Secondly, his relationship to other forms of causality, especially the Althusserian method of 'over-determination' is not clear to many in the Marxist camp who are interested in where he stands in relation to Marxist methodology. More than this, however, there is the question of the internal structure of Bourdieu's theory, and the relationship between the levels of this structure. Are elements of agency and structure to be placed at the same level of the theoretical system? This higher level of epistemological criticism is widespread and profound. Elster (1983) says, for example, that Bourdieu imposes a mixture of intentional and functional explanations on a causal account. Whatever the validity of these criticisms in the last analysis, they do constitute a serious set of distinct problems.

Thirdly, Bourdieu's use of the term 'power' occurs in such a way as to beg a series of further important questions. For example, the question has been raised as to just where the state's influence exerts itself. Bourdieu has used the state as a site where symbolic violence takes place systematically, but this sometimes seems to reduce real, material violence to a problem of signification. Wacquant (1986) has argued that if Bourdieu wishes to further his class analysis he must go beyond his work on nomination and classification. This implies a series of predominantly Marxist questions, relating social class to the role of the state, which are not provided with answers. Given that many of his readers and his critics are Marxist, it is not surprising that such questions should be raised, and no less surprising that given Bourdieu's ambiguous attitude to Marxists (though rarely to Marx) he does not answer those questions directly. A further series of queries remain, taking all these nuances into account. Is politics to be seen as a field of its own, a ghostly *deus ex machina* which works unseen behind the façade of appearance, or is it simply to be viewed as the *ultimate* form of capital, for which all other lesser currencies are finally cashed in?

The fourth major argument against Bourdieu's strategem suggests that symbolic relations are given too much weight by his analysis (Gorder 1980; Willis 1983). It is perhaps surprising in many ways that Bourdieu should suffer this particular criticism, since non-Marxist critics have frequently placed him in the materialist camp. Clearly, both criticisms cannot legitimately be voiced at the same time, and clearly also, both kinds of arguments need to confront the attempt Bourdieu has made to ignore such dichotomies in a very direct and conscious way,[4] In relation to Giroux in particular (1981), this comment is especially telling. Giroux depends on the early sources available in English on education for his establishment of critique. In a later review (1983) Giroux argues, from a different angle, that Bourdieu's conceptions of power and domination are overly mechanistic and are not properly linked to the materiality of economic forces. Charges of simple reproduction cannot be sustained when other obvious sources are tapped, most recently *Distinction*, available in French before Giroux made his comments, but the point is also clear from early ethnographic sources available in English in the 1960s. However, as we have argued above, complex arguments about determinacy do have some merit. The dominance of class conceptions in *Distinction*, for example, means that the balance between symbolic and economic strategies is ever present, and this time in a single work, rather than spread across several sources. This argument is frequently tied to the implications of a 'lack of materialism', and a lack of politics. Garnham and Williams (1980) find in Bourdieu a residual and flexible Marxism with political struggle at the very core of his work, and they do this as a result of a very thoughtful and detailed review, not of single works, but of the method as a whole. This view is authenticated by careful reference to the widespread attention he gives to such matters in many places.[5] This said, however, Bourdieu does not easily align himself with political parties or orthodox sects of the left, and he does not readily make alliances with political powers, as was evidenced at the advent of the Mitterrand government. Given this 'refusal' to be readily categorised politically as well as theoretically, it is hardly surprising that legitimate criticisms remain. One of the most poignant criticisms, and one of the most sustained is that propounded by Collectif 'Révoltes Logiques' (1984), who, in a very spirited attack complain, not that Bourdieu is *wrong* in his critique of the orthodox left in France, but that his insights are so telling that they lead to a disenchantment and a loss of imagination, which is the true power of Bourdieu's work in political critique. Not only has Bourdieu shown, along with many others, that inequalities, in education and elsewhere persist, but, they argue, he has also shown, in a thorough, sophisticated and evocative way, how difficult it is to transform such complex systems. Such complaints also arise from his refusal to replace scientific arguments with political ones – or to privilege the latter.

Fifth, while Bourdieu's work contains a powerful theory of social reproduction, it has been criticised as failing to be a theory of social transformation. These critics (see Jenkins 1982, Wacquant 1986, Willis 1983) argue that Bourdieu should be more concerned with social change, a criticism which is addressed in part above. But it is a criticism which is not targeted merely at expressive accounts of politics, but at the very heart of his method. Bourdieu is criticised by Wacquant in particular for not developing some account of collective action. In truth, perhaps, the most central and most telling of these criticisms is that within Bourdieu's method there is no real historical theory of social change (though Garnham and Williams (1980) feel they have found one). As Di Maggio (1979) comments, 'Bourdieu's is a world not of revolutions, or even of social change, but of endless transformations' (1979:1470). Rather than using accounts of class consciousness familiar to the old left, Bourdieu studies the conflict within class fractions, hence his concern to highlight the ways in which capital is transformed from one form into another, as each fraction struggles to reproduce and augment its power. At the heart of the matter is the question of whether the method of habitus and strategy, always closely connected to each other as we have shown, can account for social ruptures and qualitative changes in society, as well as the day-to-day transformations which continually occur.

In addition to criticism,[6] Bourdieu and his work have been frequently subjected to attempts at final and determinate classification. Since Bourdieu has spent much of his career attacking classifications and trying to avoid them (see Chapter 2), this activity by commentators is mildly ironic, and he has been authoritatively placed in all the major theoretical traditions.[7] Perhaps concern to have Bourdieu safely tucked away in a pigeonhole is misguided if wholly understandable. Bourdieu draws on all of his '*compagnons*' to produce an analytic method which encompasses within a single coherent framework many aspects of cultural practice. The construction of a general economy of practices situated squarely within a broad sociological tradition, draws heavily on many sources, not only those familiar to the Anglo-American world, but many also from French sources, which are rarely if ever mentioned by non-French critics.[8] Further afield, as we have seen, many others are essential to his task, including Lévi-Strauss, Foucault and Derrida, not for what he takes from them, but rather how he situates himself against them. What is clear in all this is that attempts at simple, unambiguous classification are misleading and hide more than they reveal. They are generally attempts either to welcome Bourdieu as a colleague in a specific field, with certain attendant strategies and capitals, or an attempt to dismiss him from the field, and to place him outside the struggle of a legitimate category of intellectual activity. In short, critics of this kind seek to 'name' Bourdieu in the intellectual field, to give him authority, or to deny him that authority by processes of classification. This is, of course, a very general strategy for gaining and maintaining symbolic power, a process which Bourdieu himself has spent much effort in analysing.

THE CRITICISMS THAT ENDURE

In this section, we set our own convictions concerning enduring critical commentary in relation to Bourdieu's initiatives. Many of these arguments have been touched upon above; here, we elaborate these positions more fully.

Firstly, political agnosticism. As we discuss above, Bourdieu's own politics are well-known. Clearly he lies on the progressive side of the political spectrum, placing his money on participatory democracy, extended systems of equitable distribution, open education and so on. Yet many obvious *progressiste* positions are avoided. He is patently unwilling to ally himself with the Marxist left in any of its forms, taking it upon himself to criticise not only Marxist and neo-Marxist theory, but very directly to criticise the spokespeople of the left, who, he says, constitute their followers as ways of embellishing their own statuses, rather than as a precondition for their followers' emancipation. Again, he is unwilling to follow Foucault's footsteps into a less-structured form of street politics which might appear as a natural alternative to the Marxism of earlier years. Here Bourdieu feels loyalties are too easily made and broken; much damage to the oppressed can come as a result of such adventurist moves. Neither is he willing to follow Touraine into his 'action sociology'. Yet, at the same time, Bourdieu is 'engagé'; politics is embedded in his substantive writing; it is at the heart of his method; it structures the very ordering of 'science' itself. But sometimes the impression can be given that his politics is an internal matter to the academic field – witness his early refusal to accept 'authority' and write a thesis. An attack on the classifications of the university structures has always been a preoccupation (see *Leçon sur la leçon* and, especially *Homo Academicus*) and this attack on formal authority structures attached to the claims of science is coupled with his belief that the more 'scientific' sociology is, the more politically powerful it becomes.

So, internal critique and scientifically political sociology are offered as antidotes to the more flamboyant and empty politics of the recent past. Yet politics is even more deeply embedded in Bourdieu's work than this, and perhaps even more profoundly damaging to his project. In the struggle to achieve capitals and to fight for positions in social fields, individuals and groups sometimes appear to be involved in amassing one special form of capital – a political capital, which lies behind all the other capitals in his scheme. Domination, through the mechanisms of taste, social difference, class privilege, appears as the final goal of all human struggle. It is a calculating struggle, a struggle to the death, and in a precise sense, a struggle without hope. Bourdieu's political vision, not as an individual viewing society, but as a sociologist analysing human events, has a Hobbesian quality in which the struggles are crucial (in shaping lives, moulding decisions, directing human effort) yet finally, and in a grander sense, pointless since the fields can never be altered profoundly; while the capitals will need to be struggled over, the millennium will not come into sight. This political disenchantment leads to a vision of political determinism, in which, at one and the same time, transformations are highly improbable, yet the present struggles inevitable.

Political agnosticism, an unwillingness to predict a future, has, as we have said, direct consequences for the influence Bourdieu can be expected to have in the broad field of sociology. If Sperber is right, and the present sociological climate is amenable to good scholarship, rather than the over-flashy politics of the past, Bourdieu's influence will grow in stature. Indeed, Bourdieu is not merely scholarly, but convincingly flashy in his arguments. But his unwillingness to take the prescriptive road in his politics means that the acolytes of the past will not be flocking to his door – indeed, his work has been part of the political disenchantment of a recent generation.

Secondly, we believe that a claim of tautology and functionalism can be sustained against Bourdieu's work. Capital is something that is struggled for – what is capital? Capital is that which people value and (therefore) struggle for. What is strategy and struggle about? It is the activity that people engage in, in order to gain the necessary volumes of capital to achieve their aims. These forms of theoretical circles are everywhere in Bourdieu's work, and they are both frequently convincing when coupled with engaging accounts of everyday life, as well as circular in their forms. This hermetically sealed world is also by implication, functionalist. Not that Bourdieu, in some slavish way, parrots some form of Parsonian orthodoxy concerning values, consensus and equilibrium. Bourdieu's is a dynamic functionalism – fields change their composition and their actors; the volumes and compositions of capitals may alter. Yet the needs of the system, the needs for struggle, positions and capitals remain.

This charge of tautology and functionalism can be attached to a third criticism, closely aligned to both of the preceding arguments – the criticism that Bourdieu is unwilling to provide (and unable to provide through the logic of his tautological method) an account of history, of historical transformation and therefore of the politics of transformation. In his present work (mentioned more fully below) he is constructing an account of the origins of the present intellectual field in France. Yet this reconstructive history is not typical of Bourdieu's *oeuvre*. In this regard, Marxism, for all its faults of economism, historicism and authoritarianism, which are sometimes justifiably set against it, has a decided advantage. Bourdieu is, quite reasonably, unwilling to invoke a history of societies as a history of class struggles. In consonance with this entirely plausible rejection of the Marxist account of history, and therefore implicitly of the Marxist politics embedded in this account, Bourdieu gives up more than is necessary – namely the history of social conditions. Whether his work on Manet and Flaubert will offer an antidote to these criticisms is a matter for the future to decide.

Nonetheless, this synchronic tendency in his work is damaging, because part of the explanation as to why fields take the shape that they do is inevitably missing, and the account of the social topology is thus deficient. Bourdieu goes too far in rejecting Marxist accounts of history (whichever of the variants) because his own method is clearly amenable to historical analysis.[9] To 'bend the stick' in the Marxist direction for a moment, it is clear that Bourdieu could substitute his general theory of capital for the general theory of the modes of production. Those phases of social history characterised by the feudal mode of production, could equally be analysed by looking at the forms of social and political capitals which framed those societies and the actors in them. In similar parallel fashion, the capitalist mode of production could be characterised as a form of society with qualitatively distinct forms and volumes of capitals – new rules for the game, and a new game – which directs human endeavours in new directions. Social transformations could then be characterised, not merely as a revolution in class structures, as the Marxist account would propose, but as a rupture in the old system of capitals which had prevailed in the old régime (habitus *and* social conditions), and their replacement with a new system. Indeed, Bourdieu's complex theoretical apparatus might offer a far more flexible account of these social transformations than any but the most elaborate Marxist accounts could offer. Yet this theoretical potential has not been explored, and Bourdieu's account is limited to attempts at assessing how short-term alterations take place in human affairs. Indeed, his present work itself appears (as far as brief outlines seem to suggest) to be limited to the mapping-out of various subjective components of his dynamic (habitus) and omits serious concern with social conditions, which an alternative historical method might offer.

Fourth, it is necessary to point to the meta-theoretical goals of his approach, coupled with the ambitious goals he sets for sociology. For a sociologist appropriately reflexive in his practice, it is all the more surprising to find that Bourdieu's 'method' is, in its attempt to frame systems of social life, a meta-theoretical strategy as well as an attempt at constructing a meta-methodology. By any orthodox account of theory (as a system of logically-related concepts which explain cause and effect, for example) Bourdieu's exposition of field, practice, habitus and capital inevitably takes on the mantle of a theory, even if that theory is always directed towards empirical targets. In a theoretical world of deconstruction, disaggregation and relativism, an attempt at the promulgation of general theory, even if disguised as general method, is fraught with problems. Bourdieu, of course, is on the side of a long tradition in sociology, deriving from Durkheim, which seeks to press the universalistic claims of sociology over and against the particularistic claims of psychology, literature, and now, in the present climate of relativism, against the claims of various new social categories, to call their own truths singular. In addition to this obstacle (this unwillingness of 'subject populations' to accede to the value of an imposed external truth) Bourdieu also wishes to champion the general case of sociology as a meta-science, echoing back in this instance even further than Durkheim to Comte's famous parallel attempts.

This is a particularly interesting attempt in relation to Bourdieu's comments on philosophy. In its own terms, philosophy has been construed as a second-order activity. This entails the conviction that at the highest level of abstraction philosophy can sit in judgement on all other areas of human knowledge – pronouncing them unintelligible (theology), false (astrology), conceptually confused (psychology), pretentiously vague (sociology), or progressive, i.e., acceptable as far as they go (physics and most of the other natural sciences). What Bourdieu does, of course, is to turn all this on its head. Each of these is a 'field of forces' and *so, of course, is philosophy*. Like any other discipline, it is a field of struggle where practitioners fight to transform or conserve the current field. Proponents take up positions (as utilitarians, deontologists, realists, pragmatists and the like) and act according to certain rules (paradigm cases, linguistic usage, common sense, transcendental arguments, etc.). Specific agents gather capital within the field and attract disciples whom they influence to join their 'school', and to argue with 'impeccable logic' against opposing 'schools'. There is a style of philosophical argument instantly recognisable by all who attend philosophy conferences and read philosophical journals. Despite differing points of view this 'style' must be followed for legitimacy in the field to be achieved. Thus Bourdieu offers a social analysis of the discipline whose *raison d'être* consists in denying, or at least treating as problematic, any suggestion of the importance of social context.

In developing this argument Bourdieu himself seeks to transform the fields of both philosophy and sociology: he elevates social science to the position of the second-order activity. Sociology, not philosophy, describes and analyses all the other fields (though being, of course, also recognised as a field itself) and philosophy loses its position of power. So, in Bourdieu's own terms, the struggle between philosophy and sociology is a struggle to the death. Both are now rivals within a theoretical field ('second-order activities') and they struggle for dominance, each denying the fundamental premise of the other and each seeking to control the rules of *that* game.

However, both in Bourdieu's attempt to generate a general theory of human practice, as well as to propose a meta-theoretical status for sociology in general, we can find an initiative wholly out of keeping with some of the powerful opposing currents in contemporary sociology.

These four criticisms offer enduring questions for Bourdieu's sociology, and they do not find any plausible solution in his work to date. In addition, there are several other matters which are more than passing difficulties. For example, the matter of Bourdieu's complex language is frequently raised as a criticism. These criticisms are easily dismissed by Bourdieu, but they too have an enduring quality. Bourdieu argues that complex language is necessary to reflect a complex reality – easy language is adequate for a stereotypical account of human societies to be realised, but intelligent analysis requires more. Indeed, Bourdieu, like many before him (Adorno, for example) insists that it is necessary to break with 'common sense', 'fake science' and crude explanations in order to 'bring home the corresponding social experience to those who do not or do not want, to know about it' (1984:510). Yet some paragraphs of his work, when taken out of context, are by themselves almost indecipherable even to the experienced reader of social theory, let alone the beginning student or the intelligent layperson. One enduring difficulty is with the very complex sentence structure, frequently mediated by up to six or eight conditional clauses, as if all the subtleties and nuances must be put together in one sentence. Coupled with the frequently elliptical structure of the argument, these stylistic difficulties are often considerable. It is a durable reader indeed who can read Bourdieu without preamble or exposition, and even the most sympathetic observer cannot overcome the feeling that some of this complexity is directed at protecting the writer's intellectual field rather than directed towards an explanation of the social field itself. This obscurity may not be helped by an obtuse form of referencing in which previous authors in a field are referred to by short-hand reference, often to terms they have made their own, rather than by direct reference to their names or works, which would distinguish them more clearly.

Many ideas which the French take for granted are not immediately recognisable to outsiders, nor is their phylogeny clear. Within the French tradition, the idea is not dependent upon its source, which may be deliberately unstated. For the English reader, however, errors of derivation are generally viewed more seriously. For example, linguistic philosophers would immediately recognise Bourdieu's mistaken use of Austin's work – as discussed in Chapter 7. Bourdieu criticises Austin and his supporters for searching 'in the words themselves the "illocutionary force" which they recognize from time to time in performatives' (Fr. ed. 1982:132). They, of course, did quite the opposite, turning away from 'the words themselves' to the social setting in which the words are used and the effect they are likely to have in the particular situation. Contrary to what Bourdieu implies, Austin and his followers did not try to understand language apart from the people who use it. Austin earned his reputation in philosophy by putting peoples' activities at the centre of language and he fully recognises the fact that utterances, or speech acts, had to be performed by the appropriate person – two persons are married only if an authorised person pronounces them man and wife, only the invited dignitary can launch a ship, open Parliament or christen a baby.

His lack of (to the Anglo-Saxon view) systematic referencing only adds to such confusion. There is also a lack of systematicity in Bourdieu's work – he has ranged far and wide in serendipitous fashion, from analyses of the Algerian Kabylia to the haute couture of the high bourgeoisie, from sport to art, from education to the law. In all these fields, of course, Bourdieu is perhaps trying to show how a similar logic is at work, even if the particulars are different. This is not yet clear, because, for example, the method at work in the analysis of the Kabyle is decidedly Lévi-Straussian structuralist, whereas *Distinction* is filled with reference to his own, more recently-developed method. Thus the cohesiveness of the intellectual project is lacking, which adds a further layer of confusion for the reader.

In his new work, Bourdieu may shed light on some of the arguments outlined above. In any event, it seems appropriate to end the book by indicating his current proclivities.

THE LAST WORD: NEW WORK

Bourdieu's typical form of work has been to develop concepts in a spiralling fashion, returning to earlier formulations but at another level. The preliminary ideas for all the major books are to be found in this way, and this connection with the past is characteristic of Bourdieu's present activities. Bourdieu continues, alone or with others, in many areas; in the field of law (1987), the theory of the state and education (Fr. ed. 1989), the field of housing (Bourdieu et al. 1987), the origins of the intellectual field (1988b), and the field of sport. For example he published in *Actes* a model of supply and demand for sports products (1986). This is similar to what he proposed in *Distinction* for cultural products and where he demonstrated how the adjustment in supply and demand was not the product of individual choices but of choices which were organised and orientated by the homologous position within the space of products supplied and the space of consumers of those products.

We distinguish three distinct projects, either recently or about to be published. With Monique de St Martin, he has long been working on a study of the Grandes Écoles, focusing on the methods of reproduction and failure to reproduce class position. The work has resulted in a major publication, *La Noblesse d'Etat* (Bourdieu, Fr.

ed. 1989). This study is in one way archetypal: it has a history of work and preliminary expositions stretching back twenty years. In this way, its history is also a history of the conceptual developments in his theory. Of particular note in this initiative is the study of class and strategy at two levels. Bourdieu is trying to demonstrate how schools maintain a class position within the hierarchy of tertiary institutions by following particular strategies of domination, while at the same time explaining how individuals make the choices of schools that they do, thereby reproducing or failing to reproduce both themselves and their classes. This is particularly important, because it connects several dichotomies in the Anglo-Saxon literature by subsuming them within problems of strategy – especially true in the attempt to dissolve the structure and agency elements of education and class. Mention also must be made of the broad statistical base upon which the study is partly founded, part of an ongoing critique of statistical method, as Bourdieu again presents his synthetic methods of ethnography and statistics.[10] The analysis of the data uses (somewhat surprisingly) a sophisticated method of factor analysis which allows one to uncover explanatory structures instead of trying to isolate the significance of factors which are never perfectly independent, as is the case in multiple regression analysis. (Bourdieu has also put this method into practice in constructing a mathematical model with Alain Darbel, which concerns forecasting the growth of public visits to museums (Bourdieu, Darbel and Schnapper, Fr. ed. 1966), see also note 23, pp. 84-5 above.

In 1985 Bourdieu had begun a study of the private housing market to show the way in which the culture of economic goods is interpenetrated by belief and materiality (see Bourdieu et al. 1987). The study focuses specifically upon the economic field, using housing as a specific example. Bourdieu examines empirically this 'sub-field' of the economy and the configurations of the relative strengths of economic and symbolic forces. For example, the weight of the 'brand name' and its history and fame, as a business's reputation, as the companies manoeuvre within the field of competition between companies, and impact upon profit and symbolic capital. As part of the study he also examined the power relationships among leaders who possess different economic and cultural capital. The perspective of the study stretches the theory of fields and demonstrates that the economic field is only a special case whose unique features may be understood by comparing it with other fields.

However, as a third enterprise most of Bourdieu's energies at present are taken up with a two-to-three volume work, which is an attempt to generate a broad theory of the intellectual field as a whole. The study itself is divided into three main sections. The first is an empirically-based study of the nineteenth-century literary and artistic fields. Drawing on the extensive work that he has completed in this area, Bourdieu has undertaken new studies of Flaubert and Manet, showing how these two artists were fundamentally important in shaping the contemporary intellectual field both in France and elsewhere (see Bourdieu 1987g; 1988b). Case studies focus upon the work and historical period of Flaubert, the birth and the emergence of the contemporary artistic field and the symbolic revolution accomplished by Manet. Such a focus leads Bourdieu to posit a theory of the *specific economy* of cultural objects and to clarify general properties of the artistic and literary fields. In Flaubert's work, he sees the sources of reflexivity and trajectory which are important in his own work. In Manet he finds the explosive originality which broke with all past traditions in art and made new things possible.

The second section of this larger work focuses upon a series of already-established studies concerning various fields; the fields of religion, law, politics, philosophy and science. These studies serve to pose the problem of the historical conditions of the production of discourse which claims to be universal. The third and final section of the work on the field is an attempt to formalise those theoretical propositions which are derived from the work in section 2 with respect to fundamental concepts in Bourdieu's method: those of habitus; the field as a field of forces and the field as a field of struggle; and the concept of capital in all its different forms.

In this extremely ambitious analysis, Bourdieu takes on many of the problems in his past work: the difficulties of method, of epistemology, and of adequate theorisation. As elsewhere, Bourdieu confronts these difficulties and tries to offer new answers. However, here he attempts much more, by drawing out a general theory of the field from all the specific instances of field, struggles and strategies which he has generated, and couples this with the attempt to describe nothing less than the origins of the field which we all presently inhabit. Whether this attempt is successful, and whether Bourdieu's vision will endure, can only be understood by assessing how, in Bourdieu's own terminology, the field of social theory affords it a place in the history of sociology.

NOTES

1. For example, reviews of *Reproduction in Education, Society and Culture* (1977) which tend to neglect other aspects of Bourdieu's work. See especially Archer (1984); Giroux (1981;1983); Willis (1983); Bidwell (1972); Broadfoot (1978); Bredo and Feinberg (1979). None of these authors appear to be familiar with the broader intent of Bourdieu's method nor do they appear to be familiar with works such as *Algeria 1960* or *Outline of a Theory of Practice* – both of which were available in English by 1980. More positive reviews of *Reproduction in Education, Society and Culture* and ones which attempt to use Bourdieu's methodology to some degree can be found in Gorder (1980); Hearn and Olzak (1981) and Watkins (1984).

   In the sociological literature there are several reviews of *Distinction* which take a much broader perspective on Bourdieu's general project than the above reviews of his work in education. While, in general, *Distinction* is characterised as a brilliant book, criticisms tend to focus upon the use of statistics (i.e. the presentation of data and lack of an explanation of method) see Jenkins (1983), Giddens (1986), and on Bourdieu's notion of class and class fractions as not being precise enough for general use outside of the French setting (see also Longhurst, 1986; Berger, 1986).

2. By and large these reviews focus upon class reproduction through education, which is not surprising, since until recently the most common understanding of Bourdieu's work in the English-speaking world was as an educational sociologist. Other themes which have also been reviewed are those of methodology (see Di Maggio, 1979), and most importantly the question of the dialectical opposition of objective structures and subjectivity which Bourdieu's method attempts to transcend. In general, reviews are positive (see Inglis (1979); Garnham and Williams (1980); Sulkunen (1982); Rossi (1975).

   The structure/agency debate has concerned those human geographers who have become more involved with social theory in recent years. And they feel as acutely as anyone the difficulty of relating, as one of them puts it, 'abstract generalisations about social phenomena to the features of a particular place at a particular time and to the actions of individuals' (Thrift, 1983:23).

   Quite apart from these reviews Jenkins (1982) criticises Bourdieu's 'ideological doublebind': through the processes of misrecognition, the working class helps to create its own domination by more powerful forces.

   Other points which have been major topics for discussion in reviews of Bourdieu's work are those of habitus and the field and class. Reviews (crossing several disciplines) of the concept of habitus can be found in Jackson (1983), Harker (1984) as well as in the previously mentioned Inglis (1979) and Garnham and Williams (1980). The question of class consciousness is taken up by a review of *Algeria 1960* by Stanton (1982),

Williams (1980). The concept of the field is reviewed in Cambrosio and Keating (1983).

General reviews of the concepts of habitus, field, class and capital can be found in Di Maggio (1979) and Brubaker (1985) who has 'read' or mis-read Bourdieu as a Weberian by drawing parallels between classes and status groups. Joppke also mis-reads Bourdieu in this way (1986) and in many other ways in a particularly critical review.

3. In other parallel arguments, Bourdieu is said to be contradictory, see Di Maggio (1979); Bredo and Feinberg (1979).

4. See Inglis (1979), and Giddens (1978).

5. See issues of *Actes de la recherche en sciences sociales*, the house journal of the Centre de Sociologie Européenne. In particular note numbers, 5/6 (1975); 36–38 (1981); 52 & 53 (1984); 56 (1985); 61 (1986).

6. See again Bredo and Feinberg (1979); Giroux (1983); Gorder (1980); Talbot (1972); Wacquant (1986); and Willis (1983).

7. For instance a central debate in the literature is whether he is rightly placed in the Marxist camp or not. Some of his terminology clearly derives from Marxism, a tendency hard to avoid in modern sociology. Terms such as capital are widespread: indeed his is a general theory of capital, and this has led to the conclusion that he can be safely classified as a Marxist. (See Davies (1976:133); Broadfoot (1978:75–79); Kennett (1973:328); Tyler (1977:112)). However, this view is specifically rejected by other commentators. (See Brubaker (1985), Di Maggio (1979:1169–1170); Sharp (1980:69–72); Karabel and Halsey (1977:33n.)) Some argue that Bourdieu is a structuralist (see again, Kennett (1973); Davies (1976)), while other commentators place Bourdieu firmly in the Weberian camp. (Again, note Brubaker (1986); Di Maggio (1979); Schwartz (1977); and, again, Sharp (1980).)) Yet others such as Gorder (1980) and Acciaiolo (1981) read his work as Durkheimian.

8. Such as the works of Benveniste, Canguilhem, Bachelard and Cassirer – see Chapters 2 and 3.

9. One simple reply to our criticism is available, but we find it deficient. 'Habitus' is sometimes viewed as a form of 'embodied history' – that is, habitus, or a system of dispositions, both presupposes a future (in that dispositions offer a way into the future, enabling some alternatives to develop and others to be less likely), and embodies a past, since dispositions derive from (embody) family background, history and trajectory. Even if this argument is allowed, we are no further along the path to developing an account of the history of societies beyond the individual, nor to explaining something of the nature of the historically-located field in which the dispositions of a family or a given individual developed.

10. Bourdieu has written a critique of the classifications used in coding statistics in France. This is similar to that produced by Aaron Cicourel. With reference to his previous work he says, 'I believe that one of the most misunderstood aspects of my work by Anglo-Saxons is my use of statistical data. They do not seem to be able to conceive that what they construe as faults in my work are really the types of choices that I

make in using certain data and that this choice is based within a specific logic of mathematics. Sometimes I feel like Manet who was criticized for not being "capable" of understanding the laws of perspective!' (personal communication).

Bibliography

We acknowledge the assistance obtained from the definitive Bourdieu bibliography maintained by Yvette Delsaut of the École des hautes études en sciences sociales, and the Collège de France, Paris.
This bibliography is in five parts:
A.   Books and other papers by Bourdieu in French. They are identified by the addition of 'Fr. ed.' preceding the date of publication, so as to avoid confusion with works in English.
B.   A listing of Bourdieu's articles in French which have appeared in the journal *Actes de la recherche en sciences sociales*. References to these articles in the text are identified by the addition of 'Actes' preceding the date of publication, again to avoid confusion with work in English.
C.   Works by Bourdieu available in English. These are dated to their first appearance in print in English, though many of them have been reprinted in books of readings subsequently. There are also in this listing some recent papers and documents in French.
D.   A listing of works which review, discuss or critique Bourdieu's work as a whole, or specific publications.
E.   Other works referred to in the text.

A. Books and book chapters by Bourdieu in French

Bourdieu, P. (Fr. ed. 1958) *Sociologie de l'Algérie* (Paris: PUF).
Bourdieu, P. (Fr. ed. 1967) *Architecture gothique et pensée scolastique.* Translation of E. Panofsky (Paris: Les Editions de Minuit).
Bourdieu, P. (Fr. ed. 1972) *Esquisse d'une théorie de la pratique, précéde de trois études d'Ethnologie Kabyle* (Genève: Droz).
Bourdieu, P. (Fr. ed. 1974) 'Avenir de classe et causalité du probable', *Revue française de sociologie* 15(1), 3–42.
Bourdieu, P. (Fr. ed. 1976) 'Les conditions sociales de la production sociologue; sociologie coloniale et décolonisation de la sociologie', in Moniot, H. (ed) (1976) *q.v.*
Bourdieu, P. (Fr. ed. 1977) *Algérie 60* (Paris: Les Editions de Minuit).
Bourdieu, P. (Fr. ed. 1979) *La Distinction. Critique sociale du jugement* (Paris: Les Editions de Minuit).
Bourdieu, P. (Fr. ed. 1980) *Le sens pratique* (Paris: Les Editions de Minuit).
Bourdieu, P. (Fr. ed. 1980a) *Questions de sociologie* (Paris: Les Editions de Minuit).
Bourdieu, P. (Fr. ed. 1982) *Ce que parler veut dire: l'économie des échanges linguistiques* (Paris: Fayard).
Bourdieu, P. (Fr. ed. 1982a) *Chaire de sociologie: leçon inaugurale*, faite le vendredi 23 Avril (Paris: Collège de France).
Bourdieu, P. (Fr. ed. 1982b) *Leçon sur la leçon* (Paris: Les Editions de Minuit).
Bourdieu, P. (Fr. ed. 1984) *Homo academicus* (Paris: Les Editions de Minuit).

Bourdieu, P. (Fr. ed. 1987) *Choses dites* (Paris: Les Editions de Minuit).

Bourdieu, P. (Fr. ed. 1989) *La Noblesse d'Etat* (Paris: Les Editions de Minuit).

Bourdieu, P., L. Boltanski, P. Castel, and J. C. Chamboredon (Fr. ed. 1965) *Un art moyen, essai sur les usages sociaux de la photographie* (Paris: Les Editions de Minuit).

Bourdieu, P., L. Boltanski, and P. Maldidier (Fr. ed. 1971) 'La défense du corps', *Information sur les sciences sociales* 10(4), 45–86.

Bourdieu, P., J.-C. Chamboredon and J.-C. Passeron (Fr. ed. 1968) *Le métier de sociologue* (Paris: Mouton).

Bourdieu, P., A. Darbel, J.-P. Rivet and C. Seibel (Fr. ed. 1963) *Travail et travailleurs en Algérie* (Paris–La Haye: Mouton).

Bourdieu, P., A. Darbel and D. Schnapper (Fr. ed. 1966) *L'amour de l'art, les musées d'art européens et leur public* (Paris: Les Editions de Minuit).

Bourdieu, P. and J.-C. Passeron (Fr. ed. 1964) *Les étudiants et leurs études* (Paris: Mouton).

Bourdieu, P. and J.-C. Passeron (Fr. ed. 1964a) *Les Héritiers, les étudiants et la culture* (Paris: Les Editions de Minuit).

Bourdieu, P. and J.-C. Passeron (Fr. ed. 1970) *La reproduction. Eléments pour une théorie du système d'enseignement* (Paris: Les Editions de Minuit).

Bourdieu, P., J.-C. Passeron and M. de St. Martin (Fr. ed. 1965) *Rapport pédagogique et communication* (Paris: Mouton).

Bourdieu, P. and A. Sayad (Fr. ed. 1964) *Le déracinement. La crise de l'agriculture traditionnelle en Algérie* (Paris: Les Editions de Minuit).

B. Papers in French, published in *Actes de la recherche en sciences sociales*.
Referenced in text as (Actes 1975), etc.

Bourdieu, P. and Y. Delsaut. (Actes 1975) 'Le couturier et sa griffe: contribution à une théorie de la magie', 01, 7–36.

Bourdieu, P. and L. Boltanski. (Actes 1975) 'Le titre et le post: rapports entre le système de production et le système de reproduction', 02, 95–107.

Bourdieu, P. (Actes 1975) 'L'invention de la vie d'artiste', 02, 67–93.

Bourdieu, P. and M. de St. Martin. (Actes 1975) 'Les catégories de l'entendement professoral', 03, 68–93.

Bourdieu, P. and L. Boltanski. (Actes 1975a) 'Le fétichisme de la langue', 04, 2–33.

Bourdieu, P. (Actes 1975a) 'La critique du discours lettré', 5–6, 4–8.

Bourdieu, P. (Actes 1975b) 'L'ontologie politique de Martin Heidegger', 5–6, 109–56.

Bourdieu, P. (Actes 1975c) 'La lecture de Marx: quelques remarques critiques à propos de "Quelques remarques critiques à propos de 'Lire le Capital' " ', 5–6, 65–79.

Bourdieu, P. (Actes 1975d) 'Le langage autorisé. Note sur les conditions sociales de l'efficacité du discours rituel', 5–6, 183–190.

Bourdieu, P. (Actes 1976) 'Le sens pratique', 1, 43–86.

Bourdieu, P. and L. Boltanski. (Actes 1976) 'La production de l'idéologie dominante', 2–3, 4–73.

Bourdieu, P. (Actes 1976a) 'Le champ scientifique', 2–3, 88–104.
Bourdieu, P. (Actes 1976b) 'Les modes de domination', 2–3, 122–32.
Bourdieu, P. (Actes 1976c) 'Un jeu chinois. Notes pour une critique sociale du jugement', 4, 91–101.
Bourdieu, P. (Actes 1976d) 'Anatomie du goût', 5, 2–112.
Bourdieu, P. (Actes 1977) 'La production de la croyance: contribution à une économie des biens symboliques', 13, 3–43.
Bourdieu, P. (Actes 1977a) 'Remarques provisoires sur la perception sociale du corps', 14, 51–4.
Bourdieu, P. (Actes 1977b) 'Questions de politique', 16, 55–89.
Bourdieu, P. (Actes 1977c) 'Une Classe objet', 17–18, 1–5.
Bourdieu, P. and M. de St. Martin. (Actes 1978) 'Le patronat', 20–21, 3–82.
Bourdieu, P. and M. Mammeri. (Actes 1978) 'Dialogue sur la poésie orale en Kabylie', 23, 51–66.
Bourdieu, P. (Actes 1978) 'Sur l'objectivation participante. Réponses à quelques objections', 23, 67–9.
Bourdieu, P. (Actes 1978a) 'Classement, déclassement, reclassement', 24, 2–22.
Bourdieu, P. (Actes 1979) 'Les trois états du capital culturel', 30, 3–6.
Bourdieu, P. (Actes 1980) 'Le capital social', 31, 2–3.
Bourdieu, P. (Actes 1980a) 'Lettre à Paolo Fossati à propos de la storia dell'arte italiana', 31, 90–92.
Bourdieu, P. (Actes 1980b) 'Le mort saisit le vif', 32–3, 3–14.
Bourdieu, P. (Actes 1980c) 'L'identité et la représentation. Elements pour une réflexion critique "sur l'idée de région" ', 35, 63–72.
Bourdieu, P. (Actes 1980d) 'Le Nord et le Midi: contribution à une analyse de l'effet Montesquieu', 35, 21–5.
Bourdieu, P. (Actes 1981) 'La représentation politique. Eléments pour une théorie du champ politique', 36–7, 3–24.
Bourdieu, P. (Actes 1981a) 'Décrire et prescrire. Note sur les conditions de possibilité et les limites de l'efficacité politique', 38, 69–73.
Bourdieu, P. (Actes 1981b) 'Epreuve scolaire et consécration sociale. Les classes préparatoires aux Grandes écoles', 39, 3–70.
Bourdieu, P. and Y. Delsaut. (Actes 1981) 'Pour une sociologie de la perception', 40, 3–9.
Bourdieu, P. (Actes 1982) 'Les rites d'institution', 43, 58–63.
Bourdieu, P. and M. de St. Martin. (Actes 1982) 'La sainte famille. L'épiscopat français dans le champ du pouvoir', 44–5, 2–53.
Bourdieu, P. (Actes 1983) 'Vous avez dit "populaire"?' 46, 98–105.
Bourdieu, P. (Actes 1983a) 'Les sciences sociales et la philosophie', 47–8, 45–52.
Bourdieu, P. (Actes 1984) 'Le hit-parade des intellectuels français ou qui sera juge de la légitimité des juges?' 52–3, 95–100.
Bourdieu, P. (Actes 1984a) 'Espace social et genèse des "classes" ', 52–3, 3–14.
Bourdieu, P. (Actes 1984b) 'La délégation et le fétichisme politique', 52–3, 49–55.
Bourdieu, P. and A. Bensa. (Actes 1985) 'Quand les canaques prennent la parole', 59, 69–83.

Bourdieu, P. (Actes 1985) 'Effet de champ et effet de corps', 59, 73.
Bourdieu, P., R. Chartier and R. Darnton. (Actes 1985) 'Dialogue à propos de l'histoire culturelle', 59, 86–93.
Bourdieu, P. (Actes 1986) 'La science et l'actualité', 61, 2–3.
Bourdieu, P. (Actes 1986a) 'L'illusion biographique', 62–3, 69–72.
Bourdieu, P. (Actes 1986b) 'La force du droit. Eléments pour une sociologie du champ juridique', 64, 3–19.
Bourdieu, P. (Actes 1986c) 'Habitus, code et codification', 64, 40–44.
Bourdieu, P. and M. de St. Martin (Actes 1987) 'Agrégation et ségrégation. Le champ des grandes écoles et le champ du pouvoir', 69, Sept. 2–50.
Bourdieu, P. (Actes 1987a) 'Variations et invariants. Eléments pour une histoire structurale du champ des grandes écoles', 70, Nov., 3–30.
Bourdieu, P. (Actes 1988) 'Penser la politique', 71–2, Mar., 2–3.

C. Works in English, and recent documents (some in French).

Bourdieu, P. (1962) *The Algerians* (Boston: Beacon Press).
Bourdieu, P. (1963) 'The attitude of the Algerian peasant toward time', in J. Pitt-Rivers (ed.), *Mediterranean Countrymen* (Westport, Greenwood Press).
Bourdieu, P. (1965) 'The sentiment of honour in Kabyle society', in J. Peristiany (ed.), *Honour and Shame: The Values of Mediterranean Society* (London: Weidenfeld and Nicholson).
Bourdieu, P. (1967) 'Systems of education and systems of thought', *International Social Science Journal* 19(3).
Bourdieu, P. (1968) 'Outline of a theory of art perception', *International Social Science Journal* 20(4), 589–612.
Bourdieu, P. (1968a) 'Structuralism and theory of sociological knowledge', *Social Research* 35(4), 681–706.
Bourdieu, P. (1970) 'The Berber house or the world reversed', *Social Science Information* 9(2), 151–70.
Bourdieu, P. (1971) 'Intellectual field and creative project', in M. F. D. Young (ed.), *Knowledge and Control: New Directions for the Sociology of Education* (London: Collier-Macmillan; in French 1966).
Bourdieu, P. (1971a) 'The thinkable and the unthinkable', *The Times Literary Supplement*, 15 October, 1255–56.
Bourdieu, P. (1971b) 'Systems of education and systems of thought', (Bourdieu 1967) reprinted in M. F. D. Young (ed.), (1971) q.v.
Bourdieu, P. (1973) 'The Algerian subproletariate', in W. I. Zartman (ed.), *State and Society in the Contemporary Maghrib* (London: Pall Mall Press).
Bourdieu, P. (1973a) 'The three forms of theoretical knowledge', *Social Science Information* 12(1), 53–80.
Bourdieu, P. (1973b) 'Cultural reproduction and social reproduction', in R. Brown (ed.), *Knowledge, Education and Social Change* (London: Tavistock; in French 1971).
Bourdieu, P. (1974) 'The school as a conservative force: scholastic and cultural inequalities', in J. Eggleston (ed.), *Contemporary Research in the Sociology of Education* (London: Methuen; in French 1966).
Bourdieu, P. (1975) 'The specificity of the scientific field and the social

conditions of the progress of reason', *Social Science Information* 14(6), 19–47.

Bourdieu, P. (1976) 'Marriage strategies as strategies of social reproduction', in R. Forster and P. Ranum (eds), *Family and Society: Selections from the Annales* (Baltimore: Johns Hopkins University Press; in French 1972).

Bourdieu, P. (1977) *Outline of a Theory of Practice* (Cambridge: Cambridge University Press; in French 1972).

Bourdieu, P. (1977a) 'Symbolic power', in D. Gleeson (ed.), *Identity and Structure: Issues in the Sociology of Education* (Driffield: Nafferton Books).

Bourdieu, P. (1977b) 'Economics of linguistic exchanges', *Social Science Information* (16(6), 645–68.

Bourdieu, P. (1977c) 'Afterword', in P. Rabinow *Reflections on Fieldwork in Morocco* (Berkeley: University of California Press).

Bourdieu, P. (1978) 'Sport and social class', *Social Science Information* 17(6), 819–40.

Bourdieu, P. (1979) *Algeria 1960: The Disenchantment of the World, the Sense of Honour, the Kabyle House or the World Reversed* (Cambridge: Cambridge University Press).

Bourdieu, P. (1979a) 'Symbolic power', *Critique of Anthropology* 4, 77–85 (see 1977a).

Bourdieu, P. (1979b) 'Public opinion does not exist', in A. Mattelart and S. Siegelaub (eds), *Communication and Class Struggle* (New York: International General).

Bourdieu, P. (1979c) 'Epilogue', in P. Bourdieu and J.-C. Passeron (1979), q.v.

Bourdieu, P. (1980) 'The aristocracy of culture', *Media, Culture and Society* 2(3), 225–54.

Bourdieu, P. (1980a) 'The production of belief: contributions to an economy of symbolic goods', *Media, Culture and Society* 2(3), 261–93.

Bourdieu, P. (1980b) 'Sartre', *London Review of Books* 11(22), 11–12.

Bourdieu, P. (1981) 'Men and machines', in K. Knorr-Cetina and A. V. Cicourel (eds), *Advances in Sociological Method and Methodology* (London: Routledge & Kegan Paul).

Bourdieu, P. (1983) 'The field of cultural production, or: the economic world reversed', *Poetics* 12, 311–56.

Bourdieu, P. (1983a) 'Erving Goffman, discoverer of the infinitely small', *Theory, Culture and Society* 2(1), 112–13.

Bourdieu, P. (1983b) 'The philosophical institution', in A. Montefiore (ed.), *Philosophy in France Today* (Cambridge: Cambridge University Press), 1–8.

Bourdieu, P. (1984) *Distinction: a Social Critique of the Judgement of Taste* (Cambridge, MA: Harvard University Press).

Bourdieu, P. (1984a) 'Delegation and political fetishism', *Thesis Eleven* 10/11, 56–69.

Bourdieu, P. (1985) 'The social space and the genesis of groups', *Social Science Information* 24(2), 195–220 (see also *Theory and Society* 14(6), 723–44).

Bourdieu, P. (1985a) *Propositions pour l'enseignement de l'avenir*. Élaborée à la demande de Monsieur le Président de la République par les Professeurs de Collège de France (Paris).

Bourdieu, P. (1985b) 'Recherches sur les grande écoles. Text de travail', unpublished ms.

Bourdieu, P. (1985c) Interview with C. Mahar, March 1985, unpublished ms.

Bourdieu, P. (1985d) 'A free thinker: "do not ask me who I am"'.' *Paragraph* 5, 80–87.

Bourdieu, P. (1985e) 'The genesis of the concepts of "habitus" and "field" ', *Sociocriticism* 2(2), 11–24.

Bourdieu, P. (1985f) 'The market of symbolic goods', *Poetics* 14, 13–44.

Bourdieu, P. (1986) 'The theory of the field in the space of theoretical possibilities', unpublished ms.

Bourdieu, P. (1986a) 'The forms of capital', in J. G. Richardson (ed.), *Handbook of Theory and Research for the Sociology of Education* (New York: Greenwood Press), 241–58.

Bourdieu, P. (1986b) 'From rules to strategies', *Cultural Anthropology* 1(1), 110–20. (See Lamaison (1986) in Section D.)

Bourdieu, P. (1986c) 'The struggle for symbolic order', *Theory, Culture and Society* 3(3), 35–51.

Bourdieu, P. (1986d) 'An antinomy in the notion of collective protest', in A. Foxley, M. S. McPherson and G. O'Donnell (eds), *Development, Democracy, and the Art of Trespassing* (Indiana: University of Notre Dame Press).

Bourdieu, P. (1987) 'The force of law – toward a sociology of the juridical field', *Hastings Law Journal* 38(5), 805–53.

Bourdieu, P. (1987a) 'The biographical illusion', *Working Papers and Proceedings of the Centre for Psychosocial Studies* (University of Chicago) 14, 1–7.

Bourdieu, P. (1987b) 'Revolt of the spirit', *New Socialist* 46, 9–11.

Bourdieu, P. (1987c) 'What makes a social class? On the theoretical and practical existence of groups', *Berkeley Journal of Sociology* 32, 1–17.

Bourdieu, P. (1987d) 'The historical genesis of a pure aesthetic', *The Journal of Aesthetics and Art Criticism* 46, 201–10.

Bourdieu, P. (1987e) 'Scientific field and scientific thought', paper to annual conference, American Anthropological Association, Chicago.

Bourdieu, P. (1987f) 'Legitimation and structured interests in Weber's sociology of religion', in S. Whimster and S. Lash (eds), *Max Weber, Rationality and Modernity* (London: Allen & Unwin).

Bourdieu, P. (1987g) 'The invention of the artist's life', *Yale French Studies* 73, 75–103.

Bourdieu, P. (1987h) *Questions of Sociology* (Wesleyan University Press).

Bourdieu, P. (1988) *Homo Academicus* (Cambridge: Polity Press).

Bourdieu, P. (1988a) 'Program for a sociology of sport', *Sociology of Sport Journal* 5, 153–61.

Bourdieu, P. (1988b) 'Flaubert's point of view', *Critical Inquiry* 14, 539–62.

Bourdieu, P. (1988c) 'A long trend of change', *The Times Literary Supplement*, 12–18 August, 875–6.

Bourdieu, P. (1988d) 'On interest and the relative autonomy of symbolic power: a rejoinder to some objections', *Working Papers and Proceedings of the Centre for Psychosocial Studies* (University of Chicago) 20, 1–11.

Bourdieu, P. (1988e) ' "Vive la Crise". For heterodoxy in social science', *Theory and Society* 17(5), 773–87.

Bourdieu, P. (1989) *Language and Symbolic Power* (Cambridge: Polity Press).

Bourdieu, P. (1989a) *In Other Words: Essays Towards a Reflexive Sociology* (Stanford: Stanford University Press).

Bourdieu, P. (1990, forthcoming) *The Logic of Practice* (Stanford: Stanford University Press).

Bourdieu, P. (no date) Two Bourdieu texts, translated by Richard Nice. *Birmingham Centre for Contemporary Cultural Studies, Occasional Paper* SP No. 46 ('Symbolic power' – see Bourdieu 1977a; 1979a: and 'Qualificatons and jobs' – see Bourdieu and Boltanski (Actes 1975); 1981.)

Bourdieu, P. and L. Boltanski. (1977) 'Formal qualifications and occupational hierarchies', *Reorganizing Education. Sage Annual Review, Social and Educational Change*. Vol. 1 (London: Sage).

Bourdieu, P. and L. Boltanski. (1981) 'The education system and the economy: titles and jobs', in C. C. Lemert (ed.), (1981a), q.v.

Bourdieu, P., L. Boltanski, P. Castel and J.-C. Chamboredon (forthcoming) *Photography: The Social Uses of Ordinary Art* (Cambridge: Polity Press).

Bourdieu, P., L. Boltanski and M. de Saint Martin. (1978) 'Changes in social structure and changes in the demand for educaton', in S. Giner and M. S. Archer (eds), *Contemporary Europe: Social Structures and Cultural Patterns* (London: Routledge & Kegan Paul).

Bourdieu, P. and J.-C. Passeron. (1967) 'Sociology and philosophy in France since 1945: death and resurrection of a philosophy without subject', *Social Research* 34(1), 162–212.

Bourdieu, P. and J.-C. Passeron. (1977) *Reproduction in Education, Society and Culture* (London: Sage; in French 1970).

Bourdieu, P. and J.-C. Passeron. (1979) *The Inheritors: French Students and their Relations to Culture* (Chicago: University of Chicago Press; in French 1964).

Bourdieu, P., J. C. Passeron and M. de Sant Martin. (1980) 'Pedagogy and Communication', in D. McCallum, U. Ozolins (eds), *Melbourne Working Papers 1980* (Department of Education, University of Melbourne; in French 1965).

Bourdieu, P. and J. D. Reynaud. (1974) 'Is a sociology of action possible?' in A. Giddens (ed.), *Positivism and Sociology* (London: Heinemann).

Bourdieu, P. and M. de Saint Martin. (1974) 'Scholastic excellence and the values of the educational system', in J. Eggleston (ed.), *Contemporary Research in the Sociology of Education* (London: Methuen; in French 1970).

Bourdieu, P. and M. de Saint Martin. (1986) *Structures objectives et représentations subjectives du champ des institutions d'enseignement supérieur* (Paris: Centre de sociologie Européenne; mimeo).

Bourdieu, P. et al. (1987) *Eléments d'une analyse du marché de la maison individuelle* (Paris: Centre de sociologie Européenne; mimeo).

Bibliography 233

D. References discussing or reviewing Bourdieu's work

Acciaiolo, G. L. (1981) 'Knowing what you are doing: a review of Pierre Bourdieu's "Outline of a Theory of Practice" ' *Canberra Anthropology* 4(1), 23–51.

Accardo, A. (1983) *Initiation à la sociologie de l'illusionnisme social* (Bordeaux: Editions le Mascaret).

Amiot, M. (1981) 'Comparing Baudelot and Establet with Bourdieu and Passeron', in C. C. Lemert (ed.), (1981a), q.v.

Archer, M. (1984) 'Process without system' (A review of Bourdieu and Passeron (1977), *European Journal of Sociology* 21(1), 196–221.

Baudelot, C. and R. Establet. (1981) 'France's capitalistic school: problems of analysis and practice', in C. C. Lemert (ed.), (1981a), q.v.

Berger, B. M. (1986) Review essay: 'Taste and discrimination', *American Journal of Sociology* 91(6), 1445–53.

Bidet, J. (1979) 'Questions to Pierre Bourdieu', *Critique of Anthropology* 4(13/14), 203–8.

Bidwell, C. E. (1972) Review of 'Reproduction', *American Journal of Sociology* 77(5), 990–92.

Bisseret, N. (1979) *Education, Class Language and Ideology* (London: Routledge & Kegan Paul).

Bogart, L. (1987) Review of 'Distinction', *Public Opinion Quarterly* 51, 131–4.

Bredo, E. and W. Feinberg. (1979) 'Meaning, power and pedagogy: Pierre Bourdieu and Jean-Claude Passeron, "Reproduction in Educaton, Society and Culture" ', *Journal of Curriculum Studies* 11(4), 315–32.

Broadfoot, T. (1978) 'Reproduction in education, society and culture', *Comparative Education* 14(1), 75–82.

Brubaker, R. (1985) 'Rethinking classical theory: the sociological vision of Pierre Bourdieu', *Theory and Society* 14(6), 745–75.

Carnoy, M. (1982) 'Education, economy and the state', in M. W. Apple (ed.), *Cultural and Economic Reproduction in Education* (London: Routledge & Kegan Paul), 103–6.

Collectif (1988) *Lectures de Pierre Bourdieu* (Caen: Cahiers du LASA), numéro spécial.

Collectif 'Révoltes Logiques', (1984) *L'Empire du sociologue*. Cahiers Libres 384 (Paris: Editions La Découverte).

Davies, B. (1976) *Social Control and Education* (London: Methuen).

Di Maggio, P. (1979) Review essay: 'On Pierre Bourdieu', *American Journal of Sociology* 84(6), 1460–74.

Di Maggio, P. (1982) 'Cultural capital and school success', *American Sociological Review* 47(2), 189–201.

Di Maggio, P. and M. Useem. (1982) 'The arts in class reproduction', in M. W. Apple (ed.), *Cultural and Economic Reproduction in Education* (London: Routledge & Kegan Paul).

Douglas, M. (1981) 'Good taste: review of Pierre Bourdieu, "La Distinction" ', *The Times Literary Supplement* 13 February, 163–9.

Elster, J. (1983) *Sour Grapes: Studies in the Subversion of Rationality* (Cambridge: Cambridge University Press).

Foster, S. W. (1986) 'Reading Pierre Bourdieu', *Cultural Anthropology* 1(1), 103–10.

Frank, A. W. (1980) Review of 'Outline', *Contemporary Sociology – A Journal of Reviews* (2), 256–7.

Frow, J. (1987) 'Accounting for tastes: some problems in Bourdieu's sociology of culture', *Cultural Studies* 1(1), 59–73.

Garnham, N. (1986) Extended review: Bourdieu's 'Distinction', *The Sociological Review* 34(2), 423–33.

Garnham, N. and R. Williams. (1980) 'Pierre Bourdieu and the sociology of culture: an introduction', *Media, Culture and Society* 2(3), 209–23.

Giddens, A. (1978) Review of 'Outline', *Political Studies* 26(1), p. 176.

Giddens, A. (1986) 'The politics of taste – review of "Distinction" ', *Partisan Review* 53(2), 300–305.

Giroux, H. (1981) *Ideology, Culture and the Process of Schooling* (Brighton: Falmer Press).

Giroux, H. (1982) 'Power and resistance in the new sociology of education: beyond theories of social and cultural reproduction', *Curriculum Perspectives* 2(3), 1–13.

Giroux, H. (1983) 'Theories of reproduction and resistance in the new sociology of education: a critical analysis', *Harvard Educational Review* 52(3), 257–93.

Gorder, K. L. (1980) 'Understanding school knowledge: a critical appraisal of Basil Bernstein and Pierre Bourdieu', *Educational Theory* 30(4), 335–46.

Harker, R. (1984) 'On reproduction, habitus and education', *British Journal of Sociology of Education* 5(2), 117–27.

Harker, R. (1984a) 'Bourdieu on education', *Education Research and Perspectives* 11(2), 40–53.

Hawthorn, G. (1977) Review of 'Outline', *New Society* 41(776), 356.

Hearn, J. C. and S. Olzak. (1981) 'The role of college major departments in the reproduction of sexual inequality', *Sociology of Education* 54(3), 195–205.

Hoffmann, S. (1986) 'Monsieur taste', *New York Review of Books* 33(6), 45–8.

Honneth, A. N. (1986) 'The fragmented world of symbolic forms: reflections on Pierre Bourdieu's sociology of culture', *Theory, Culture and Society* 3(3), 55–66.

Honneth, A. N., H. Kocyba and B. Schwibs. (1986) 'The struggle for symbolic order – an interview with Pierre Bourdieu', *Theory, Culture and Society* 3(3), 35–51.

Honneth, A. N. and B. Schwibs. (1985) Interview with P. Bourdieu. (mimeo) (our translation – A. Visser).

Inglis, F. (1979) 'Good and bad habitus: Bourdieu, Habermas and the condition of England', *The Sociological Review* 27(2), 353–69.

Ingram, D. (1982) 'The possibility of a communication ethic reconsidered: Habermas, Gadamer and Bourdieu on discourse', *Man and World* 15, 149–61.

Jenkins, R. (1982) 'Pierre Bourdieu and the reproduction of determinism', *Sociology* 16(2), 270–81.

Jenkins, R. (1983) *Lads, Citizens and Ordinary Kids* (London: Routledge & Kegan Paul).

Jenkins, R. (1986) Review of 'Distinction', *Sociology* 20, 103–5.

Johnson, D. (1980) Review of Bourdieu and Passeron (1979), *New Society* (900), 30.

Joppke, C. (1986) 'The cultural dimensions of class formation and class struggle: on the social theory of Pierre Bourdieu', *Berkeley Journal of Sociology* 31, 53–78.

Judt, T. (1989) 'Elite formations – review of La Noblesse d'Etat', *The Times Literary Supplement* August 18–24, (No. 4705), 889.

Karabel, J. and A. H. Halsey (eds) (1977) *Power and Ideology in Education* (Oxford: Oxford University Press).

Kennett, J. (1973) 'The sociology of Pierre Bourdieu', *Educational Review* 25(3), 237–49.

Knorr, K. D. (1977) 'Producing and reproducing knowledge; descriptive or constructive', *Social Science Information* 16, 669–96.

Lakomski, G. (1984) 'On agency and structure: Pierre Bourdieu and Jean-Claude Passeron's theory of symbolic violence', *Curriculum Inquiry* 14(2), 151–63.

Lamaison, P. (1986) 'From rules to strategies: an interview with Pierre Bourdieu', *Cultural Anthropology* 1(1), 110–20.

Lamont, M. and A. Lareau. (1987) 'Cultural capital in American research: problems and possibilities', *Working Papers and Proceedings of the Centre for Psychosocial Studies* (Chicago: University of Chicago Press).

Lareau, A. (1987) 'Social class differences in family–school relationships: the importance of cultural capital', *Sociology of Education* 60, 73–85.

Lemert, C. C. (1981) 'Literary politics and the *champ* of French sociology', *Theory and Society* 10, 645–69.

Lemert, C. C. (ed.) (1981a) *French Sociology: Rupture and Renewal Since 1968* (New York: Columbia University Press).

Lienard, G. and E. Servais. (1979) 'Practical sense', *Critique of Anthropology* 4(13/14), 209–19.

Littleton, C. S. (1979) Review of 'Outline', *American Anthropologist* 81(1), 181–2.

Longhurst, B. (1986) Review of 'Distinction', *British Journal of Sociology* 37, 453–4.

Luong, H. V. (1985) Review of 'Ce que parler veut dire', *American Anthropologist* 87, 946–7.

McCleary, D. (1989) Extended review of Bourdieu's 'Choses dites', *The Sociological Review* 37(2), 373–83.

Montefiore, A. (1982) Review of 'Le sens pratique', *Journal of Modern History* 54(4), 775–6.

Murphy, R. (1982) 'Power and autonomy in the sociology of education', *Theory and Society* 11, 179–203.

Nice, R. (1978) 'Bourdieu: a "vulgar materialist" in the sociology of culture', *Screen Education* 28, 23–33.

Nice, R. (1985) Interviewed by C. Mahar. (mimeo).

Ostrow, J. M. (1981) 'Culture as a fundamental dimension of experience –

a discussion of P. Bourdieu's theory of human habitus', *Human Studies* 4(3), 279–97.

Peristiany, J. (ed.) (1965) *Honour and Shame: The Values of Mediterranean Society* (London: Weidenfeld & Nicholson).

Pinto, L. (1974) 'La théorie de la pratique', *La Pensée* 178, 54–76.

Rose, D. (1986) Review of 'Distinction', *American Ethnologist* 13, 163–4.

Rosenblum, B. (1984) 'Culture and class are a matter of taste' (Review of *Distinction*). *San Francisco Chronicle* Dec. 23.

Rossi, I. (1975) 'Review of 'Esquisse d'une théorie de la pratique', *American Anthropologist* 77(4), 931–3.

Sainsaulieu, R. (1981) 'On reproduction', in C. C. Lemert (ed.) (1981a), q.v.

Schatzki, T. R. (1987) 'Overdue analysis of Bourdieu's theory of practice', *Inquiry* 30, 113–15.

Schiltz, M. (1982) 'Habitus and peasantization in Nigeria: a Yoruba case study', *Man* 17(4), 728–46.

Schwibs, B. (1985) 'Bernd Schwibs gespräch mit Pierre Bourdieu', *Neue Sammlung* 3 (Stuttgart: Klett-Cotta).

Sharp, R. (1980) *Knowledge, Ideology and the Politics of Schooling: Towards a Marxist Analysis of Schooling* (London: Routledge & Kegan Paul).

Sohlich, W. (1984) 'Prolegomenon for a theory of drama reception; Peter Brook's "Measure for Measure" and the emergent bourgeoisie', *Comparative Drama* 18(1), 54–81.

Stanton, G. (1982) Review of 'Algeria 1960', *Africa* 52(2), 121.

Sulkunin, P. (1982) 'Society made visible: on the cultural sociology of Pierre Bourdieu' *Acta Sociologica* 25(2), 103–15.

Swartz, D. (1977) 'Pierre Bourdieu: the cultural transmission of social inequality', *Harvard Education Review* 47(4), 545–55.

Talbott, J. E. (1972) Review of the French edition (1964) of Bourdieu and Passeron (1979), *History of Education Quarterly* 12(4), 551–61.

Thompson, J. B. (1984) *Studies in the Theory of Ideology* (Cambridge: Polity Press).

Van Esterik, P. (1986) Review of 'Distinction' (Bourdieu, 1984), *American Anthropologist* 88(2), 456–7.

Vogt, P. (1980) Review of Bourdieu and Passeron (1979), *American Journal of Education* 88(3), 383–6.

Wacquant, L. J. D. (1984) 'Symbolic Violence and the Making of the French Agriculturist: Review Essay on Pierre Bourdieu and Sylvain Maresca'. ORSTOM, New Caledonia. (mimeo).

Wacquant, L. J. D. (1987) 'Symbolic violence and the making of the French agriculturalist: an inquiry into Pierre Bourdieu's sociology', *Australian and New Zealand Journal of Sociology* 23(1), 65–88.

Wacquant, L. J. D. (1989) 'Toward a reflexive sociology. A workshop with Pierre Bourdieu', *Sociological Theory* 7(1).

Warner, M. (1985) Review of 'Distinction' (Bourdieu, 1984). *MLN* 100(5), 1133–5.

Watkins, P. E. (1984) 'Culture, cultural resources and the labor market – a study of a Christian Brothers College', *Australian Journal of Education* 28(1), 66–77.

Willis, P. (1983) 'Cultural production and theories of reproduction', in L. Barton and S. Walker (eds), *Race, Class and Education* (London: Croom Helm).

Wilson, E. (1988) 'Picasso and pâté de foie gras: Pierre Bourdieu's sociology of culture', *Diacritics* Summer, 47–60.

Zolberg, V. (1986) 'Taste as a social weapon', *Contemporary Sociology* 15(4), 511–15.

E. Other references used in this text

Agee, J. and W. Evans. (1960) *Let Us Now Praise Famous Men* (Boston: Houghton Mifflin).

Asad, T. (ed.) (1973) *Anthropology and the Colonial Encounter* (New York: Humanities Press).

Augé, M. (1982) *The Anthropological Circle: Symbol, Function, History* (London: Cambridge University Press).

Baron, S. (1985) 'The study of culture; cultural studies and British sociology compared', *Acta Sociologica* 28, 71–86.

Barthes, R. (1977) 'The death of the author', in *Image-Music-Text* (Glasgow: Fontana/Collins; in French 1968).

Bauman, Z. (1988) 'Is there a post-modern sociology?', *Theory, Culture and Society* 5, 217–37.

Benveniste, E. (1969) *Le vocabulaire des institutions Indo-Européennes II* (Paris: Les Editions de Minuit).

Benveniste, E. (1974) *Problèmes de linguistique générale II* (Paris: Gallimard).

Benzecri, J.-P. (1969) 'Statistical analysis as a test to make patterns emerge from clouds', in S. Watanabe (ed.) *Methodologies of Pattern Recognition* (New York: Academic Press), 35–74.

Benzecri, J.-P. (1974) 'La place de l'apriori', *Encyclopédie Universalis* (Section Organum), Paris.

Berger, J. (1972) *Ways of Seeing* (Harmondsworth: Penguin Books).

Bernstein, R. J. (1972) *Praxis and Action* (London: Duckworth).

Best, D. (1980) 'The objectivity of artistic appreciation', *Brtish Journal of Aesthetics* 20(2), 115–27.

Bhaskar, R. (1975) *A Realist Theory of Science* (Leeds: Leeds Books).

Bhaskar, R. (1979) *The Possibility of Naturalism: A Philosophical Critique of the Human Sciences* (Brighton: Harvester Press).

Bloch, M. (1983) *Marxism and Anthropology* (Oxford: Oxford University Press).

Bloor, D. (1983) *Wittgenstein: A Social Theory of Knowledge* (London: Macmillan).

Bolton, D. (1979) *An Approach to Wittgenstein's Philosophy* (London: Macmillan).

Bowles, S. and H. Gintis. (1976) *Schooling in Capitalist America* (New York: Basic Books).

Brand, G. (1979) *The Central Texts of Ludwig Wittgenstein* (Oxford: Basil Blackwell).

Cambrosio and Keating (1983) 'The disciplinary strike – the case of chrono-biology', *Social Studies of Science* 13(3), 323–53.

Casey, J. (1966) *The Language of Criticism* (London: Methuen).

Cassirer, E. (1961) *The Philosophy of Symbolic Forms* (tr. by R. Manhem) (New Haven: Yale University Press; in German 1923–9).

Centre for European Sociology. (1972) *Current Research* (Paris: Ecole pratique des haute études, Maison des sciences de l'homme).

Charbonnier, G. (1969) *Conversations with Claude Lévi-Strauss* (London: Jonathan Cape).

Chomsky, N. (1979) *Language and Responsibility* (tr. John Viertal) (Brighton: Harvester Press).

Clark, T. (1973) *Prophets and Patrons* (Cambridge, MA: Harvard University Press).

Clifford, J. (1988) *The Predicament of Culture* (London: Harvard University Press).

Clifford, J., and G. E. Marcus. (1987) *Writing Culture: the Poetics and Politics of Ethnography* (Berkeley: University of California Press).

Codd, J. A. (1982) 'Interpretive cognition and the education of artistic appreciation', *The Journal of Aesthetic Education* 16(3), 15–33.

Collingwood R. G. (1938) *The Principles of Art* (Oxford: Clarendon Press).

Collins, R. (1988) *Theoretical Sociology* (San Diego: Harcourt Brace Jovanovich).

Copans, J. (ed.) (1974) *Critiques et politiques de l'anthropologie* (Paris: Maspero).

Craib, I. (1984) *Modern Social Theory: From Parsons to Habermas* (Brighton: Wheatsheaf).

Crick, M. et al. (1984) 'Anthropological imperialism; comments', *Australian Anthropological Society Newsletter*, December, 17–27.

Croce, B. (1922) *Aesthetics* (tr. by D. Ainslie) (London: Macmillan) 2nd edition.

Duby, G. (1980) *The Three Orders: Feudal Society Imagined* (Chicago: University of Chicago Press).

Ducasse, C. J. (1929) *The Philosophy of Art* (New York: Dial).

Dumont, L. (1957) 'For a sociology of India', *Contributions to Indian Sociology* 1, 7–22.

Durkheim, E. (1956) *Education and Sociology* (Boston: Free Press).

Ehrmann, J. (ed.) (1970) *Structuralism* (New York: Doubleday).

Encrevé Designe, P. E. (1983) In *Encyclopédie Universalis*, 614–16.

Fabian, J. (1983) *Time and the Other: How Anthropology Makes Its Object* (New York: Columbia University Press).

Freeman, D. (1984) *Margaret Mead and Samoa; the Making and Unmaking of an Anthropological Myth* (Harmondsworth: Penguin).

Geertz, C. (1973) *The Interpretation of Cultures* (New York: Basic Books).

Geertz, C. (1985) 'Waddling in', *The Times Literary Supplement*, 7 June 1985, no. 4288, 623–4.

Geertz, C. (1988) *Works and Lives: the Anthropologist as Author* (Cambridge: Polity Press).

Giddens, A. (1976) *New Rules of Sociological Method* (London: Hutchinson).

Giddens, A. (1979) *Central Problems in Social Theory* (London: Macmillan).

Giddens, A. (1981) *A Contemporary Critique of Historical Materialism* (London: Macmillan).

Giddens, A. (1982) *Profiles and Critiques in Social Theory* (London: Macmillan).

Giddens, A. (1984) *The Constitution of Society* (Berkeley: University of California Press).

Goldthorpe, J. (1980) *Social Mobility and Class Structure in Modern Britain* (London: Oxford University Press). -

Gombrich, E. (1960) *Art and Illusion* (New York: Pantheon).

Gramsci, A. (1971) *Selections from Prison Notebooks* (London: Lawrence & Wishart).

Hall, S. and T. Jefferson. (1976) *Resistance Through Rituals: Youth Subcultures in Post-war Britain* (London: Hutchinson).

Harker, R. (1975) 'Streaming and Social Class', in P. D. K. Ramsay (ed.), *The Family and the School in New Zealand Society* (Melbourne: Pitman).

Hollingdale, R. J. (1973) *Nietzsche* (London: Routledge & Kegan Paul).

Holtzman, S. H. and C. M. Leitch (1981) (eds), *Wittgenstein: To Follow a Rule* (London: Routledge & Kegan Paul).

Jackson, M. (1983) 'Knowledge of the body', *Man* 18(2), 327–45.

Jarvie, I. C. (1964) *The Revolution in Anthropology* (London: Routledge & Kegan Paul).

Jessop, B. (1985) *Nicos Poulantzas* (London: Macmillan).

Johnson, T., C. Dandeker and C. Ashworth. (1984) *The Structure of Social Theory* (London: Macmillan).

Kolenda, K. (1973) *Philosophy's Journey: A Historical Introduction* (New York: Addison Wesley).

Langer, S. K. (1953) *Feeling and Form* (New York: Scribners).

Langer, S. K. (1957) *Philosophy in a New Key*. 3rd edition, (Cambridge, MA: Harvard University Press; first published 1942).

Leach, E. (1957) 'The epistemological background to Malinowski's empiricism', in Raymond Firth (ed.), *Man in Culture; an Evaluation of the Work of Malinowski* (London: Routledge & Kegan Paul), 119–38.

Lebart, L., A. Morineau, and K. M. Warwick. (1984) *Multivariate Descriptive Statistical Analysis: Correspondence Analysis and Related Techniques for Large Matrices* (New York: John Wiley & Sons).

Lemert, C. (1986) 'French sociology: after the patrons, what?' *Contemporary Sociology* 15, 689–92.

Lévi-Strauss, C. (1960) *The Scope of Anthropology* (London: Jonathan Cape).

Lévi-Strauss, C. (1966) *The Savage Mind* (London: Weidenfeld & Nicholson).

Lévi-Strauss, C. (1972) *Structural Anthropology* (Harmondsworth: Penguin; in French 1958).

Lévi-Strauss, C. (1973) *Tristes Tropiques* (Harmondsworth: Penguin).

Marcus, G. E., and D. Cushman. (1982) 'Ethnographies as texts', *Annual Review of Anthropology* 11, 25–69.

Marcus, G. E., and M. J. Fischer. (1986) *Anthropology as Cultural Critique:*

an Expermental Moment in the Human Sciences (Chicago: Chicago University Press).

Marshall, G., D. Rose, C. Vogler and H. Nenby. (1985) 'Class, citizenship and distributional conflict in modern Brtain', *British Journal of Sociology* 36(2), 259–84.

Merton, T. (1973) *Contemplation in a World of Action* (Garden City: Doubleday).

Moniot, H. (ed.) (1976) *Le mal de voir* (Paris: Union Générale d'Edition).

Needham, R. (1974) *Remarks and Inventions: Sceptical Essays about Kinship* (London: Tavistock).

Nietzsche, F. (1927) *The Philosophy of Nietzsche* (New York: Modern Library).

Nietzsche, F. (1954) *The Portable Nietzsche* (Walter Kaufman (ed.); New York: Viking Press.)

Nietzsche, F. (1967) *The Will to Power* (Walter Kaufmann (ed.); New York: Random House).

Panofsky, E. (1955) 'Iconography and iconology: an introduction to the study of renaissance art', in *Meaning in the Visual Arts* (New York: Doubleday).

Payne, G. and J. Payne. (1983) 'Occupational and industrial transition in social mobility', *British Journal of Sociology* 34(1), 72–92.

Poulantzas, N. (1968) *Pouvoir politiques et classes sociales* (Paris: PUF).

Read, H. (1943) *Education Through Art* (London: Faber).

Rabinow, P. (1985) 'Discourse and power; on the limits of ethnographic texts', *Dialectical Anthropology* 10, 1–14.

Robey, D. (ed.) (1973) *Structuralism: An Introduction* (Oxford: Clarendon Press).

Roseberry, W. (1984) 'Balinese Cockfights and the seduction of anthropology', *Social Research* 49, 1013–28.

Sahlins, M. (1976) *Culture and Practical Reason* (Chicago: University of Chicago Press).

Sahlins, M. (1981) *Historical Metaphors and Mythical Realities: Structure in the Early History of Sandwich Island Kingdoms* (Ann Arbor: University of Michigan Press).

Said, E. (1979) *Orientalism* (New York: Random House).

Santayana, G. (1896) *The Sense of Beauty* (New York: Scribner).

Saussure, F. de. (1974) *Course in General Linguistics* (London: Fontana/Collins; originally published in 1916).

Sayer, A. (1984) *Method in Social Science: A Realist Approach* (London: Hutchinson University Library).

Scruton, R. (1974) *Art and Imagination* (London: Methuen).

Simpson, F. A. (1950) *Chatham Exiles: Yesterday and Today at the Chatham Islands* (Wellington: A. H. and A. W. Reed).

Singer, M. (1984) *Man's Glassy Essence: explorations in semiotic anthropology* (Bloomington: Indiana University Press).

Solomon, R. C. (1972) *From Rationalism to Existentialism: The Existentialists and Their Nineteenth Century Background* (New York: Humanities Press).

Sperber, B. (1986) 'Interviewed by Roy Boyne', *Theory, Culture and Society* 3(3).

Thrift, N. (1983) 'Time-Geography as a way of life'. Paper to ISA Conference, Canada.

Turner, V. W. (1982) *From Ritual to Theatre; The Human Seriousness of Play* (New York: Performing Arts Journal Publication).

Wilby, P. (1979) 'Habermas and the language of the modern state', *New Society*, 22 March, 667–9.

Williams, R. (1973) 'Base and superstructure in marxist cultural theory', *New Left Review* 82, 3–16.

Williams, R. (1981) *Culture* (London: Fontana).

Willis, P. (1978) *Profane Culture* (London: Routledge & Kegan Paul).

Willis, P. (1980) 'Notes on method', in S. Hall et al. (eds), *Culture, Media, Language* (London: Hutchinson), 88–95.

Wittgenstein, L. (1974) *Philosophical Investigations* (tr. G. E. M. Anscombe; Oxford: Basil Blackwell).

Wolff, J. (1981) *The Social Production of Art* (London: Macmillan).

Wright, E. O. (1978) *Class, Crises and the State* (New York: Verso).

Wright, E. O. (1985) *Classes* (London: Verso).

Young, M. F. D. (ed.) (1971) *Knowledge and Control: New Directions for the Sociology of Education* (London: Collier-Macmillan).

Name Index

Subject Index